STATE AND LOCAL GOVERNMENT

STATE AND LOCAL GOVERNMENT

2003–2004

Edited by Thad L. Beyle

University of North Carolina
at Chapel Hill

A Division of Congressional Quarterly Inc.
Washington, D.C.

Congressional Quarterly Inc.

Congressional Quarterly Inc., an editorial research service and publishing company, serves clients in the fields of news, education, business and government. It combines the specific coverage of Congress, government and politics contained in the *CQ Weekly* with the more general subject range of an affiliated service, the *CQ Researcher.*

Under the CQ Press imprint, Congressional Quarterly also publishes college political science textbooks and public affairs paperbacks on developing issues and events, information directories and reference books on the federal government, national elections and politics. Titles include the *Guide to the Presidency,* the *Guide to Congress,* the *Guide to the U.S. Supreme Court,* the *Guide to U.S. Elections* and *Politics in America.* CQ's A–Z collection is a reference series that provides essential information about American government and the electoral process. The *CQ Almanac,* a compendium of legislation for one session of Congress, is published each year. *Congress and the Nation,* a record of government for a presidential term, is published every four years.

CQ publishes *CQ Today* (formerly the *Daily Monitor*), a report on the current and future activities of congressional committees. An online information system, CQ.com on Congress, provides immediate access to CQ's databases of legislative action, votes, schedules, profiles and analyses. Visit www.cq.com for more information.

ISSN: 0888-8590
ISBN: 1-56802-804-0

CQ Press
1255 22nd Street, N.W.
Suite 400
Washington, D.C. 20037

(202) 729-1900; toll-free, 1-866-4CQ-PRESS (1-866-427-7737)

www.cqpress.com

Printed and bound in the United States of America

07   06   05   04   03   5   4   3   2   1

♾ The paper used in this publication exceeds the requirements of the American National Standard for Information Sciences—Permanence of Paper for Printed Library Materials, ANSI Z39.48-1992.

Cover: Rich Pottern
Index: Joan Stout

The Library of Congress cataloged the first edition of this title as follows:

Beyle, Thad L.
    State government.

    Bibliography: p.
    Includes index.
    1. State governments—Addresses, essays, lectures. I. Congressional
Quarterly Inc. II. Title.

JK2408.B49   1985   320.973   85-9657

Contents

I. POLITICS AT THE TURN OF THE CENTURY

II. POLITICS: DIRECT DEMOCRACY

VI. GOVERNORS AND THE EXECUTIVE BRANCH

VII. STATE AND LOCAL BUREAUCRACIES AND ADMINISTRATION

VIII. STATE COURTS

IX. LOCAL GOVERNMENT

Boxes, Tables, and Figure

BOXES

TABLES

FIGURE

Preface

The states have acquired considerable importance over the past four decades. Their growth—as measured by the reach of policies and programs, the size of budgets and bureaucracies, as well as states' overall responsibility to their citizens—is unprecedented. Their problems, too, are unprecedented, and the changes in the federal system now occurring in federal programs and budgets pose new and important challenges for the states to address. And with the advent of terrorism in our own land, the need to plan and then carry out "homeland security" programs has added to their burdens.

This increased visibility and influence is tied to a major shift in how our federal system of government operates. In the late 1970s, the national government began cutting back in ever-increasing proportions its commitment to handle the domestic issues facing the country. State governments were asked to shoulder more of the domestic policy burden while the federal government tried to cope with the national debt and issues of national defense.

The states' response to the fiscal challenges of the 1980s became an issue of national as well as local importance. It fell mainly to state governments to take up the slack created by a federal government pulling back on support for domestic programs. The states were able to meet this challenge in an expanding economy in which revenue estimates were always too low and extra funds were usually available.

Toward the end of the 1980s there were signs that this buildup of budgets and programs based on ever-increasing revenues was coming to an end. And end it did. The early 1990s brought a tough twist for state leaders as the economy went into recession. Adding to the melee, the 1992 elections saw the national government refocus its attention on deficit reduction and large-scale cutbacks in the armed forces. Then came the major changes brought on by the 1994 elections, which gave control of Congress to the Republicans. State leaders became fearful that the federal budget would be balanced on the backs of the states, causing even more problems for the states. Then, as the 1996 elections grew closer, Congress passed, and the president signed into law, a major welfare reform bill that would have a significant impact on the states.

During the rest of the 1990s, as the national and individual state economies grew in strength, states found themselves with budget surpluses. State revenues were outrunning state expenditures, and governors and legislatures were deciding what to do with budget surpluses. Taxes were cut in some states, and more expenditures were seen in most. This was a return of the "good times," when policy decisions were much easier to make.

But now, as we move through the first decade of the twenty-first century, the troubles of the early 1990s have returned with a vengeance. Our booming economy is no longer booming, and all states are seeing tax revenues fall while demands for assistance rise. Many states are facing growing deficits, and state leaders wonder how they will maintain current service and infrastructure levels in the future. In many places local leaders are facing the need to raise local taxes to make up for what the states have cut back on. And these local officials fear it will only get worse at the local level.

Despite this shifting between bad news and good news, many seeking political careers see the states as where the action is and where those seeking to have an effect on government and policymaking turn. The states are also important rungs on our national political career ladder, as four of the past five presidents have been governors.

According to Carl Van Horn of the Eagleton Institute of Politics at Rutgers University, over the past few decades state governments have undergone a quiet revolution. This revolution, in which "states reformed and strengthened their political and economic houses," now finds the states occupying "a more important role in American life" as they pioneer "solutions to some of the country's most difficult problems and demonstrate effective leadership."[1]

State governments are no longer sleepy backwater operations located in far-off capitals

where few people know or care what they are doing. In many ways, it might be better to look at state governments as big-time organizations comparable to some of the world's largest nations or our country's largest corporations. From this perspective, the roles of state leaders in governing the states could be compared with those of leaders who govern large nations or run large corporations. They are big, complex organizations with a range of operations and goals—and they warrant the attention of both national and international policymakers.

The 2003–2004 edition of *State and Local Government* includes recent articles that define and analyze these state issues and agendas. Short background essays introduce the articles and highlight developments.

The organization of this book parallels that of most state government texts. First is politics: the most recent election results and the roles of direct democracy, interest groups, political parties, and the media. Next are institutions: legislatures, governors, bureaucracies, and state courts. The final two sections focus on local governments and some issues of primary concern to both state and local governments.

There are many to thank for assistance in developing this book. Among them are Grace Hill, of CQ Press, for her support, and Kerry Kern for her fine editorial hand. This is our nineteenth compilation, and we are still learning. Any errors you find are mine. I hope you will send your comments and suggestions so that we might be able to improve the 2004–2005 edition.

Note

1. Carl Van Horn, "The Quiet Revolution," in *The State of the States,* 3d ed., ed. Carl Van Horn (Washington, D.C.: CQ Press, 1996), 1.

STATE AND LOCAL GOVERNMENT

I. POLITICS AT THE TURN OF THE CENTURY

State officials continue to debate the timing of U.S. elections. Some argue that national, state, and local elections should be held at different times to keep separate the issues, candidates, and political concerns of each level. Following this argument, national elections for president, vice president, U.S. senators, and U.S. representatives would be held in even years, as they are now; exactly which year would depend on the length of the term—that is, representatives every two years, presidents every four years, and senators every six years. State-level elections for governor and other executive officials, state legislators, and state constitutional amendments and referendums would be held in "off-years" (nonpresidential election years) or possibly in odd-numbered years. And local elections would be at another time, preferably not in conjunction with either state or national elections.

Others advocate holding all elections at the same time to maximize voter interest and turnout and, not inconsequentially, to increase the importance of the political party as the main determinant of voters' decisions from the top of the ballot to the bottom. But there is not a single Republican party or a single Democratic party to influence voters' choices. At least fifty different Republican and Democratic state parties reflect the unique political culture, heritage, and positions of the fifty states. Add to that the increasing numbers of independents and split-ticket voters, and it is clear that the political party rationale does not hold up in the practical world of politics.

Neither side of the timing argument has predominated. During the 2000 presidential election year, forty-six states elected their legislatures and eleven elected their governors. Of these eleven states, New Hampshire and Vermont elect their governors to two-year terms, which means that their gubernatorial elections alternate between presidential and nonpresidential election years. Indeed, most states hold their gubernatorial elections in even, nonpresidential years, as in 2002, when thirty-six governors were elected, along with most legislatures; or in odd years, as in 2003, when Kentucky, Louisiana, and Mississippi are holding theirs, and in 2001, when New Jersey and Virginia held theirs.

A major reason why some states have shifted their elections to nonpresidential years is because the personalities, issues, and concerns evident in presidential elections often spill over into state-level contests. While presidential elections are stirring events that bring the excitement of politics to the American populace and lead to higher turnout among voters, some state officials fear that the "coattail effect" of the national elections will change the results of their elections and, most importantly, obscure the state issues that voters should consider on election day.

But there are other politics involved. For example, the Kentucky legislature recently drew up a proposed amendment to that state's constitution that would permit the governor to seek a second term and allow the governor and lieutenant governor to run as a team. It passed narrowly in 1992. However, legislative leaders killed a proposed provision that would have shifted the election timetable for governors to match that of legislators. The reason: "Because they feared that it would somehow weaken the power of the legislators if members ran the same time the governor did."[1]

Trends in Recent State Elections

Gender. In the past two decades, women have been increasingly successful as candidates for top-level state offices. After the 1998 elections all five statewide elected officials in Arizona were women. They were sworn into office in January 1999 by U.S. Supreme Court Justice Sandra Day O'Connor—another Arizonan and the first woman appointed to the top federal court.[2] These women can attribute their success to better fund raising, aid from other office holders who are women, more active financial support and counseling from female corporate executives, and more active support for top female candidates from men.[3] Following the 2002 elections there were five women serving as governor.

To some observers, this set of victories by women represents the third wave of recruitment of women into state politics. The first wave, up to the early 1970s, consisted of women winning as widows, wives, or daughters of established male politicians. The second wave, through the 1970s, consisted of women active in civic affairs shifting their volunteer work and contacts into political affairs. The third wave now evident is of women who have moved up the political ladder by defeating other candidates while keeping their eyes on a higher political goal such as becoming a legislative leader, much as men have. In other words, the third wave consists of upwardly mobile politicians who happen to be women.[4]

Abortion. In July 1989, midway through the New Jersey and Virginia gubernatorial races, the U.S. Supreme Court announced a major decision on abortion.[5] In effect, the Court began the process of reversing the standard set in an earlier decision, *Roe v. Wade* (1973), which had provided women the right under the U.S. Constitution to choose an abortion within a certain time period. This earlier decision also had the effect of giving governors and "state legislators the opportunity not to choose sides in a wrenching political debate."[6]

The impact of the 1989 decision was almost immediate as candidates for office in the states were asked their positions on the issue: were they prolife or prochoice? In both New Jersey and Virginia the abortion issue hurt the Republican candidates for governor because they held prolife views—in contrast to the more prochoice views of the Democratic candidates. But as the Republicans began to feel the heat of

the rapidly growing ranks of the prochoice activists—even from within their own party— and as they saw the numbers in their polls rising against them, they waffled on the issue, moving away from their previous prolife stand. That strategy seemed to hurt them even more.

Abortion politics continues to be a difficult problem for politicians. In the 1994 elections, exit polls found that between 8 and 18 percent of the voters indicated abortion was one of the two issues of greatest concern to them in voting.[7] Following the 1994 elections, twenty of the nation's governors were prochoice, and ten had a mixed record on the issue. In the 1995 state legislative sessions, at least thirteen states considered legislation calling for parental consent and notification and at least sixteen others considered mandating a waiting period.[8]

Independence. Voters in the states are becoming more independent in their voting choices. Increasingly, they are splitting their votes between party candidates. From the party politician's point of view, though, they are not becoming more independent, but rather more unreliable. Whether caused by ticket splitting or unreliable voting, the impact of this type of voting can be significant. Some examples make the point.

A look at the way voters chose their candidates in the 1992 races points out how common ticket splitting is in the states. The fact that independent presidential candidate Ross Perot received 19 percent of the vote nationwide indicates that nearly one-fifth of the voters had to have split their ballots if they voted for anyone else in the election. In Indiana, incumbent governor Evan Bayh (D) won with 63 percent of the vote while incumbent U.S. senator Dan Coats (R) won with 58 percent of the vote—a swing of twenty-one points. In 1994, Vermont governor Howard Dean (D) won with 70 percent of the vote, U.S. senator Jim Jeffords (R) won with 50 percent, and at-large congressman Bernard Sanders (I) won with 50 percent. In the 2000 elections in West Virginia, veteran Democratic senator Robert Byrd won with over 79 percent of the vote while George W. Bush won the state's electoral votes with 53 percent—a swing of thirty-two points. The Democratic candidate for governor, Robert Wise, barely won by two percentage points.

The results of such split-ticket voting are evident in the winners of state-wide elections. There are few states in which all statewide elected officials are members of just a single party.

As of March 1, 2003, Republicans controlled both houses of twenty-one legislatures to the sixteen that Democrats controlled. Twelve other states had split partisan control, including three states having a tie in one of their legislative chambers.[9]

Add to these twelve split partisan-control states the eight Republican governors facing Democratic-controlled legislatures and the eight Democratic governors facing Republican-controlled legislatures, and you have twenty-eight states with a "power-split" in state leadership. A power-split is defined when a governor is the member of one party and one or both houses of the state legislature are controlled by the other party.

In the 1990 gubernatorial elections, two states elected independent candidates: Walter Hickel in Alaska and Lowell Weicker Jr. in Connecticut. Both were former Republican office holders, but this time they ran as independents, defeating not only Democratic candidates but Republican candidates as well. Like the 1992 Perot voters, enough voters in these two states turned aside the two major party candidates for a leader free of normal party ties. In 1994 Maine voters also rejected both major party candidates and elected independent Angus King as governor. In 1998 King was reelected, and the political world and many in the state of Minnesota were startled to find that a former professional wrestler—Jesse "the

Body" Ventura, who ran on the Reform Party ticket—was elected governor of that state.

Race. Virginia's 1989 gubernatorial race was significant for more than how abortion affected that state's politics. The Commonwealth's voters elected the nation's first elected black governor, Lt. Governor L. Douglas Wilder (D). Even though Wilder won, public opinion polls—even polls taken as voters exited the voting booths—showed him winning by a much wider margin than was ultimately the case. This phenomenon of inflated public opinion strength skewing projections has occurred elsewhere when a minority candidate was running for a major office. This indicates that a new and subtle form of racism exists in which voters are reticent to admit that they will vote or just have voted against a minority candidate; hence the difference between how they say they voted and the actual vote totals.

Issues in State Politics

Issues in state campaigns vary considerably, not only from state to state but also among offices being contested. For example, campaigns for state legislative seats tend to focus on the individual candidate as he or she seeks to achieve name recognition among voters. Some candidates shy away from taking a position on specific issues, preferring instead to endorse economic development, reduction of crime, better education, and other broad issues. Others use specific issues such as anti-abortion, tax repeal, or growth limits to achieve the name recognition they need to win.

On the whole, however, candidates prefer to take a position on broad issues rather than commit themselves to something specific that could alienate potential supporters. As *State Policy Reports* has pointed out,

Campaigns rarely reveal candidate positions on the difficult questions of state policy. The easy question is whether candidates are for lower state and local taxes, better educational quality, higher teacher pay, and protecting the environment while stimulating economic growth. The candidates generally share these objectives. The hard question is what to do when these objectives collide as they often do.[10]

As a result, the average voter has a hard time discerning where the candidates stand on specific issues, and attempts to survey state legislative candidates on specific issues usually are not successful. But some issues are just too controversial and intrude into everyone's radar scope at election time. Abortion, as has already been noted, is one of these issues.

Another set of issues revolves around the question of representation: more precisely, the staying power of incumbents and the need to redraw many state legislative and congressional district lines following a U.S. census. The incumbency question has become an important issue in many states—a sort of "throw all the rascals out" perspective stemming from scandals and a realization that incumbents usually win. This drive has seen the successful passage of term-limit referendums limiting elective service in some of the states. Thus, constitutional provisions in these states now restrict an incumbent's stay in office if the voters won't. More efforts are planned in other states, even though the constitutionality of such added provisions is usually contested in the courts and several states that adopted term limits in the 1990s are now repealing them.

No issue is as intensely and personally political to state legislators as what many must do following each census—redraw district boundaries for themselves, as state legislators, and for U.S. representatives to achieve equal representation. The definition of equality is flexible and changing, however. And the issue is intensely personal because it has much to do with the legislators' chances of winning another election to the legislature, and intensely political because each party is trying to maximize its gains and minimize the gains of the opposition party. Add lawsuits and court decisions to the mix and this issue can have a long and unsettling life.

This section provides some perspective on the politics dominating our states early in the twenty-first century. Alan Ehrenhalt of *Governing* discusses the "Myths and Realities of Statehouse Power." Tim Storey of the National Conference of State Legislatures reviews the 2002 election results for state legislatures that presented the states with a lot of changes, and R. Doug Lewis of The Election Center explores the changes that states have and will need to continue making in the efforts at election reform. Both of their articles were from *Spectrum: The Journal of State Government*. Finally, Anya Sostek of *Governing* presents us with a portrait of one of the state officials trying to cope with electoral reform.

Notes

1. Malcolm Jewell, "Amendment Changes Elections," *Kentucky Journal* 5:1 (March 1993): 16.

2. Beverly Medlyn, "'Fab Five' Give Arizona Something to Brag About," stateline.org, February 3, 1999. In addition to the governor, the other offices were secretary of state, attorney general, superintendent of public instruction, and state treasurer.

3. Meg Armstrong, "WSEG Campaign News," *Women in State Government Newsletter*, May 1986, 4.

4. Comments of Celinda Lake, Candidate Services Director of the Women's Campaign Fund, at a National Conference of State Legislatures seminar as reported by David Broder, "Hard-Earned Credentials Give Female Candidates an Edge," (Raleigh) *News and Observer*, September 15, 1986, 13A.

5. *Webster v. Reproductive Health Services* (1989).

6. Wendy Kaminer, "From *Roe* to *Webster*: Court Hands Abortion to States," *State Government News* 32:11 (November 1989): 12.

7. "More Election Vignettes: Abortion," *The American Enterprise* 6:1 (January 1995): 110–111.

8. "Abortion and Govs," *The Hotline* 8:121 (March 17, 1995): 10–11.

9. Web site, National Conference of State Legislatures, *www.ncsl.org*, March 27, 2003.

10. *State Policy Reports* 2:20 (October 31, 1984): 13.

Myths and Realities of Statehouse Power

by Alan Ehrenhalt

When George W. Bush ran for president two years ago, it was with the help of some high-profile supporters at the statehouse level: Eight of the 10 most-populous states were governed by Republicans. In 2004, it won't be quite the same. Democrats took a serious bath in the elections last month, but they managed to climb out of the tub clutching the statehouse in half of the Top 10 and, even more remarkably, in 13 of the Top 20. As of next January, more Americans will be living under Democratic governors than under Republicans—at least 20 million more, as a matter of fact.

We all know why this is important: The more governorships a party controls, especially in the large states, the more of an advantage it has in seeking the White House. All the experts agree on it.

And all of them seemed to be repeating it before and after Election Day. "To have governors in these statehouses, in these large electoral states, is crucial," declared Democratic National Committee chairman Terry McAuliffe. "The Midwest will be critical," conceded Republican consultant Scott Reed. "It will be tougher to win with Democratic governors setting the agenda in those states."

Just how much difference can a governor make for his party's presidential nominee? Most commentators seem pretty much in agreement on this as well: 2 to 3 percentage points. This sounds plausible, until you stop and reflect that this is their answer to almost any question about the importance of any factor in elections. What can you expect to gain from a get-out-the-vote effort? 2 to 3 points. How much bounce can you expect from a strong debate performance? 2 to 3 points. What's the likely impact of a presidential visit on an off-year Senate race? 2 to 3 points.

If I were a little more cynical, I might suspect that the experts had hit upon a foolproof way to sound perceptive without actually knowing much. A couple of percentage points is a small enough number to seem plausible to almost anyone, and just precise enough to be convincing. That's not a criticism, of course. I may want to try this ploy myself sometime soon.

The beauty of such prognostications is that they are very hard to disprove. But they do

---

Alan Ehrenhalt is executive editor of *Governing*. This article is reprinted from *Governing* (December 2002): 6, 8.

submit to at least a rough kind of historical analysis. Just for fun, I tried it. When the last presidential election was held, in 2000, Republicans held the governorship in eight of the nation's 10 largest states. Bush won three of them—if you include Texas, where he himself was the governor, and Florida, where nobody even knows what happened. If you don't include Texas and Florida, Bush carried exactly one out of the GOP's Big Eight.

An aberration, you might say. But then I looked at 1996. The list of megastates was slightly different at that time, but Republicans still controlled the governorship in eight of them. Bob Dole carried one. If this is the kind of juice governors possess in presidential politics, it's been running a little thin lately.

Admittedly, the methodology isn't foolproof. Perhaps one should focus on individual states rather than the entire map at once. Bush carried Ohio in 2000 by a little more than 150,000 votes. A portion of this might possibly be attributable to the "governor's bonus" afforded him by the presence of Republican Bob Taft in the statehouse. Then again, it might not. At some point, the whole subject becomes so fuzzy as to cease being very interesting. About all you can say with confidence is that it helps to have the governor on your side if he is your brother, the result is extremely close and he is in charge of counting the votes. Otherwise, you shouldn't expect too much.

What's interesting is how journalists, consultants and other experts seem determined to find some connection between governors and presidential politics, however tenuous it might be. Second only to the "governors bonus" theory about presidential elections is the "new faces" theory. You hear this one all the time. After all, the theory goes, four of the last five men to win the White House emerged from gubernatorial ranks. Take a good look at the incoming governors of this year, and you will

see the presidential and vice presidential nominees of tomorrow.

Well, not tomorrow, exactly. Some time in the distant future would be more like it. Bill Clinton made it to the White House in 1992, but that was 14 years after his first election as governor of Arkansas. Fourteen years also elapsed between Ronald Reagan's initial gubernatorial victory in California and his victory for president. Even Michael Dukakis had to wait 14 years before being nominated to head the Democratic ticket—albeit unsuccessfully—in 1988. (Seems to be something in the 14-year apprenticeship, doesn't there? Maybe 2004 will be the year for Pete Wilson.)

George W. Bush made it to the White House after six years running Texas, but he was able to do that because he was a Bush, not because of anything he did as governor. In the entire 50-plus years of postwar history, only Jimmy Carter's election in 1976 provides any real evidence for the "new faces" doctrine. Carter can legitimately be said to have built on his record and contacts in one term as governor of Georgia to vault himself quickly onto the national political scene. But that's a slender thread to hang a cliché on.

It's even more slender when you consider governors as potential vice presidents. In the past 80 years, only one sitting governor has been elected vice president. That was Spiro Agnew in 1968. Before Agnew, you have to go all the way back to Calvin Coolidge. Stories about the new crop of governors producing fresh material for the next national ticket are no doubt flattering to the governors themselves. But they hardly have any historical basis at all.

Well then, if governors don't determine presidential results in their states, and they don't make quick, dramatic leaps into presidential politics, what makes gubernatorial elections worth devoting so much space to? Here's an answer that's so simple it tends to be overlooked: Governors are important not because they are electoral power brokers, or because they are future presidents, but because they make policy. They make national policy. It's arguable that they have been making more of it lately than Congress has.

Over the past decade, as Congress has mired itself ever more deeply in partisan gridlock, creative governors have moved in to fill the policy vacuum, sometimes out of ambition, sometimes out of sheer desperation.

After Congress failed to enact a health care program in the early 1990s, Vermont under Howard Dean began to enact one on a piecemeal basis that eventually grew to take in much of the middle class as well as the uninsured poor. Maryland's Parris Glendening all but invented the concept of Smart Growth, sold it to his legislature and then pushed it onto the national agenda effectively enough to generate new laws in states all over the country. The one legislative action of the 1990s most often cited as a genuine congressional accomplishment—passage of the welfare reform act of 1996—was, in fact, a derivative of experiments launched in Wisconsin under Tommy Thompson, and then tried in other places and judged to work.

It would be easy to come up with a much longer list. The 1990s produced a large crop of statehouse entrepreneurs in both parties who not only wanted to influence the national agenda but knew how to go about it. Virtually all of them are gone now, or will be next month, either through voluntary retirement, term limits or, in the case of Georgia's Roy Barnes, electoral defeat.

So if the era of gubernatorial activism is to continue, it will have to be in the hands of a new generation of activists. As it happens, a huge new generation is about to be sworn in— 24 of them, which would be the largest number of new governors to come in to office together in decades. They are the gubernatorial equivalent of the Baby Boom generation.

And they are being born into a situation far different from the one their predecessors were familiar with. Dean, Glendening, Thompson and their contemporaries had budget surpluses and significant amounts of cash to play with; the incoming Class of 2003 will be confronting the biggest state fiscal crisis in decades. Nearly every state is burdened by a tax system that doesn't generate enough revenue to meet its costs, and a combination of fixed spending commitments, foremost among them Medicaid, that are impossible to repudiate. And virtually all of these new governors campaigned for the office on promises not to raise taxes, or to cut spending in the few big categories where they have discretion, such as the schools.

But who's to say that austerity won't be as good a crucible for creative policy as prosperity. Faced with the need to break with precedent and find new ways to live within their means, at least a few members of the statehouse Baby Boom will turn out to be genuine innovators. And the experiments that succeed will force their way into national debate. That's the way things work now: Ideas flow up from the state capitals, not down from Washington.

And that's what makes governors interesting and makes their elections worth paying attention to. Treating them as adjuncts to presidential campaigns is not only useless—it misses the crucial point about how the American political system currently works.

2002 State Legislative Elections

by Tim Storey

When the book is closed on the 2002 legislative elections, Democrats will likely want to hide it on a high, out-of-the-way shelf to be forgotten. For Republicans, though, the story of the November 2002 elections is a page-turner with a happy ending destined for a prominent spot on the coffee table. In terms of total state house seats held by each party, Republicans nudged past the Democrats last fall for the first time in 50 years. The GOP emerged holding 21 state legislatures, more than it has controlled in five decades. While the GOP enjoyed a good election night, there were some bright spots for Democrats as well, and the final analysis shows that legislatures are still very evenly divided and likely to stay that way for the foreseeable future.

By every measure, this was a big election year for states. In addition to 36 governors' races, elections took place for more than 6,214 total legislative seats, or more than 85 percent of all seats in the 50 states. The total number of seats to be elected was up slightly from the usual 80 percent because 2002 was the first election following redistricting using the 2000 census data. In a handful of states like Illinois and Texas, senators run on a staggered schedule with either half or one-third of the body up

every two years. Some of those states also require that all members stand for election after redistricting with the result being that elections in years ending in "2" are the biggest in each decade. Forty-six states had regular legislative elections in 2002. Not holding elections were Louisiana, Mississippi, New Jersey and Virginia, who conduct legislative elections in odd numbered years. No regular senate elections were held in Kansas, New Mexico and South Carolina, only house races, so the total number of chambers holding elections last November was 89.

Mid-Term Election Trend. History has proven the party of the president has a difficult time gaining state legislative seats in mid-term elections. Since 1938—and possibly before, since records are not available—the president's party has lost an average of more than 350 seats in every midterm election cycle. Although that trend nearly ended in 1998, when, during Bill Clinton's second mid-term election, Democrats lost only one seat. Tucked comfortably into the

Tim Storey is a program principal in the Legislative Management Program of the National Center of State Legislatures. This article is reprinted from *Spectrum* (winter 2003): 7–11. Reprinted with permission from *Spectrum*.

2002 Gubernatorial Elections

Six eligible incumbent governors decided not to seek another term in 2002. Two governors decided to seek another office: Jeanne Shaheen (D-New Hampshire) ran unsuccessfully for a U.S. Senate seat, while Howard Dean (D-Vermont) began a campaign for the 2004 Democratic nomination for president. Two governors decided to retire after their first terms: George Ryan (R-Illinois) and Jesse Ventura (Reform-Minnesota). Two "accidental" governors, who succeeded to the governorship when the incumbent governor was appointed to a position in the Bush Administration, found little support for their own candidacies and retired from the governorship: Jane Swift (R-Massachusetts) and Mark Schweiker (R-Pennsylvania). These six seats added to the 14 other open seats meant that there were 20 open gubernatorial seats up in 2002.

Four incumbent governors lost their bids to serve a second term, a 25-percent non-success rate. The four losing incumbents were Don Siegelman (D-Alabama) Roy Barnes (D-Georgia), Jim Hodges (D-South Carolina) and Scott McCallum (R-Wisconsin). The three unsuccessful Democrats were from the deep South, which continues the South's move toward the Republican side of the aisle; the one unsuccessful Republican was an "accidental" governor who was not able to win the office on his own.

The remaining 24 races were won by candidates new to the gubernatorial office. They were equally split between the two parties–12 Democrats and 12 Republicans.

Source: Thad Beyle, *Spectrum* (winter 2003): 12.

wake of President George W. Bush's 65 percent popularity, Republicans netted more than 175 total seats in this cycle, including 2001 off-year elections in New Jersey and Virginia. The last time Democrats had a net gain in legislative seats was in 1996 when Bill Clinton won his second term.

Pundits emphasized that President Bush's strong approval rating almost certainly helped Republicans in legislative races down the ticket. The GOP also waged a stronger than usual "get out the vote" effort in several key states like Georgia, Missouri and New Hampshire helping boost Republicans running for all offices.

Regional Analysis. 2002 saw the GOP continue to chip away at the Democrats' traditional power base in the South. Democrats have lost southern seats in every legislative election cycle since 1982. That year they held 83 percent of all the seats in the region. Although it is still the strongest region for the Democrats,

only 56 percent of Southern legislative seats now belong to Democrats.

Republicans are strongest in the Midwest where they hold 58 percent of all legislative seats. Democrats find themselves at their lowest point in the Midwest since 1962. Democrats gained a net of five seats in the West where the party continues to creep upwards. Democrats are also still strong in the East where they claim 53 percent of all the seats. This includes controlling four of the six New England state legislatures

Redistricting. One of the most important factors in the 2002 elections was redistricting, which probably had more to do with the outcome of the elections than any traditional issue—more than education, roads or health care, and maybe even the economy. The U. S. Constitution mandates redistricting of all state legislative districts after the decennial census. This ensures that all districts are roughly equal in population and comply with the constitutional principle of one-person/one-vote. Before the 2002 elections, all but two of the states holding elections had completed the redistricting process. Maine and Montana did not have new districts in place for the 2002 election, but both of those states will do redistricting in time for 2004 elections.

In 11 of the 12 legislative chambers where party control switched in this first post-redistricting election cycle, either a commission or a court drew the new lines. Redistricting plans drawn outside the legislature leave the majority party in a more vulnerable position than if the legislature draws its own lines. In the 25 states where the legislature adopted its own redistricting plan, there were no party control changes. The only exception was the Georgia Senate, where a Democratic plan helped elect four Democrats who subsequently switched to the GOP, delivering control of the chamber to the Republicans.

Leaders. About a third of legislative leaders will not be serving in leadership roles next year. Some 120 leadership changes are expected when lawmakers convene in January 2003, including at least 46 Senate presidents, Senate presidents pro tem and House speakers. This comes close to the sweeping leadership changes in 1994 when 138 leadership posts changed.

Conclusion

Even though 2002 was a good year for the GOP and they continue to show strength in state legislative elections, state governments remain evenly divided between the two major parties. The most prominent issue facing almost all of the legislators who won in 2002 will be budget shortfalls. A recent NCSL fiscal survey indicates that states face a combined $18 billion budget shortfall before the end of 2003 fiscal year. 2004 does look even worse. Simply put, the state fiscal outlook is gloomier than it has been in over a decade, so many of the newly elected legislators may wonder why they sought to enter the field at such a challenging time. And no matter what course states plot through the fiscal straits that lie ahead, it is certain that most of them will have to identify bipartisan solutions given the even partisan balance that exists across the land.

Trends in State Elections: 2002 and Beyond

by R. Doug Lewis

State and local governments will be faced with a dramatic shift of elections responsibility as a result of the federal Help America Vote Act of 2002 (HAVA). It is imperative that state legislatures and local government officials recognize the changes required by the law and plan their responses to facilitate compliance.

The learning curve for states and local governments is likely to be significant, but since the 2004 elections have to be conducted under the new law, the learning cycle has to be immediate. There is little luxury of time to work out long-term strategies. Written state plans required by law will need to be developed quickly in early 2003 if there is to be any chance that states can be in compliance by 2004.

Voter Registration

Some provisions of HAVA take place immediately. For instance, on January 1, 2003, voters who register by mail need to provide positive identification of who they are before they can vote. In 2004, the voter registration form must include a question on citizenship and age. Further requirements in the law mandate all voter registrations must include either a driver's license number or the last four digits of the voter's Social Security number. If the voter has

neither of those, the state must provide a unique identification number for that person.

From a practical standpoint, election officials are unlikely to look at these requirements separately. They will need to redesign the voter registration forms to include such information and make the forms available almost immediately.

Voter Databases

States are mandated to develop, own and maintain a central statewide voter database that is interactive with local elections jurisdictions. The new law indicates it wants those databases ready by 2004, but it grants until 2006 for compliance.

Some states have already developed a voter database with information accumulated from local governments in whatever software format they have it. Many officials now believe that anything less than states providing local jurisdictions with identical software to be used for accumulation of voter registration information

---

R. Doug Lewis is executive director of The Election Center, Houston, Texas. This article is reprinted from *Spectrum* (winter 2003): 5–6. Copyright 2003 The Council of State Governments. Reprinted with permission from *Spectrum.*

Web Sites to Visit

Here are some starting points if you want more details on the states individually or collectively:

http://stateline.org	A daily review of media coverage of issues, events, and activities in the fifty states. It also contains some comparative data on the states.
http://csg.org	The national state government perspective from the Council of State Governments.
http://ncsl.org	The national state legislative perspective from the National Conference of State Legislatures.
http://nga.org	The national state gubernatorial perspective from the National Governors' Association.
http://www.electionline.org	The Election Reform Information Project Web site provides links to all major election reports along with daily news about developments.
http://state.al.us	The state of Alabama's Web site and entry point to the range of information available from all of Alabama's agencies and programs. This specific address is for Alabama [al]. For other states, use their zip code abbreviation [ak → wy]

Remember to check for links to other interesting Web sites containing information on the states when you visit a specific state agency or program's Web site.

Source: Thad Beyle.

is the only answer allowed by the law. This is likely to cause furor from local governments who have traditionally designed and maintained their own voter registration programs.

Opponents of giving up local databases to a central state-owned and maintained database will argue that such a database is unlikely to work and that voters will be disenfranchised. Opponents contend that moving to a state database will cause errors and inefficiencies—if not an outright shutdown of the local process. They point to several states that have attempted statewide voter databases that are error-filled or dysfunctional for use as an effective tool in conducting elections.

Proponents of the single statewide database argue that Kentucky, Louisiana, Michigan, Oklahoma, South Carolina and Virginia—

among others—have very functional statewide databases and that their local officials find them useful and accomplish the desired task of cutting down on duplications.

Regardless of how officials at state and local levels feel about the requirements and which is the correct means of compliance, if the discussion of whether a state is going to require a single, central piece of software gets bogged down in arguments between local and state governments, meeting the deadlines of the law on this provision will prove difficult, if not impossible.

Funding

The HAVA legislation is about reordering priorities and indicates the federal government will provide funding to accomplish those goals.

Books to Visit

Here are some starting points if you want more specific information on the fifty states:

Barone, Michael, and Grant Ujifusa. *The Almanac of American Politics, 2002*. National Journal, 2001.

Council of State Governments. *The Book of the States, 2003*. Council of State Governments, 2003.

Gray, Virginia, and Russell L. Hanson. *Politics in the American States: A Comparative Analysis*. 8th ed. CQ Press, 2003.

Hovey, Kendra A., and Harold A. Hovey. *CQ's State Fact Finder 2003*. CQ Press, 2003.

Remember to check bibliographies and footnotes for other interesting publications containing information on the states.

Source: Thad Beyle.

The law specifies that state officials certify to the federal government that they comply with federal disability laws and National Voter Registration Act provisions (where applicable) before they can qualify to receive money under HAVA.

Whatever funding is done by Congress on HAVA, however, the chief state election official will have a significantly increased responsibility of supporting local governments in implementing and ensuring compliance with HAVA. The key concept for policymakers and implementation administrators to understand is that it is states that will become responsible for assuring the compliance with the law and the measurement of progress under the law.

Questions and Concerns

Does the state plan to get rid of punch cards and lever machines in order to qualify for voting system buyout incentives under Title I of the Act? If one jurisdiction in the state wants to receive money under the provisions for buyout, does the Act require that all jurisdictions within the state to do likewise? It is unclear if

using federal funds to buy one new voting system for a local jurisdiction requires all jurisdictions in the state to immediately provide one voting device fully accessible to voters with disabilities per polling site.

Has the state adopted a legal definition, or given the state's chief election official the authority to define, what actually constitutes a vote so that all jurisdictions in the state are using the same criteria in counting votes? These definitions have to be according to each generic type of voting equipment (e.g. optical scan, paper or punch card ballot, lever machine or direct recording equipment—DRE).

Will the state receive and spend all of the money at the state level? Or will the state develop plans with each of the local election jurisdictions and pass money through to the local jurisdictions? This is a major decision and has far-reaching impact. If the state chooses to keep all of the money at the state level, and then spends that money buying a statewide voting system, developing a statewide voter database, requiring state training or certification of local

Journals to Visit

Here are some starting points for analyses of trends, problems, politics, and policies occurring in the states and their local communities:

Governing (See especially the April supplement, *State and Local Sourcebook*.)	Congressional Quarterly—monthly
Spectrum	Council of State Governments—quarterly
State Government News	Council of State Governments—monthly
State Legislatures	National Conference of State Legislatures—monthly
State Policy Reports	State Policy Research—biweekly
State Politics and Policy Quarterly	Academic journal—quarterly

Source: Thad Beyle.

election officials, and providing funds for making voting equipment and polling sites fully accessible to people with disabilities, how will those decisions be made and supported by the political system? Will legislators be willing to withstand the political heat from county commissioners and local elections administrators because they are not receiving a more direct funding method?

If the state is to be responsible for how the funds are spent and accountable to the federal government for compliance, should the states even engage in pass-through funding? Such pass-through funding is permissible under HAVA, but is this a correct choice? Further, if the state decides to do pass-through funding, is it to be based on a specific formula or is it to be on a needs-assessment basis? If it is the latter, who and how are decisions made to determine needs? Also, if pass-through funding is chosen, how does the state assure compliance with HAVA since the state is responsible? While the law doesn't set many specific penalties for noncompliance, other than repayment of the funds

sent to the state, can political figures stand up to the political pressures of noncompliance by a local jurisdiction or jurisdictions?

Since the law essentially forces most states to change their voting equipment to "touch screen" or DRE equipment (at least one device per precinct for use of the disabled and other voters), should the state become the technical experts by hiring technical programming staff and equipment maintenance staff? If not, how do local jurisdictions afford such expertise? What of the other costs of fully electronic equipment, such as special storage facilities? Also, since all electronic gear has a percentage of failure rates, who is to do the pre-election and post-election tests? Should that be a state function (such as performed by Georgia, Oklahoma and Rhode Island) or the responsibility of local jurisdictions?

Provisional voting is required of all states. Provisional voting is to be offered to any voter who asserts that they meet the requirements of voting within the state and jurisdiction but does not appear on the official voter rolls. Qualifying the provisional voters and the voter's ballot after the election takes time, however. California, for example, uses a full 28 days after an election to verify the eligibility of provisional ballot voters. Under HAVA, most states now have two weeks or less to complete an election and certify the results. Are legislatures going to change the number of days allowed to verify voter eligibility? Without such verification time, provisional voters may be denied the opportunity to have their vote counted. Are states prepared to handle the extensive lawsuits that are likely to result from too few days to qualify provisional ballots?

The new law makes the state responsible for developing a complaints procedure so that voters can notify the state immediately of anything they believe is wrong with a local elections process or operation. How will states structure such a process? Does it require starting with the local jurisdiction or bypassing it and making decisions at the state level?

Conclusion

State governments have to be aware that significant changes are forced due to the Help America Vote Act. While the law makes the chief election officer of each state responsible for implementation, no state can be successful without the support of its governor and state legislature. There needs to be recognition among all that elections, of necessity, must be conducted through local jurisdictions for the foreseeable future. Cooperation between state and local governments is vital to the continued health of America's democratic process. The legislation has the capacity to force great conflict between state and local governments unless unusual care and cooperation are fostered by all.

The end result could be not election reform, but failed elections, and those unintended consequences are simply unacceptable. Americans must have faith in their electoral process. Without it, they cannot believe in the government that results from the process. State governments have a new and large responsibility that must be carefully examined and carefully implemented. The alternative of chaos and confusion, with voters angry and distrustful of the electoral process itself, is too great a risk.

Machine Politics: Deploying—
Not Just Debating—New
Voting Technology

by Anya Sostek

Since the presidential election debacle in November 2000, Cathy Cox, Georgia's secretary of state, has been a zealous crusader for election reform. Against all odds, she successfully pushed an ambitious proposal past the legislature in time for the 2002 election. Cox's basic plan—putting touch-screen voting machines in every single Georgia precinct—has resulted in the most significant and far-reaching change anywhere in the country.

In many states, election reform degenerated into myriad study commissions, internal bickering and most of all, a long wait for Congress to pass an election-reform bill. In Georgia, Cox didn't let that happen. From the very start, she was hell-bent on getting new machines, reasoning that all momentum would be lost unless she acted immediately.

In the weeks after the 2000 election, Cox's office put together a report on Georgia's election performance. The results weren't pretty. The report estimated that bad election technology had spoiled 94,000 votes in Georgia, more than in Florida and almost double the national average. Election technology in Georgia ran the gamut, from paper ballots to lever machines to punch cards to optical scans, and the report showed serious flaws in all sys-

tems. Although Cox was committed to getting high-tech, touch-screen voting machines, she knew that most counties wouldn't change machines unless the state paid for them.

When she first went to the legislature with cost estimates on touch-screen machines, Cox says, "they told me that I was out of my mind." But in the following months, the price of the machines came down and the court ruled that bonds could be used to finance the upgrades. Despite a tough budget year, she was able to get the legislature to issue $54 million worth of bonds to buy 19,000 high-tech machines. Under the federal government's election-reform bill, most of the money will be reimbursed—something Cox argued for when she testified twice before Congress.

Not everyone agrees with Cox's methods—the value of touch-screen machines and the issue of statewide control over the election process are still up for debate—but few could dispute the accomplishment of overhauling a whole state's election system almost single-handedly. "For her to convince the legislature, get the funds and sell it to 159 county officials

Anya Sostek is an associate editor for *Governing*. This article is reprinted from *Governing* (November 2002): 33.

Election Reform

1. Ensure nondiscriminatory equal access to the elections system for all voters, including elderly, disabled, minority, military, and overseas citizens.

2. Encourage the adoption and enforcement of Election Day rules and procedures to ensure equal treatment of all voters.

3. Modernize the voting process as necessary, including voting machines, equipment, voting technologies and systems and implement well-defined, consistent standards for what counts as a vote throughout the election process ensuring accurate counts and minimal voter error.

4. Encourage states to adopt uniform state standards and procedures for both recounts and contested elections, in order to ensure that each vote is counted and to provide public confidence in the election system.

5. Provide election officials with increased funding to implement the recommendations of this resolution.

6. Conduct aggressive voter education and broad-based outreach programs.

7. Expand poll worker recruitment and training programs by adopting the innovative practices of other states and localities, with the ultimate goal of providing a satisfactory Election Day experience for all voters.

8. Maintain accurate voter registration rolls with a system of intergovernmental cooperation and communication.

9. Enhance the integrity and timeliness of absentee ballot procedures.

10. Adopt and adhere to the voluntary Federal Voting System Standards for voting systems.

11. Provide for continuous training and certification for election officials.

12. Collect data and election information on a regular and consistent basis to provide a nexus for public consumption and systemic improvements.

Source: National Association of Secretaries of State, "Election Reform," *Spectrum* (winter 2002): 37, 32.

is pretty remarkable," says Doug Chapin, director of the Election Reform Information Project. "If you had to pick a list of five people identified with election reform—not just because of what they said but what they did— she would be on it."

Cox, a lawyer and former state legislator from rural Georgia, first made history just by winning election to the secretary of state's office in 1998. With the exception of school superintendent, no other statewide office had ever been occupied by a woman. Although Cox exudes Southern charm, political insiders know that she can be as tough and aggressive as a street fighter—which is a good thing,

because her duties as secretary of state also include those of boxing commissioner.

This month, her handiwork will be put to the test. Rather than rolling out the machines in a special election or a primary, Georgia is doing it in the general election. With characteristic attention to detail, Cox also secured $4 million in cash for training—a particularly prescient move in light of Florida's numerous troubles with inconsistent poll-worker training in its September 2002 primary. That money includes 13 full-time staff members who do nothing but demonstrate the machines at grocery stores, churches and senior centers.

There's one other small detail that Cox hopes works out for her on Election Day: She's up for reelection and she'd like to win. In her opinion, her reelection campaign is the ultimate referendum on the new machines. "I wouldn't try to do this with my name on the ballot unless I was 1,000 percent sure of it," she says. "We will show the rest of the nation that this is the way to vote."

II. POLITICS: DIRECT DEMOCRACY

Voters in many states do more than choose candidates for state offices; they also vote directly on particular issues. Rather than have their elected representatives make the policy decisions, the voters themselves decide. This is called *direct democracy.* The concept of direct democracy has had a long history in the Midwest and West and at the local level in New England communities, where citizens and leaders often assemble in town meetings to determine the town budget as well as other policy issues.

There are three specific vehicles for citizens to use in states with direct democracy: *initiative, referendum,* and *recall.* In over one-third of the states, citizens may stimulate change in state constitutions by initiating constitutional amendments to be voted on in a statewide referendum. In nearly two-fifths of the states, an initiative provision allows proposed laws to be placed directly on a state ballot by citizen petition; the proposal is then enacted or rejected by a statewide vote. Three-fourths of the states have a referendum provision in their constitutions that refers acts passed by the state legislature to the voters for their concurrence before they become law. Most amendments to state constitutions are referred to the voters for approval; only in Delaware can the legislature amend the constitution without referring the proposed change to the people. In sixteen states, a recall provision allows voters to remove a state elected official from office through a recall election.[1] The most recent state to adopt the recall was New Jersey in the 1993 election when the voters approved it by a 3-to-1 margin.[2]

The importance of the voters' right to recall an elected official was demonstrated in Arizona in the late 1980s. The words and actions of Governor Evan Mecham, elected in 1986, so angered many Arizonans that a recall petition was circulated to remove him from office. This successful drive was part of the series of events that led to Mecham's removal

from office in April 1988, after he had served only seventeen months.

Mecham had won a three-candidate race by gaining only 40 percent of the general election vote. This political situation led to voter approval of a 1988 constitutional amendment calling for a runoff election should no candidate receive a majority vote in the general election—that is, no more plurality vote governors. However, the 1988 Arizona legislature failed to adopt the so-called "Dracula clause" in that state's constitution that would have barred Mecham, as an impeached official, from ever seeking or holding office again. He did seek the governorship in 1990 and drew enough votes in a third place finish to force the top two contenders into a February 1991 runoff. This again proves reforms often have unintended consequences.

Immediate Effects

The effects of direct democracy can be far reaching, affecting not only the state that has the initiative, referendum, or recall provision, but also other states and the broader political milieu in which state government operates. Some examples illustrate this phenomenon.

When California voters adopted Proposition 13 in 1978, they sent a message to elected officials across the country. This successful initiative put the brakes on state and local governments in California by restricting their ability to fund governmental programs and services. The initiative reduced property taxes to 1 percent of property value (a 57 percent cut in property tax revenues); future assessments were limited to an annual increase of only 2 percent; and a two-thirds vote of the state legislature was required for the enactment of any new state taxes.

The voters' message to state and local governments was clear: "We have had enough! We want less government, fewer programs, and greatly reduced taxes." This message—from what had been considered the most progressive electorate and state government among the fifty—prompted a widespread reevaluation of the goals of state and local governments. To what extent should elected officials expect the taxpayers to pay to achieve these goals?

More recently, the issue is term limits. Since 1990, nineteen states have imposed term limits on some of their elected officials in response to a general feeling that incumbents have too much of an advantage in any political campaign. Since the power of incumbency seems to be insurmountable in many states, the way to beat incumbents is to allow them to serve only a set number of terms or years. Starting with successes in three states in 1990 (California, Colorado, and Oklahoma), the movement spread to Washington state, where in 1991 the proposal was defeated by a narrow margin. In 1992, while everyone's eyes were on the presidential race, term limits were adopted in fourteen states, including Washington state, where it had reappeared on the ballot a second time.[3] Since then, the term limit movement has had some successes and some setbacks.

The vehicles used for winning these term limit victories are the initiative, which gets the issue on the ballot, and the referendum, which allows the people, not the legislature, to vote on the issue. Waiting for a state legislature to propose limits on its members' terms would appear to be fruitless, so success has been achieved through direct democracy (except in Utah). However, when the term limit movement meets up with states that do not employ direct democracy, it may well be stopped in its tracks unless some other vehicle can be found, or unless the political mood for term limits is so strong that a legislature must act.

One of the most interesting aspects of the term limit effort has been the level of government at which it has been directed. There would seem to be a strong argument that citizens can vote to limit the terms of elected representatives in state and local government by amending their state's constitution, although nothing is ever certain in our political system. But there has been a real constitutional question as to whether they can limit the terms of their federal representatives to the U.S. Senate and House of Representatives. This question was settled in a 5–4 U.S. Supreme Court decision on May 22, 1995, which rejected state efforts to restrict federal officials' terms.[4] Any change in the term limits of federal officials requires amendment of the U.S. Constitution, which sets only age, U.S. citizenship, and residency requirements.[5] This is not an easy task, as there is little support among the members of either chamber of Congress to propose an amendment to limit their own terms.

In 1996, the proponents of term limits took a new tack. Voters in fourteen states were asked to support a measure calling on any candidates for congressional office to seek to have such an amendment pass once they are elected. If they declined to do so, and won, this would be duly noted on the ballot the next time they ran. These measures succeeded in nine states, but were defeated in five others. However, an immediate challenge to this constitutional provision saw the Arkansas Supreme Court strike down this "scarlet letter" notation. In February 1997, the U.S. Supreme Court let that ruling stand without comment, a position reaffirmed by the U.S. Circuit Court of Appeals in March 1999 regarding the Nebraska "scarlet letter" provision.

Some Trends

In the first eighty years of the twentieth century there were about five hundred separate initiatives placed on state ballots, an average of about six a year. Following the 2002 elections, there had been 1,976 initiatives considered by the voters in twenty-four states since 1902. Oregon was the leader with 321 initiatives (16 percent) followed by California with 270 (14 percent).[6] In 1996, there were at least 90 citizen initiatives on the ballots of 20 states, in 1998 there were 64 in 16 states, and in 2000 there were 72 in 17 states. [7]

The initiative and referenda processes are not only becoming more prevalent in the states but more complex and expensive as well. The amount spent to qualify, support, or oppose the thirteen 1992 California referenda measures was over $40 million, with the opponents of a measure to increase a business tax spending nearly $10 million—"the largest amount ever spent to support or oppose a single state measure."[8] In 1988, the cost of fighting for or against the twenty-nine referenda on the 1988 general election ballot in California was $100 million, or $4 per capita.[9] Initiative and referenda politics are big business.

There is often a conservative ideological basis to these initiatives and referenda. That was true in the tax reduction efforts of the late 1970s, and was certainly true in some of the initiatives that came before the voters in the 1990s: term limits, minority rights for homosexuals, and removing affirmative action programs. Money, coordination, petition circulators, and other needs associated with running a successful initiative campaign have been emanating from sources on the right side of the political spectrum.[10]

In this section we learn from M. Dane Waters, president of the Initiative & Referendum Institute, more about this process of direct democracy. In these columns from *Campaigns & Elections* and *Spectrum* he raises the interesting question about state's rights in the initiative process and looks at results of the 2002 elections in regards to initiatives and referenda. A report from his Iniative & Referendum Institute discusses the impact of money on this direct democracy process.

Notes

11. *The Book of the States,* 1994–95 (Lexington, Ky.: Council of State Governments, 1994), 23, 294–308.

12. "Election Results: Full Reports, State by State," *USA Today,* November 4, 1993, 4A.

13. For an in-depth discussion of term limits, see Gerald Benjamin and Michael J. Malbin Jr., *Limiting Legislative Terms* (Washington, D.C.: CQ Press, 1992).

14. *U.S. Term Limits v. Thornton* (1995).

15. See Article I, Section 2, clause 2, and Section 3, clause 3, of the U.S. Constitution for these requirements.

16. "Initiative States Ranked in Order of Use, 1898–2000," National Conference of State Legislatures, *www.ncsl.org,* March 28, 2003.

17. Elaine Stuart, "Voters Make Laws," *State Government News* (December 1996): 31.

18. "Initiatives Can Be Expensive," *State Legislatures* 20:1 (January 1994): 9.

19. "The Long Ballot in California," *State Policy Reports* 6:15 (August 1988): 27–28.

10. Discussion with Dave Kehler, April 20, 1993. See also Stuart Rothenburg, "Transplanting Term Limits: Political Amobilization and Grass-Roots Politics" (pp. 97–113), and David J. Olson, "Term Limits in Washington: The 1991 Battleground" (pp. 65–96), in Benjamin and Malbin.

States' Rights and the Initiative Process

by M. Dane Waters

The line between the federal government and the states over who has the ultimate authority over the day-to-day lives of the citizens who live within a state's borders is constantly being defined. The Civil War was fought over this issue, and it has been a topic of courtroom drama for generations. It is clearly the role of the federal government to provide for national security, conduct foreign policy and conduct a host of other activities designed to facilitate some uniformity among the states so as to ensure that we don't end up in another civil war (even though some people would support the secession of Texas from the Union), but when federal law should supersede state law is of constant debate and without true definition.

Even though most Americans in theory support the concept of states' rights and dread the overreaching hand of the federal government, many argue as to where the line actually exists between the power of the states and the authority of the federal government. This line is being tested more and more often—not by laws passed by state legislatures—but by laws passed by the people, using the initiative process.

Since the inception of the initiative process in 1898 in South Dakota, the citizens have been placing laws on state ballots that were clearly designed to "push the envelope" between what is allowable legislation by the states and what is not allowed because it could be argued that it violates some federal statute. The prohibition and women's suffrage movements in the early twentieth century are notable examples as well as gay rights, term limits and abortion rights in the last decade. These issues have been pushed utilizing the initiative process and have lead to numerous legal challenges designed to help "define" the line between states' rights and the role of the federal government. The verdict has been mixed, and to this day no clear line exists that can be followed by the citizens in the states wishing to adopt change utilizing the initiative process.

However, though court challenges have been pursued to try and establish the "line," never before has the federal government been so vigorous in attempting to flex its muscle. Last month, Attorney General John Ashcroft instructed the Drug Enforcement Agency

M. Dane Waters is founder, president, and cochair of the Initiative & Referendum Institute in Washington, D.C. This article is reprinted from *Campaigns & Elections* (April 2002): 32.

(DEA) to enforce federal controlled substance laws that state it is "a felony violation of federal law to cultivate, distribute or possess with intent to distribute marijuana. . . ." The enforcement of this law effectively overturns citizen-sponsored and -adopted initiatives in eight states that legalized the dispensing of marijuana for medicinal purposes. Not only did Ashcroft effectively overturn the citizen-adopted medical marijuana laws, he also ordered the DEA to revoke the licenses of Oregon physicians who prescribe lethal doses of drugs to terminally ill patients. This action, once again, effectively overturned a citizen-sponsored initiative that had been adopted twice by the voters of Oregon. Federal Judge Robert Jones intervened and extended for five months an order prohibiting the DEA from taking action in Oregon.

These two examples will be critical moments for states' rights and will go a long way in helping define "the line" between the power of the states and the reach of federal statutes.

There is no doubt that regardless of the outcome of the litigation and legal action by the federal government regarding the role of states in regulating "controlled substances," reformers at the state level will continue to push reforms utilizing the initiative process that test the line and definition of states' rights. This next election cycle will definitely contain initiatives that fit this description.

Early reformers knew that even though statewide initiatives proposing women's suffrage might be illegal under federal law, they were necessary in getting the public and the federal government to focus on this important reform. Reformers of today are no different. They may know that they are "pushing the envelope" in placing on the ballot initiatives that conflict with federal statutes, but they also realize that it is the only way to get the people and the federal government to focus on their reforms.

I personally think this is good for democracy. The active participation of the citizens in highlighting reforms they believe in—utilizing the initiative process—exemplifies the freedoms that our soldiers are defending today. Resolving conflicts between state and federal laws is critical in establishing and defining the proper role of the federal government. The initiative process has served and will serve a critical role in facilitating this debate and defining the line between the states and the federal government.

2002 Initiatives and Referenda

by M. Dane Waters

On Election Day 2002, voters cast their ballots on 202 statewide ballot measures in 40 states and approved approximately 62 percent of them. Fifty-three were placed on the ballot by the people, and 149 were placed on the ballot by state legislatures. Of the measures placed on the ballot by the people, 47 percent were approved—slightly higher than the 100-year average of 41 percent. In looking at the measures placed on the ballot by state legislatures, voters continued the trend of passing those at a higher percentage than citizen measures by adopting almost 66 percent of them. Interestingly, there were 30 percent fewer initiatives on the ballot than 2000 and the fewest number since 1986.

Ballot Initiatives

Drug Policy. Coming into the 2002 election cycle, drug policy reformers had enjoyed a tremendous winning record, but they suffered a clean sweep defeat on their statewide initiatives (they did win a local measure in Washington, D.C. and one in San Francisco). Ohio voters chose not to adopt Issue One that would have allowed for treatment instead of incarceration of non-violent drug offenders while Nevadans chose to vote down Question 9 that would have legalized marijuana for recreational purposes. In a surprising outcome, voters voted down Proposition 203 in Arizona that would have legalized medical marijuana. Two closely watched drug related initiatives in South Dakota were defeated. Amendment A would have allowed a criminal defendant to argue the merits of the law and possibly be found innocent because the jury found the law itself to be bad public policy. Measure 1 would have legalized industrial hemp (cannabis).

Many have argued that the reason this election cycle has proven to be more difficult for the drug policy movement than previous elections is due to the extraordinary step by John Walter (President Bush's drug policy advisor) and Asa Hutchison (head of the Drug Enforcement Administration) in actively campaigning against these measures—a move that many believe may lead to litigation regarding the federal government's involvement in political

M. Dane Waters is the founder, president and cochair of the Initiative & Referendum Institute, Washington, D.C. This article is reprinted from *Spectrum* (winter 2003): 20–21. Copyright 2002 The Council of State Governments. Reprinted with permission from *Spectrum* and M. Dane Waters.

campaigns. Regardless of the outcome of this election cycle, there is little doubt that the drug policy reform movement will continue to utilize the initiative process in its quest to raise awareness of the reforms they are seeking.

Animal Rights. Animal rights advocates fared well on Election Day. The animal protection movement emerged in the 1990s as a dominant issue at the ballot box; this election cycle was no exception. Voters in Oklahoma approved an initiative outlawing cockfighting while voters in Florida voted to ban the use of gestation crates for pregnant pigs. On the losing side was an Arkansas initiative that would have made cruelty to animals a class D felony instead of the current class A misdemeanor. The Florida win will help energize the movement to ban gestation crates across the country leading to more ballot measures on this issue in the near future.

Education Reform. Another favorite at the ballot box has been education reform, and this election cycle continued the trend. Five initiatives are especially worth noting. In California, Arnold Swartzenegger's Proposition 49 won handily. The initiative will "increase state grant funds available for before and after school programs." This impressive victory will no doubt give the "Terminator" the political prestige he wanted to launch his rumored gubernatorial campaign.

In Colorado and Massachusetts voters decided on initiatives that would require children to be taught by using the English language in the classroom. These two initiatives follow wins on this issue in Arizona and California. The surprising thing about these two initiatives is where they won and lost. This issue, which is usually personified as a conservative issue, won handily in the liberal state of Massachusetts (Question 2) but lost in conservative Colorado (Amendment 31). This just goes to show that voters can't be expected to vote straight party ideology when voting on ballot measures.

Floridians dealt with two high-profile education initiatives. Measure 8, requiring "every four-year-old child in Florida be offered a high quality pre-kindergarten learning opportunity," won by a narrow margin as did Measure 9. Measure 9 will "provide funding for sufficient classrooms so that there be a maximum number of students in public school classes." Measure 9 had become a big issue in the governor's race with candidate Bill McBride throwing strong support behind it while Gov. Jeb Bush was caught in an unfortunate candid moment saying that he had already thought of several "devious ways" to keep the measure from going into [e]ffect.

Election Reform. One of the biggest losers on Election Day was election reform. In California and Colorado, voters said no to initiatives that would have put in place what is commonly referred to as "same day voter registration." Three other Colorado initiatives are also worth noting. Amendment 29, which would have changed the way candidates are placed on the primary ballot by requiring nominating petitions instead of relying on nominating conventions, was defeated. Amendment 28, which would have allowed for mail ballot elections, was defeated as well. The third, Amendment 27, was victorious. Amendment 27 will "reduce the amount of money that individuals and political committees can contribute."

One of the more telling signs of the political feelings of the electorate was exemplified in Idaho where voters gave a controversial endorsement to a measure that would abolish term limits in Idaho. However, this victory for state lawmakers is being overshadowed by persistent stories of voter confusion over which way to vote on the ballot measure.

Gaming. Several ballot measures dealing with expanding gaming or creating a lottery were put before the voters but, as is usually the case, they didn't fair well. In Arizona, three initiatives were voted on that dealt with gaming.

Propositions 200 and 202 dealt with expanding Indian gaming and dictating where and how the proceeds should be divided had mixed results. Proposition 200 was soundly defeated while Proposition 202 passed. The other initiative, Proposition 201, would have allowed for "non-tribal gaming" in the state and was defeated overwhelmingly. In Idaho, voters decided to allow video gaming on Indian land and voters in North Dakota decided to "direct the legislative assembly to authorize the state to join a multi-state lottery."

Tax Reform. Since 1978's Proposition 13 in California cut property taxes, tax reformers have used the initiative process religiously; this election cycle was no different. However, it wasn't exactly a banner year for tax cut advocates. The voters of Massachusetts voted down Question 1 that would have abolished their state income tax, while voters in Arkansas defeated an initiative that would have abolished certain taxes on their food and medicine. Regardless of these outcomes, tax cutters will be back in future elections to carry on the legacy California's Proposition 13.

Honorable Mentions. Voters also showed their resolve to maintain the norm with the defeat of two high-profile measures in Oregon—Measure 23 would have called for universal health care and Measure 27 would have called for the labeling of genetically modified foods. These defeats do not necessarily mean that voters don't support these reforms—it's just that given the uncertainty of the times these are items that they feel can be addressed in the future—but not now. Smoking was another area that voters spoke out on. In Florida the voters adopted Amendment 6 that will ban smoking in all public places. In Missouri, voters chose not to increase cigarette taxes, while in Arizona the voters decided to make cigarette taxes $1.18 a pack—more than double the current rate. As to social policy, not much was on the ballot this

election cycle with the exception of banning same sex marriage in Nevada. Nevadans voted once again (by law amendments must be voted on twice before becoming law) to adopt the ban.

Referenda

Over the last couple of election cycles, and especially since the fiscal impact of Sept. 11, state legislatures have been looking at ways to increase revenues in their states. At least 40 states will have budget deficits this year, and in this election cycle, lawmakers were hoping that the voters would "ease their pain" and give them more money to spend. In short—the verdict is mixed. Tennessee lawmakers were hoping to establish a lottery, and voters decided to help them by passing Amendment A-1. In Louisiana, Montana, and South Carolina, voters were asked to give lawmakers greater latitude in investing in the stock market. The voters for the most part said no, with the exception of one measure in South Carolina—essentially telling lawmakers that the stock market is too risky to be investing public funds. As to bonds, California voters adopted the largest bond measure in the state's history; Proposition 47 will raise $13 billion for an across-the-board overhaul of the state's public school facilities. Other bond measures across the country seamed to fare well also.

Conclusion

So what did we learn from the voters? Primarily, faced with uncertain economic times and the possibility of war, voters chose to be cautious and maintain the status quo, with one obvious exception—education reform. The reason for this, many argue, is that during tough fiscal times voters feel that big ticket road projects and other costly non-education-related items can wait until economic times are better and they are more comfortable approving them. What can't wait is the education of their kids.

What Impact Does Money Have in the Initiative Process?

by the Initiative & Referendum Institute

In recent years, economic interest groups with vast financial resources have used the initiative process with increasing frequency. Such groups often spend millions of dollars to promote their political causes, taking their cases directly to voters. These expensive, high profile campaigns have lead many observers to conclude that by spending vast sums, narrow, wealthy economic interest groups are now able to use the initiative process to pass laws at the expense of broader citizen interests. But can this point be proven? In short, no.

There is no doubt that individuals, industry sectors and special interest groups with large sums of money are using the initiative process to seek reforms they want—but this isn't new. In the early days of the initiative process, businesses with an interest in selling alcohol and other spirits to the masses used the initiative process to try and overturn prohibition laws—but they were rarely successful. In the 1920s and 30s, the chiropractic industry used the initiative process, with varying degrees of success, to get states to allow them to practice. In the 1980s and 90s, denturists (the people who make dentures, etc.) used the initiative process to try and get state laws changed so that they, in addition to dentists,

could be licensed to make and sell dentures to the public. They felt that dentists had a monopoly and so they tried to stop it—but they were only moderately successful. Since 1912, gambling and lottery interests have used the initiative process to expand their industry. However, after spending tens of millions of dollars over a 90-year period, the industry has only been successful in passing less than 25% of the initiatives they attempted. This is why the industry has chosen not to pursue initiatives to expand their interests. They realize that money alone will not pass an initiative.

In the last decade alone, numerous wealthy individuals have tried to enact reform through the initiative process only to lose after spending millions of dollars. George Soros, Gene Sperling and Peter Lewis spent millions of dollars in 2000 to try and get a drug policy reform initiative passed in Massachusetts only to be defeated. Dick DeVos (the founder of Amway), along with several other wealthy individuals spent almost $30 million dollars in the 2000 election cycle to try and get school choice initiatives adopted—they too were left empty

---

This article is reprinted from iandrinstitute.org (March 16, 2003).

handed on election night. In yet another example, millionaire Ron Unz, the successful architect of the California and Arizona initiatives to require that schools teach in English only (with some exceptions), saw his campaign finance reform initiative handily defeated in California in 2000—after spending a substantial amount of his own money. Numerous more examples can be given, but in short, just because you have money doesn't mean you can buy a law at the ballot box. But let's look [past] the anecdotal examples and look at the academic research that has been conducted in this area.

Professor Liz Gerber of the University of California, San Diego and arguably one of the most well respected academics in the study of the initiative process, wrote a book on the role and influence of money in the initiative process. For the book, *The Populist Paradox* (Princeton University Press, 1999), she analyzed surveys of interest group activities and motivations, as well as campaign finance records from 168 different direct legislation campaigns in eight states. Her research found that ". . . economic interest groups are severely limited in their ability to pass new laws by initiative. Simply put, money is necessary but not sufficient for success at the ballot box. By contrast, research found that citizen groups with broad-based support could much more effectively use direct legislation to pass new laws. When they are able to mobilize sufficient financial resources to get out their message, citizen groups are much more successful at the ballot box, even when economic interest groups greatly outspend them."

Additional research by political scientists Todd Donovan, Shaun Bowler, David McCuan, and Ken Fernandez found that while 40% of ALL initiatives on the Californian ballot from 1986–1996 passed, only 14% of initiatives pushed by special interests passed. They concluded, "[o]ur data reveals that these are indeed the hardest initiatives to market in California,

and that money spent by proponents in this arena is largely wasted." This research complements political scientist Anne Campbell's research on special interest–backed initiatives in Colorado from 1966 to 1994. Her research found that during those 28 years, only ONE initiative pushed by special interests was successful at the ballot box.

This is not to say, however, that wealthy economic interest groups have no influence on initiatives appearing on the ballot. They have been very successful in blocking initiatives they do not like. Not because they are buying a "no" vote, but because voters are 1) predisposed to vote against any new law—regardless of if it is proposed by the people or the state legislature and 2) are more likely to vote no and maintain the status quo when confronted with a new law that they are uncertain about. This is supported by the fact that only 41% of all the statewide initiatives to appear on the ballot have been approved by the citizens.

Regardless of the fact that research shows that money can't buy a new law at the ballot box, there have been numerous attempts at regulating the amount of money spent on ballot measure campaigns. In most cases, the proposed laws have attempted to limit the amount of money corporations could spend in either support or opposition of ballot measures. However, state and federal courts, including the U.S. Supreme Court in 1977, have consistently ruled that states cannot limit the amount of money in ballot measure campaigns. Their basic logic has been that you can't corrupt a piece of paper (the ballot measure) and therefore there is no need in limiting the amount of money spent on these campaigns. This is where they apply a different standard in those cases pertaining to contributions to candidate campaigns—the courts have upheld contribution limits to candidates because of the possibility of corruption. *In short, any attempt to regulate the amount of money in ballot measure campaigns would be viewed as unconstitutional given the current case law.*

There is no doubt that there will continue to be large sums of money associated with initiative campaigns. But it is important to understand why. The main reason is the growing regulation of the initiative process by state legislators. They have been swayed by the rhetoric that money has corrupted the initiative process—even though there is no academic research to support this viewpoint. Their new regulations are the cause for the growing amount of money in initiative campaigns. More regulation just means that initiative proponents will just spend more money to overcome these hurdles. The loser in this scenario is the average citizen. They do not have the resources to overcome these hurdles and therefore are locked out of the process. If legislators are concerned about wealthy individuals and special interest[s] being the only ones using the process, then they should make the process more accessible to those individuals without access to large sums of money.

III. POLITICS: PARTIES, INTEREST GROUPS, AND PACS

Politics in the American states is changing. Political parties, once the backbone of the U.S. political system and the chief force in state government, are becoming less influential, or so say many observers. As Malcolm Jewell and David Olson point out, "It has become a truism that party organizations are declining in importance, and there is no reason to anticipate a reversal of that trend."[1] Whether they are in decline or have just assumed new roles, most observers agree political parties are an adaptable and durable force in the states, as they "remain the principal agencies for making nominations, contesting elections, recruiting leaders, and providing a link between citizens and their government."[2]

But what are political parties? This question must be addressed before the reasons for these different interpretations can be understood. Are they the organizations from precinct to national convention—*the party in organization?* Are they the individuals who run, win, and control government under a party label—*the party in office?* Or are they the voters themselves, who identify more with a particular party and vote accordingly—*the party in the electorate?* Political parties are all three, diverse in definition and ever-changing in their impact on state government.

Perhaps the clearest signal that parties sway voters less than they once did is the rise of split-ticket voting. In state and local elections in 1956, only 28 percent of the voters who identified themselves as either Democrats or Republicans did not vote the straight party line but split their tickets by voting for candidates of both parties; in 1980, 51 percent split their tickets.[3] In 1986, 20 percent of those identifying themselves as Democrats and 17 percent of those identifying themselves as Republicans voted for the U.S. Senate candidate of the opposing party.[4] This divided party voting and its impact is discussed in further detail in the introduction to Part I.

What's Happened to the Parties?

Various explanations have been offered for the decline of political parties. Direct primaries—the means by which party voters can participate directly in the nomination process rather than have party leaders select candidates—certainly have curtailed the influence of party organizations. By 1920 most of the states had adopted the direct primary.[5] No longer could party organizations or party bosses rule the nominating process with an iron hand, dominate the election campaigns, and distribute patronage positions and benefits at will. The ability to circumvent official party channels and appeal directly to the electorate greatly increased the power of individual candidates. A candidate's personality has taken on new importance as party affiliation has become less influential in gaining votes.

In the current environment, parties are challenged by the mass media, interest groups, independent political consultants, and political action committees—vehicles that perform many of the historic functions of the political party. Public opinion polls, rather than party ward and precinct organizations, survey the "faithful." Today,

. . .[P]olitical consultants, answerable only to their client candidates and independent of the political parties, have inflicted severe damage upon the party system and masterminded the modern triumph of personality cults over party politics in the United States.[6]

One analyst argues, however, that the rise of the political consultant has opened up the political process through the use of polls and other techniques. Now candidates can talk about the issues voters are concerned about without the "party communications filter."[7]

Candidates have also changed, and some of these changes do not help the parties. For example, we are seeing more independent candidates running for office. These independents are no less political than other candidates, but are simply independent of the two major parties. At the national level, the 1992 and 1996 presidential runs by Texas billionaire Ross Perot is an example of this phenomenon. At the state level, two governors elected in 1990, Walter Hickel of Alaska and Lowell Weicker of Connecticut, both ran and served as independents, as did Angus King of Maine, elected in 1994 and 1998, and Jesse Ventura of Minnesota, also elected in 1998. There will be others.

More important is the rise of the self-starting candidate with both fiscal and political resources of his or her own. These candidates can afford to run for office on their own, needing the party only for its nomination to get on the ballot. Such "candidate-centered campaigns are becoming more prevalent at the state level," and as they do, "party-line voting is declining."[8] Alan Ehrenhalt argues that "political careers are open to ambition now in a way that has not been true in America in most of this century."[9] He believes these self-starting candidates are motivated by their personal ambition, which drives their entry into politics. Because the candidates can "manipulate the instruments of the system—the fund raising, the personal campaigning, the opportunities to express themselves in public—[they] confront very few limits on their capacity to reach the top."[10]

The 1994 elections, across the states, present an interesting contrast to the trends mentioned above. The sweeping victories of Republicans at all levels of government suggested the possibility that parties are not quite as moribund as many think. This possibility seemed especially plausible because the Republicans banded together with a common set of positions on certain issues, making their candidacies more party based than individually based. The results of the 1996 and 1998 elections reversed the 1994 results to some extent, as many candidates resumed more individually based campaign styles.

To most citizens, parties are important only during the election season. Our system is unlike that of most European countries, where there are rigid election schedules in which campaigning is limited to a specific time period. The American state and local government election season is generally thought to start around Labor Day in early September and run until election day in early November. Cynics believe that this is too long, and that in most voters' minds the season really begins at the end of the World Series in late October. Of course, the candidates have been at work for months, even years, getting ready for this unofficial election season, but the impact of other events often conspires to distract the electorate. (Of course, in 1994, due to the professional baseball strike, there was no World Series, and it thus was not a factor. Some have suggested that the loss of the World Series also had an effect on the fans, who, unable to vent their emotions during the games, did the next best thing by venting their anger at politicians.)

Signs of Party Resurgence

Yet not everyone is ready to declare the parties moribund. As noted, the party process is still the means of selecting candidates for national, state, and, in some cases, local office.

Control of state legislatures is determined by which party has the majority, with the exception of the non-partisan Nebraska legislature. Appointments to state government positions usually go to the party colleagues of state legislators or of the governor.

Although the party in organization and the party in the electorate are weaker than they once were, the party in office may be gaining strength, argues Alan Rosenthal. Legislators are increasingly preoccupied with winning reelection. The "art of politicking" may be superseding the "art of legislating."[11] Party caucuses have begun to play an important role in selecting the legislative leadership, assigning committee and other responsibilities, and establishing positions on issues.

In fact, the party in organization may not be as weak as many think. Since the 1960s, budgets and staffs have grown in size, staffs have become more professional, party services and activities have increased, and elected leaders may be even more involved in party affairs.[12] Now, some feel that the money these state parties can raise and the campaign services they provide to their candidates and local affiliates have made them a strong force in state politics.[13] In a few words, these state parties have become "service" organizations, serving those who are running for office under the party label.

Of course, party politics differ in each state. As Samuel C. Patterson writes, "In some places parties are strong and vigorous; in other places, they are sluggish; in yet others, moribund. But, on balance, the state parties appear remarkably vibrant."[14]

Interest Group Politics

Are interest groups an evil that must be endured or are they a necessary part of the governing process? Is their impact on state government primarily beneficial or harmful? Perhaps most importantly, do the interests that groups seek to advance or protect benefit the whole state or only the lobbies themselves? State officials, pressured by a myriad of interest groups, wrestle with these questions and reach different answers.

Interest groups' influence on the political process varies from state to state. Business groups are by far the most predominant; the influence of labor groups pales in comparison. Thus, the interest group structure of most states is business-oriented and conservative.

Lately, however, groups representing government employees, local government officials, and the public interest (for example, Common Cause and environmental protection groups) have increased their visibility and effectiveness in state politics.

An interest group's effectiveness depends on the representatives it sends to the state legislature and executive branch agencies—the so-called professional lobbyists. Who are these people? Usually they have served in government and are already known to those they seek to influence. Their ranks include former agency heads, legislators, and even governors in private law practice who have clients with special interests. Some of the most effective lobbyists represent several interests.

The relationship between political parties and interest groups in the states tends to vary by state and often by region. In some states there are both strong party and interest group systems (Illinois, Michigan, and New York). In some other states both the party and interest group systems are relatively weak (South Dakota and Vermont). And in some southern and western states there is an inverse relationship of weak party and strong interest group systems. Two observers of interest groups in the states suggest "the party-[interest] group relationship does undergo constant change both across the states and within particular states."[15]

Theoretically, in a competitive, two-party state, the stakes are more likely to be out in the open as one party fights the other for control. Conversely, in the noncompetitive, one-party state, the stakes are less easy to see as interest groups do battle with each other to maintain or change the status quo. Again, in theory, the power of the party flows from the voters through their elected representatives; the power of interest groups is derived from their numbers, money, and lobbying skill. But in practice the relationship is not as clear as this explanation would suggest. In fact, once the parties organize state government, state politics usually becomes the special quarry of interest groups—except, of course, on distinctive, party-line issues (such as selecting the leadership), or when there are other institutions with political strength, such as the governor or the media.

One Person, One Vote

Following the decennial U.S. census in the "0" year of the decade, there is an overtly political issue that the members of the state legislatures in most all states must focus upon. Due to changes in population, new district lines must be drawn for congressional and state legislative districts. Legislatures used various devices such as the gerrymander (excessive manipulation of the shape of a legislative district to benefit a certain incumbent or party) or silent gerrymander (district lines were left intact despite major shifts in population).[16] Both types of legislative legerdemain resulted in underrepresentation of minorities and those living in the cities.

As a result of this misrepresentation, the U.S. Supreme Court ruled in the landmark decision *Baker v. Carr* (1962) that federal courts had the power to review legislative apportionment in the states. Two years later, in *Reynolds v. Sims,* the Court ruled that both houses of a state legislature must be apportioned on the basis of population—that is, "one person, one vote." And in the *Davis v. Bandemer* (1986) case, the Court gave political parties standing in court suits over apportionment if a particular political party felt gerrymandered unfairly. And which party won't feel treated unfairly if it does not get the legislative apportionment plan that helps it the most? In *Colgrove v. Green* (1946), the Court indicated that it wanted to stay out of the "political thicket" of apportionment; forty years later it jumped squarely into that thicket.

Redistricting is always one of the most politically charged issues that state legislatures find on their agendas, since it directly affects the legislators themselves and is so overtly political. Each party tries to maximize its potential strength in future elections, and concurrently reduce the power of the opposition.

In the round of redrawing the lines following the 1990 Census, several of the states were compelled to create districts with enough minority strength to ensure that a minority representative would be elected. In essence, some of the states were compelled to use a "racial gerrymander" to increase the number of minorities in Congress and in state legislatures. The result has led to a new legislature computer game called "shapes," which replaces the older and neater game of "blocks."[17] "Blocks" used counties, townships, cities, and voting districts as the building units (or "blocks") for creating districts. In "shapes," computers are used to create new districts that maximize the representation prospects of minorities.

While use of blocks usually resulted in neat, box- or rectangular-like districts, the latest shapes to emerge from the computers are considerably more difficult to define. The Texas legislature created what looked like a snowflake district in Houston and the Illinois legislature developed a district that was likened to an earmuff in Chicago. The North Carolina legislature added the so-called "I-85" district that sat astride an interstate highway running from Durham to west of Charlotte and was likened to a snake.

The basic redistricting game remains the same: trying to provide equal representation for all citizens. But in some cases the legislatures had to work harder to ensure that some citizens got the representation they should have. Without such torturous and directed line-drawing activities, some minorities would remain submerged in majority-dominated districts. Put simply, their candidates would never win. However, some argue that this type of redistricting actually reduces the overall power of such minorities because their presence in other districts is reduced in order to "pack" them into a minority-majority district.

This situation is slowly being resolved by the U.S. Supreme Court, as lawsuits challenging racial gerrymandering in several states have been appealed to that court over the past decade. The plaintiffs in these cases are generally members of the majority white race arguing that in creating districts in which minorities will win, the legislature has violated their rights. In June 1995, the Court struck down Georgia's congressional district map as racial gerrymandering violating the Constitution's guarantees of equal protection under the law.[18] In 1996, North Carolina's "snake" district was rejected by the U.S. Supreme Court. The Court directed the North Carolina legislature to redraw the district before the 1998 elections.[19] The partisan split control legislature was able to develop a new plan with new district lines for the 1998 elections. But that too was rejected by the Court, the congressional primaries were postponed, and the legislature had to redraw the district lines for the third time in a decade. Then, on April 5, 2001, in a 5 to 4 split decision, the Supreme Court upheld the state legislature's plan for the 12th district, as it was no longer the product of a racial gerrymander, just regular politics.[20]

While it is clear that the U.S. Supreme Court has reversed its direction and no longer calls for creation of minority race-majority districts, some observers suggest that the Supreme Court wants to get out of the redistricting game entirely. To do this, the five-member majority is willing to let the states decide how to draw these districts as long as they do not make those decisions solely on the basis of race. But the "rules of the game" could change once again as the composition of the court changes. The "swing vote" in the most recent case, Justice Sandra Day O'Connor, has been rumored to be ready for retirement, as are one or two other members of the current bench. With just a 5 to 4 majority in the most recent decision, the answer to how the Supreme Court views the state legislatures' efforts to redistrict following the 2000 census will lie in the hands of President George W. Bush, who will appoint any

replacements for retiring justices, and the U.S. Senate, which will confirm them. A Republican president appointing, and for now a one-vote Republican majority U.S. Senate confirming, indicates just how "politically dicey" the politics of changing the composition of the U.S. Supreme Court could be.

[But in early July 2003, Justice O'Connor indicated that she was not going to retire now, nor had any other justice indicated that they were about to leave. So, the intense politics that would attend the nomination and confirmation of any new Supreme Court justices has been put off for a while.]

The Role of State Governments

State governments have two main roles vis-à-vis the other actors in state politics: they set the "rules of the game" in which parties and interest groups operate, and then they regulate their financial activities. The rules govern the nomination and election processes and the ways in which interests are allowed to press their demands. However, the rules change at a glacial pace because those who know how to play the game fear that change will upset the balance of power—or at least their spot in the power system. In fact, it often takes a lawsuit by someone outside that power system to change the rules or a scandal to tighten financial reporting requirements.

Recently, the states have adopted policies that increase their regulatory role regarding political parties. Public disclosure and campaign finance laws are more strict, and political action committees (PACs) are monitored with a more watchful eye due to their increased activity. Some of these regulations have been successfully challenged in the courts. For example, the Republican Party of Connecticut won its fight to allow some nonparty members, that is, independents, to vote in their primary despite a contrary state law, and California found its ban on pre-primary party endorsements invalidated.[21]

Importantly, since the 2000 presidential election, states are also in the spotlight as they run our elections. They buy the voting machines, print the ballots, and set the rules for voting and counting the ballots. Much attention has been focused on the states in an attempt to have them "clean up" their voting processes so that we do not have to experience another such difficult electoral aftermath. Some of the problems are covered in Section I.

This section provides some insights into politics at the state level. Alan Greenblatt of *Governing* indicates how business is getting more active—and investing more money—in various state political campaigns. Michael Jonas of *CommonWealth* describes how one interest group in Massacusetts is trying to change its image. Finally, Alan Rosenthal of *Spectrum: The Journal of State Government* provides an assessment of the performance of political parties in the state legislatures.

Notes

1. Malcolm Jewell and David Olson, *American State Political Parties and Elections* (Homewood, Ill.: Dorsey Press, 1982), 280.

2. John F. Bibby and Thomas M. Holbrook, "Parties and Elections," in *Politics in the American States,* 7th ed., eds. Virginia Gray, Russell L. Hanson, and Herbert Jacob (Washington, D.C.: CQ Press, 1999), 108.

3. David E. Price, *Bringing Back the Parties* (Washington, D.C.: CQ Press, 1984), 15.

4. Survey by ABC News, November 4, 1986, reported in *Public Opinion* 9:4 (January–February 1987): 34.

5. Price, *Bringing Back the Parties,* 32.

6. Larry Sabato, *The Rise of Political Consultants: New Ways of Winning Elections* (New York: Basic Books, 1981), 3.

7. Walter DeVries, "American Campaign Consulting: Trends and Concerns," *PS: Political Science and Politics* 12:1 (March 1989): 24.

8. Stephen A. Salmore and Barbara G. Salmore, "The Transformation of State Electoral Politics," in *The State of the States,* 3d ed., ed. Carl Van Horn (Washington, D.C.: CQ Press, 1996), 51.

9. Alan Ehrenhalt, *The United States of Ambition* (New York: Times Books, 1992), 272.

10. Ehrenhalt, 273.

11. Alan Rosenthal, "If the Party's Over, Where's All That Noise Coming From?" *State Government* 57:2 (Summer 1984): 50, 54.

12. Timothy Conlan, Ann Martino, and Robert Dilger, "State Parties in the 1980s: Adaptation, Resurgence, and Continuing Constraints," *Intergovernmental Perspective* 20:4 (Fall 1984): 23.

13. Bibby and Holbrook, "Parties and Elections," 83.

14. Samuel C. Patterson, "The Persistence of State Parties," in *The State of the States,* 2d ed., ed. Carl Van Horn (Washington, D.C.: CQ Press, 1993), 169.

15. Clive S. Thomas and Ronald J. Hrebenar, "Interest Groups in the States," in *Politics in the American States,* 7th ed., eds. Gray, Hanson, and Jacob.

16. The term "gerrymander" originated in 1812, the year the Massachusetts legislature carved a district out of Essex County that historian John Fiske said had a "dragonlike contour." When the painter Gilbert Stuart saw the misshapen district, he penciled in a head, wings, and claws and exclaimed: "That will do for a salamander!"—to which editor Benjamin Russell replied: "Better say a "Gerrymander"—after Elbridge Gerry, the governor of Massachusetts. Congressional Quarterly's *Guide to U.S. Elections,* 2d ed. (Washington, D.C.: Congressional Quarterly, 1985), 691.

17. Kimball W. Brace and Doug Chapin, "Shades of Redistricting," *State Government News* 34:12 (December 1991): 6–9.

18. *Miller v. Johnson* (1995).

19. *Shaw v. Reno* (1996).

20. *Hunt v. Cromartie* (2001). Note that since Jim Hunt is no longer governor of North Carolina, the court indicated that the case would be retitled to reflect the name of the new governor, Michael Easley. So look for *Easley v. Cromartie* (2001) when the case is officially published. Linda Greenhouse, "Justices Permit Race as a Factor in Redistricting," *New York Times* (April 19, 2001).

21. Patterson, "The Persistence of State Parties," 197. The two mentioned court cases that concerned this issue were *Tashjian v. Connecticut* (1986) and *Secretary of State of California v. San Francisco Democratic Central Committee* (1989).

Where Campaign Money Flows

by Alan Greenblatt

Mike Cox, a Wayne County prosecutor, has clear ideas about what activities the attorney general of Michigan should target. Prosecuting criminals tops his list, naturally. Another primary mission he ticks off is enforcement of child support payments. The lack of it in Michigan—the state ranks as third from worst in collecting outstanding "deadbeat dad" payments—has Cox, this year's Republican nominee for attorney general, complaining that the present AG has neglected these core chores in favor of running after corporations with showy consumer-protection cases. "There are a lot of attorneys general who got hooked into getting cute stories instead of doing the heavy lifting," Cox says.

Such talk, not surprisingly, has won Cox enthusiastic fans in the Michigan business community. But it's not Cox's get-tough rhetoric that has endeared him to business groups so much as his opposition to pursuing the type of anti-corporate lawsuits that have made state attorneys general into the business groups' fearsome enemies. State attorneys general, including the current occupant of the office in Michigan, Democrat Jennifer Granholm, are building on their high-profile wins combating Microsoft Corp., tobacco companies and Mer-

rill Lynch to join together to take on other Wall Street securities firms, drug companies and environmental polluters.

Clearly, a lot of regulatory action has shifted from the federal government to the states through the efforts of attorneys general pursuing consumer-friendly lawsuits. It's also increasingly obvious that the businesses that are being sued—or fear being targeted—don't like it and intend to do something about it. Business groups are hoping to stop state lawsuits before they start by electing allies and defeating candidates for attorney general who are perceived as hostile toward them and too friendly toward consumers or labor. Accordingly, they are now pouring millions of dollars into attorney general races that in the past they might have ignored. "Historically, at least with the advent of business PACs in the late 1970s, attorney general races were off most business people's radar screens," says Bob LaBrant of the Michigan Chamber of Commerce. Now, he says, "there's greater incentive to get involved in an attorney general race because of the increased involvement of attorneys general across the

Alan Greenblatt is a staff writer for *Governing*. This article is reprinted from *Governing* (November 2002): 44, 46.

country in litigation against the business community."

Righteous Anger

One of the great philosophical divides in American politics lies between those with opposing views of how business should be regulated. There are those who believe that businesses have a right to conduct their affairs with a minimum of interference from state governments, which can only hinder their productivity and profits. There are others who believe just as strongly that conducting business in a state is a privilege that confers with it a number of responsibilities that the state has the duty to enforce. The majority of state attorneys general over the past few years have acted as if they were members of the "privilege" camp, and that's what's fueled the rise of groups such as the U.S. Chamber of Commerce's Institute for Legal Reform, designed to combat what the business sector sees as excessive regulatory activism on the part of the AGs.

Attack ads—$200,000 worth of them—sponsored by the chamber were widely viewed as having tipped the balance in a close Indiana race two years ago. "It was planned perfectly. It just came out of nowhere," recalls Karen Freeman-Wilson, the Democratic attorney general unseated in that contest. Freeman-Wilson served only a short time but had investigated tobacco and gasoline retailers and come down hard on nursing home operators. "Certainly I earned their interest," she says of the ad campaign.

Bill Pryor, the attorney general of Alabama, sees the motivating force behind the business groups' involvement in attorney general campaigns as a means of protecting "the free market and the rule of law." Pryor says that many of his Republican colleagues—and that includes Pryor himself—"are more committed to the traditional role of attorney general as chief law enforcement officer. We don't think

that the court system ought to be used as a regulatory vehicle."

Republicans have traditionally fared poorly in state attorney general races, winning only about one-third of the time since 1968. To remedy that problem, Pryor helped found in 1999 the Republican Attorneys General Association, a partisan organization run under the auspices of the Republican National Committee. At that time, there were only a dozen Republican attorneys general. Now there are 16, and RAGA is eyeing a half-dozen races that have been left open this year by Democratic retirements. (A Democratic counterpart organization was set up this past summer and hoped to raise $1 million by year's end at dinners featuring current attorneys general.)

RAGA does not take in or disburse money directly, but its efforts have led to huge donations to the Republican National State Elections Committee from businesses that fear state lawsuits. Microsoft, for example, said in 2000 that it gave RAGA $10,000 through the Elections Committee, a figure dwarfed by donations from tobacco companies, insurers and the gun lobby. Pryor considers it important for the Republican Party to recruit competitive candidates for attorney general since so many end up becoming favorites to run for governor and the U.S. Senate. But his main concern, he says, is ensuring that there is a healthy debate over the proper role for attorneys general to play while they serve in that office. "I think it's fair to say that some of the lawsuits filed by state attorneys general have been designed to increase the scope of government, including the revenues flowing to government and regulation of the marketplace," Pryor says. "That should concern anyone who believes our free market functions better with limited government."

Radioactive Money

Since there are plenty of people who do share that concern, the Republican candidates for attorney general in each of the last two Texas races have each received hundreds of thousands of dollars from donors in litigious industries, including developers and insurance companies. As much as a quarter of their haul came from individuals and PACs associated with a pair of Texas groups founded to combat "lawsuit abuse." In both those races, the GOP candidate was viewed as primarily a pro-business candidate, while the Democratic hopeful had worked as a trial lawyer. "The idea of having a plaintiffs' attorney managing the state's law firm is something we find troubling," notes Jeff Clark, executive director of the Texas chapter of the National Federation of Independent Business, a small-business lobby. As Margaret Justus, spokeswoman for this year's Democratic nominee, Kirk Watson, points out, every season is open season for business to beat up on trial lawyers. Justus posits that Watson's record as a tech-friendly mayor of Austin can help him counteract the hostility his legal career might engender in the business sector. Clark and other Texas business lobbyists aren't buying that argument. Bill Hammond, president of the Texas Association of Business, calls campaign contributions from trial lawyers "radioactive."

But if the business lobby seeks to tar Watson because of the company he keeps, Watson's campaign is questioning the association of his GOP opponent, former state Supreme Court Justice Greg Abbott, with business groups. The leading client of the law firm where Abbott draws his checks used to be Enron, before that company's implosion. Kenneth Lay, the discredited former head of Enron, used to sit on the board of Texans for Lawsuit Reform, which advocates limits on product-liability cases. Watson is also making hay out of the fact that

three of the attorneys at Abbott's firm have represented Farmers Insurance Group. Fast-rising homeowners insurance premiums are a hot political issue in Texas, and the state is suing Farmers for alleged price gouging. The Watson camp thinks Abbott would have a clear conflict of interest in the case if elected attorney general. Abbott dismisses the charge as scurrilous, pledging to uphold the law against insurance companies.

Still, there is no question that there are dangers for candidates who embrace business interests too ardently during the current season of corporate scandals. Ohio state Senator Lee Herington, a Democrat, has built his campaign for attorney general on the premise that the state government has become too cozy with business. "Corporations have kind of taken over in Ohio," Herington says. "I think the public is going to get engaged in this campaign and they're going to understand these corporate excesses, and the Republicans are not going to win this race." Whether Herington can turn the tide in a state where Democrats have been shut out of statewide offices in recent years remains doubtful.

Regardless of the success or failure of the Herington campaign, however, big-business regulation is going to remain a mainstay issue of state attorney general elections for the foreseeable future. That, in turn, means that business groups will be contributing to these campaigns in a way that they had not done in the past. "These are generally low-visibility races," says Chad Kniss, who has studied state attorney general elections at the University of Kansas. "If you conclude that the visibility of the races is on the increase and more money is being spent on the AG contests, this is a radical change in the nature of elections for that office."

Changing Their Name, but Not Their Stripes

by Michael Jonas

Formed in 1987 as a liberal counterweight to Citizens for Limited Taxation, the Tax Equity Alliance for Massachusetts has made the case for public spending and progressive taxation with the same zeal its foes have brought to their anti-tax crusades. But after 15 years in the tax-battle mosh pit, TEAM is getting a makeover. Shedding its name—and well-known acronym—for a wonkier moniker, the organization-formerly-known-as-TEAM has recast itself as the Massachusetts Budget and Policy Center.

Leaders of the group say the name change simply brings the title in line with the work. "Over the last several years we've expanded to work on far more issues than just taxes or just tax equity," says executive director James St. George. The organization's recent research reports include an examination of growing income disparities between the state's top and bottom wage earners and an analysis of state budget growth in the 1990s.

The new Massachusetts Budget and Policy Center is part of a network of liberal-leaning groups in 23 states receiving funding from the Ford Foundation, the Charles Stewart Mott Foundation, and the Annie E. Casey Foundation to produce budget and tax analyses with a particular focus on low-income and other vulnerable groups. (TEAM will still exist, on paper at least, handling more direct political and lobbying work, but is not expected to consume much of the four-person staff's time.)

Citizens for Limited Taxation executive director Barbara Anderson, who says the TEAM acronym should have stood for "tax everything and more," sees the name change as an effort to camouflage the group's left-wing image. "I think they're trying to get away from TEAM because people aren't into liberals anymore," says Anderson.

The organization's leaders say it's more because the battleground has changed. Now that the anti-tax fervor of a decade ago has cooled—and CLT's star has dimmed—they felt the time was right to take a step back from the pitched battles of the past.

"When we first started TEAM we were very much in a political mode," says co-founder Susan Shaer. The focus now, she says, is on "the long-term need for long-term thinking. People

Michael Jonas is an associate editor at *CommonWealth*. This article is reprinted from *CommonWealth* (fall 2002): 26–28.

are looking for information that goes beyond this year's ballot."

The new tack is a far cry from the hurly-burly of a dozen years ago, when Anderson and Jim Braude, TEAM's first director, turned the battle over a 1990 tax-rollback ballot question into a high-profile road show, carpooling together to debates across the state where they went at each other with a fervor that seems to have vanished from the political landscape.

Which is not to say the group plans to just ruminate from the sidelines. "I certainly hope that no one will believe we have moved away from being staunch defenders of valuable public investments and public services," says St. George. With an eye toward the state's continuing grim budget picture, he says, "In the near-term future, closing a variety of tax loopholes and [levying] additional tax increases are far preferable to continued cuts in education, health care, and other services important to Massachusetts and her citizens." Thus, the policy-speak from the new Massachusetts Budget and Policy Center still has a strong echo of the old TEAM spirit.

Is the Party Over? Trends in State Legislative Parties

by Alan Rosenthal

When asked to think about the future, I am reminded of the story told about former U.S. senator Theodore Francis Green from Rhode Island. At a crowded reception on Capitol Hill, he took out his appointment book and started leafing through the pages. Noticing the veteran senator's apparent confusion, another guest asked, "Are you trying to figure out where you go from here, Senator?" "No," said Green, "I'm trying to figure out where I am now."

It is tough enough to figure out where we are presently, let alone speculate about the future. In either case, however, it is helpful to start in the past to determine where we have come from. The task here is to explore how political parties in state legislatures have been evolving in recent years, particularly in terms of their performance. Where are they now in comparison to where they were then?

In considering political parties, a distinction can be drawn among the party-in-the-electorate, the party-as-organization and the party-in-government. It is necessary to recognize also that legislative parties differ in the 50 states and 99 legislative bodies (Nebraska's legislature is non-partisan, so the legislative party as such does not exist there). Some legislatures are overwhelmingly Democratic or overwhelmingly Republican. In these states parties in the legislature mean less, but even here parties count. As states become more competitive, the minority party in the legislature gains members, organizes, and takes on an electoral role. Differences exist, not only among the states, but also between chambers. Because they are larger and members' terms are shorter, houses generally tend to be organized more on a partisan basis, while senates are smaller, more individualistic and power is more diffuse.

Assessing Legislative Parties

Americans do not distinguish among national, state and local parties nor do they have much of an idea of congressional or legislative parties, and recent studies show anti-party sentiments have been increasing in recent decades. About 60 percent of those surveyed in a national sample think political parties have

Alan Rosenthal is a professor with the Eagleton Institute of Politics at Rutgers University. This article is reprinted from *Spectrum* (fall 2002): 5–9. Copyright 2002 The Council of State Governments. Reprinted with permission from *Spectrum*.

too much power (as compared to 5 percent who think they do not have enough). Almost half the sample is dissatisfied with the two-party system as such and would like to have a new national party running candidates for office. One out of five respondents felt there was no hope at all and wanted parties banned from politics entirely.[1]

To assess the public's critical view of the political parties, we shall examine how, and how well, the legislative parties in the states have been performing two general functions—representation and governance. The first—representation—is primarily, but by no means exclusively, an external matter, one that connects the legislative parties to the electorate. The second—governance—is primarily, but by no means exclusively, an internal matter, one in which the legislative parties fulfill law-making functions and institutional obligations.

The Parties and Representation

In the systems of representative democracy that exist in the states, people are represented in three principal ways. First, they are represented by individuals they elect to serve in the legislature, who are nearly all Democrats or Republicans. Second, they are represented by one or, more likely, a number of the interest groups that are organized to promote their agendas, many of which lean toward one party or toward the other. Third, they are represented by the political parties, with whom most people affiliate. Regardless of the party of the legislators who represent their own districts, people's values and interests are also expressed by the Democratic party on the one hand or the Republican party on the other, or sometimes by both.

Affiliation

If the political parties are to fulfill their representation function, they must have members or a following to represent. They do, per-

haps not to the extent they did 40 or 50 years ago, but still to a significant extent. Despite a decline, party identification is still extremely important. Currently one-quarter to one-third of voters consider themselves Independents, but many of these lean toward either the Democratic or Republican Party. The other two-thirds to three-quarters of the voters divide between the two parties in varying proportions, depending on the state. As far as registration goes, according to 1998 data for 28 states, 78 percent of eligible voters register as either Democrat or Republican, 20 percent register as Independent or miscellaneous, and fewer than 2 percent as members of third parties.

Identification structures voting decisions for most people.[2] Those who identify Democratic are apt to vote Democratic, and those who identify Republican are apt to vote Republican. In the 2000 presidential election, for example, nine out of 10 people who identified as Republicans voted for George W. Bush and nearly the same proportion of people who identified as Democrats voted for Al Gore. If party cues are important in high-visibility contests like presidential elections, they are even more important in low-visibility contests like state legislative elections, where people have virtually no other cues to guide them. Whatever the level of election, party ID and voting behavior are closely connected.

Competition

Because their support is about equally divided, the parties are extraordinarily competitive today, both at the national and state levels. In the 2002 elections, about 40 seats in the U.S. House are up for grabs. Thus, either party has a chance to win control of the entire U.S. House.

At the state level, anywhere from two to four out of every five districts is relatively safe for an incumbent of one party or the other, but races in the remaining districts decide which party will control the senate or house in the

Party Control of the State Legislatures, 1982–2003

Partisan Control by Number of States

Year	Democrat	Republican	Split*
1982	34	10	5
1984	26	11	12
1986	28	9	12
1988	29	8	12
1990	30	6	13
1992	25	8	16
1994	18	19	12
1996	20	18	11
1998	19	17	13
2000	18	17	14
2002	17	17	15
2003	16	21	12

Source: Data compiled from biennial volumes of *The Book of the States* published by The Council of State Governments.

* Ties are counted as split control.

states. Of the 98 legislative chambers (excluding non-partisan Nebraska) in the 50 states, almost 60 percent are competitive. That is, each party has won control during the past 20 years and/or the margin is close enough so that each has a chance to win control in the period ahead. Some chambers have been solidly Democratic over the 20-year period. Both chambers in Alabama, Arkansas, Hawaii, Massachusetts and Rhode Island are examples. Some chambers have been solidly Republican; both chambers in Idaho and Wyoming are examples. Several, such as New York, with a Republican senate and Democratic assembly, have been split. But from 1982–1990 to 1992–2000, more legislative bodies have become competitive.

Some legislatures are still dominated by one party. In Alabama, Arkansas, Hawaii, Louisiana, Maryland, Massachusetts, Mississippi, Oklahoma, Rhode Island and West Virginia Democrats are on top. In Idaho, Montana, North Dakota, Utah and Wyoming Republicans are on top. The rest of the legislatures are competitive. Before 1994, as many as 24 legislatures had been under almost continuous Democratic control, while only Republicans continuously controlled a few legislatures. However, in the 1994 election the GOP took control of the U.S. Senate and U.S. House (the latter body for the first time in almost 50 years), and it made huge gains in the states as well. Since then control has been almost equally divided between the two parties, with another dozen or so legislatures split.

The Contest

Probably the major organizational change in the state party system in the past 25 years has been the increased role of the legislative party in election campaigns. With the loosening of state and local party organization in most places, the diminution of patronage and the weakening of party-leadership control of the nominating process, a vacuum was created. In about two-thirds of the states, the legislative parties have moved into this vacuum. As the party-in-government took on the new assignment of ensuring that it won power, the line between campaigning and governing blurred.

This happened even though legislative campaigns, like congressional ones, were becoming "candidate-centered" instead of "party-centered." That is, candidates have been taking it on their own to run, putting together personal organizations, war chests and campaign management. "Candidate-centered" campaigns are still the norm, because most races are not really in doubt and, therefore, are not targeted by the legislative parties. In the less competitive races the individual candidates play the major role, but in the relatively few competitive races, the legislative parties play the major role. Too much is at stake for the parties to leave it to individual candidates.

Legislative campaign committees, under the direction of legislative party leaders, are now the principal source of party assistance to legislative candidates in tough races. Legislative leaders and their committees have become full-service organizations, involved in recruitment, training, research, press, polling, strategy and phone banks. Perhaps their major role has been in raising and allocating campaign funds. The money leaders raise goes to the candidates who can put it to best use: incumbents from marginal districts who are targeted by the opposition and challengers running for open seats or against incumbents who are beatable.

Legislative party efforts have had significant payoffs. Able candidates are recruited, party resources are distributed effectively, money is used strategically and individual members become more insulated from contributors (while party leaders become more exposed). No longer do the legislative parties have to rely on the state parties or, more importantly, on the governor (in the case of the governor's party). The legislative party, as a conse-quence of becoming a campaign organization, has gained greater independence.

Mobilization and Education

In the old days, local parties, in some but by no means all the states, did a good job of mobilizing voters. People were brought into politics and found roles there for themselves, not the least of which were working in campaigns and voting in elections. "Voter mobilization and the extension of the bounds of participation in the political system," according to political scientist William Crotty, "are functions of the individual parties and the party system more generally."[3] The appeal of "mobilizing parties" is that they "promote democracy by broadening the political process," according to Gerald Pomper. They register and turn out voters, educate citizens, bring new people into office, and "by extending participation—and thereby enlarging peaceful conflict—these parties change both the focus and outcome of political debate."[4]

There can be little doubt that the legislative parties today do little to mobilize people, encourage participation or educate the mass public. They fail to turn out voters generally, as a gradual but persistent decline in voting indicates. The parties have not broadened, to any great degree, the base of contributors to campaigns, which includes only about 5 percent of the population.[5] In most legislative districts today, while individual candidates may go door-to-door, legislative parties employ polling, direct mail, radio, newspapers and sometimes television advertising. They do not recruit volunteers. Nor do they have as an objective turning out voters; rather, they want only their voters or their likely voters to go to the polls. Their objective is to win, not to broaden participation. When participation increases, it is usually a byproduct of a competitive election.

Nor are the legislative parties especially interested in education. Their appeals are designed to reinforce, persuade, and/or activate, not educate. Again, the goal is winning. Campaign advertising is criticized for being too negative, and it probably is. Yet, as far as the legislative parties are concerned, it gets the job done. Today mobilization is a job undertaken by political interest groups, rather than by political parties. In the larger states and on key items, economic, professional, and ideological groups engage in grass roots and issue campaigns, as well as in voter mobilization efforts. Interest groups appear to have greater mobilizing appeal than do political parties.

Choice

Democrats and Republicans agree on a number of issues. On some key matters, however, they differ. In view of the fact that they represent the interests of competing social and economic groups and their activists have conflicting views, the legislative parties can be expected to differ on policy. Indeed, they do. In the legislature, Democrats tend to support government action, while Republicans emphasize private initiatives and less of a government role. Democrats are more inclined to tax and regulate than are Republicans. One can see differences at the state legislative level on budgets, taxes, the environment, and even education. There is little doubt, therefore, that the parties do differ on policy matters and offer contrasting approaches in a number of areas. Thus, the electorate is offered a meaningful choice between contending programs. From a public policy standpoint, it matters just about everywhere whether Democrats or Republicans have control.

Accountability

Legislators as individuals can be held accountable for their performance. They have to run every two years, as in the case of most houses, or every four years, as in the case of most senates. Even if they represent districts that are considered statistically safe, they can be challenged from within their own party in a primary or can be upset by an opponent in a general election. The legislative parties collectively are probably even more accountable for their actions than are their candidates individually. If the majority party or its members displease enough voters, after the election the old minority will be a new majority.

Legislative party accountability, of course, has less meaning in those states where one party dominates. No matter what, the minority party has no chance of winning. But these are also the states where legislative parties are less substantial organizations.

The Parties and Governance

At one time, several degrees separated the legislative process from election campaigns, but today they are virtually intertwined. "Inside" the legislature constantly reaches out, while "outside" constantly reaches in.

Structure

The way the legislature is structured has changed, in part because of the expanding role of the legislative parties and the more competitive electoral environment. The structural significance of the party is demonstrated by how the legislature is organized for purposes of lawmaking. Normally, the majority party controls the organization of the body. Except in occasional instances of bipartisan coalitions, the majority caucus selects the speaker of the house or the president or president pro tem of the senate. With few exceptions, members of the majority are appointed to chair standing committees on which the majority party has a majority of members.

Although legislative party leaders may appear to have acquired more power as a result of their raising and allocating campaign funds, in fact their positions are less secure than they used to be. Their members now expect them to raise funds diligently, distribute them broadly and win elections continuously. If legislative party leaders lose seats in an election, they risk losing their leadership positions as well. In any case, power is more dispersed in legislative bodies than formerly, especially in the 17 term-limited legislatures. The caucus is a key mechanism in the legislative process in three out of four legislative chambers in the states. When it meets on practically a daily basis during a legislative session—as in Minnesota, New Jersey, Ohio, Vermont and Washington—it tends, along with leadership, to set the agenda and establish policy for the party. The majority party caucus sets the agenda for the chamber as a whole. The legislative party caucus brings greater coherence to the lawmaking process than would otherwise be the case.

Elections influence the process significantly. Unable to control the legislative agenda, the minority party tends to place a lot of its attention on the election and positioning itself vis-à-vis the majority on issues. And electoral considerations help shape the way the majority party organizes and manages the legislature. New and vulnerable members are given assignments on key standing committees and positions that make it easier for them to raise campaign funds from affected interest groups or to bring bacon home to their constituents. They are given bills to carry that will play well in their districts and other opportunities to strengthen themselves as candidates for reelection. Moreover, they are released from voting with their caucus's position, if such votes potentially can hurt them in the district.

Perhaps one-third of the states now have partisan staff to serve the legislative party and its members. Officially, such staffers will not be involved in campaigning (except on their own, not the legislature's, time). Unofficially, one of their main jobs is to advance the electoral prospects of their legislative party members. Whatever their involvement in campaigns, members of partisan staffs approach issues from a partisan perspective, tend to emphasize partisan differences and look for opportunities to score partisan points.

Lawmaking

Governing is the goal, but in order to achieve it—and to exercise power and advance policy—the legislative parties have to win control of the senate or of the house. So much of what they do, qua legislative parties, is influenced by the next election. They try to be responsive to the voters, the independents and leaners as well as their stalwarts, taking into account what positions could net them votes and which could cost them votes. Each party, in the processes of lawmaking, wants to position itself advantageously. None of this is new, but because of competition the weight of electoral considerations is greater than before.

Lawmaking, especially on controversial issues (including nearly always the budget and taxes), nowadays is characterized by three principal activities, each of which is party-related. The first, having to do with the substance of policy, involves debate and deliberation on the merits of an issue. Frequently, the parties disagree on substance. The second, having to do with the enactment of policy, involves discussion and execution of a strategy by which successive majorities can be won at the various stages of the process. Often this is done within the majority (without seeking votes from minority members) through intra-party negotiations, trades, payments and compromise. Third, which is electorally related, involves discussion and execution of a strategy whereby substance and process are tailored to take into account the reaction of voters. This goes on as measures are shaped and reshaped. The first two activities probably have not changed much in intensity in recent years, but the third activity appears to be more important than it used to be.

Consensus

A major job of the legislature is to resolve conflict and build consensus. That appears to have become more difficult, in part because of the increased strength and expanded role of the legislative parties.

Factional politics threaten the parties internally. The Republicans are divided into more and less conservative groupings, while Democrats are mostly moderates but with liberal wings as well. Still, the main division is between the parties and not within them. Despite internal tensions, the legislative parties manage to build substantial consensus within the caucus. Members appreciate that retaining or winning control depends on their accomplishing something. And inducements are available to encourage individuals to stay with their party if at all politically possible.

Sharp competition makes consensus-building between the legislative parties even more difficult than it would be otherwise. Not only are fundamental philosophical or policy differences sometimes involved, but so is electoral competition. Thus, the function of many legislative bodies has been shifting toward crystallizing rather than resolving, divergent partisan views. This trend may render the deliberation and negotiation parts of the process less important, while the exploitation of issues for the purpose of partisan electoral gain becomes more important.

Institutional Maintenance

Legislators of both parties ought to be concerned with the legislature as an institution. The legislative process provides the mechanism for resolving conflict and is of critical importance in a representative democracy. The institution and the process require care. In the best of times not many legislators in any legislative body are institutionally inclined. As a rule, legislative leaders and more senior members are more inclined to take an institutional perspective than are back-benchers and more junior members.

The new role of the legislative parties has made maintenance of the well being of the institution an even harder job. Leaders are more preoccupied with campaigns and elections. With campaigns infusing the process, civility is on the decline. Because the environment has changed, socializing across party lines (or even within party lines) is much diminished. Few members have inclination or time to devote to the legislature as such. If they do, it ranks low on their list of priorities. As far as the legislative parties per se are concerned, winning control and enacting a program are the objectives. The institution is relevant in so far as it serves party purposes.

Conclusion

The two major political party systems may not please citizens and are deficient in the judgment of a number of political scientists, but they have proven to be very resilient. Third parties, for example, have made almost no headway at all. After the election of 2000, out of 7,421 state legislators only the 49 in Nebraska and 15 in the other 49 states were not either Democrats nor Republicans. Since 1982 only once did third-party legislators number more than 20 (22 in 1992). National third-party candidates have had little lasting impact on the system.

Electoral rules make it difficult for third parties to emerge in most places, but the fact is that the two-party system generally has worked well in our representative democracy. If we take as criteria the various aspects of party performance of the functions of representation and governance, then the development of legislative parties during the past 25 years overall has strengthened the system. Legislative parties have done yeoman work in advancing representation, while their record in governance is somewhat more mixed. To summarize the argument presented here, Table 2 provides an assessment (based on judgment, not any science) of party performance in recent years.

Legislative Party Performance

Function	Excellent	Good	Poor
Representation			
Affiliation	x		
Competition	x		
Contest	x		
Mobilization and Education			x
Choice	x		
Accountability	x		
Governance			
Structure	x		
Lawmaking		x	
Consensus Building		x	
Institutional Maintenance			x

In taking on responsibility for campaigns, in what have become very competitive environments, the legislative parties have paid great attention to their constituencies. Thus, their job of representation—their connections and their responsiveness—is much improved. The only weakness here is mobilization and education, which are neglected except insofar as these activities are part of a campaign strategy or are byproducts of intense competition. If campaign finance laws become more restrictive, limiting the funds that can be raised and spent but still encouraging party-building activities, mobilization and education may become more important in the future. In the meantime, however, interest groups are picking up the slack and are mobilizing their members during and between elections.

The campaign orientation of the legislative parties has affected the way they perform their governance function. They are more responsive than they have ever been to interest groups, constituencies and electorates. Con-sensus-building still is one of the major achievements in the process, but on some major issues it is more likely to occur within legislative parties than between them. The real loser, as a result of the transformation of legislative parties into campaign organizations, is the legislature itself. It is not receiving the attention it requires if it is to remain strong. Moreover, it is more of a battlefield as the parties maneuver in committee and on the floor for electoral advantage.

For all its accomplishments, the contemporary legislative-party system may be out of balance. It is more democratic than it used to be, mainly because the legislative parties are electorally focused and consequently very sensitive to their various constituencies. But the increased democratization of the system, by emphasizing the political at the expense of other considerations, may have taken a toll on governance. And it surely has sapped the strength of the legislature as an institution. With some fine-tuning, a better balance could be created. But such engineering seldom occurs, and when it does, it frequently has consequences that are both unintended and unwanted.

As for the future, who knows? Anything is possible, given American politics, state legislatures and political parties. For the present, however, the legislative parties are very much alive and doing a reasonably good job.

Notes

1. John R. Hibbing and Elizabeth Theiss-Morse, *Stealth Democracy* (New York: Cambridge University Press. 2002), 96, 98, 101–102.

2. See especially Larry M. Bartels, "Partisanship and Voting Behavior, 1952–1996," *American Journal of Political Science* 44 (January 2000): 35–50.

3. William Crotty, "Democracy and the Future of Political Parties in America" in *The Future of American Democratic Politics: Principles and Practices,* ed. Gerald M. Pomper and Marc D. Weiner. (New Brunswick, N.J.: Rutgers University Press, forthcoming.

4. Gerald M. Pomper, "The Fate of Political Parties," paper dated June 2002.

5. Crotty, "Democracy and the Future of Political Parties in America."

IV. MEDIA AND THE STATES

"The media" is a broad term that needs to be broken into its components for us to understand better how the media operate in the states. There are the print media, the daily and weekly newspapers we read; the television stations, which provide local and national news; the radio stations, which offer a large variety of formats; and the wire services, which provide the backbone of news stories to the other media. And there is increasing use of a new form of information collection—the Internet.

In fact, it is the wire services and the daily newspapers that set the agenda for television and radio, although TV and radio stations pick and choose what they want to cover. Look at your state's or city's major morning paper and compare the main stories on the front page with what you hear on the early morning radio news. Go into any radio or television station and watch how closely they follow and use the information coming over the wire services. A recent study indicates that state elected officials find newspapers and the wire services the two most politically significant media in the states. This is in contrast to the general perception that newspapers and TV are the most important media at the national level.[1]

There are assets and liabilities to each medium. For example, newspapers can cover a broad range of items and concerns, making them attractive to many readers. In fact, some critics argue that newspapers may be covering too many types of stories and may be losing their focus and concern over larger public issues. Television is a "hot" medium because stories are expressed through pictures, which is an easier way for most people to absorb the news. However, TV is limited by its own technology because it depends on pictures to carry the message; how does one take a picture of taxes? A study conducted in the mid-1970s of forty-four newspapers and television stations in ten cities found that newspapers allocated more space to stories on state government than

did television stations. Newspapers also gave stories on state government greater prominence (front page location) than did the television stations (lead story status).[2] But Bill Gormley, the study's author, argued that even with this newspaper coverage, "few give [state government] the kind of coverage it needs."[3]

Gormley cited the comments of others who had misgivings about the media's coverage of the states. Political scientist V.O. Key Jr. argued in 1961 that the media "may dig to find the facts about individual acts of corruption but the grand problems of the political system by and large escape their critical attention."[4] Former North Carolina governor Terry Sanford (D, 1961–1965) questioned, "Who, in some 40 states or more, can say he begins to understand state government by what he reads in the newspapers?"[5]

State Media Structures

There is great variety in the media structures across the states, just as there is great variety in population size, population centers, and economic complexity. For example, New Jersey sits within two major media markets—the northern part of the state receives broadcasts from the New York City metropolitan area, and the southern part receives broadcasts from the greater Philadelphia metropolitan area. Radio, TV, and cable stations emanating from those major markets dominate what is seen or heard in New Jersey, and there are few strong New Jersey-based media outlets to combat this. News about New Jersey must fight for a spot in these media outlets.

West Virginia also faces this problem: as much of the state is served by media markets in Cincinnati, Pittsburgh, and Washington, D.C. West Virginia lacks its own major media outlet because its terrain makes it impossible for any station to reach all parts of the state. In his 1980 reelection bid, Governor John D. "Jay" Rockefeller IV (D, 1977–1985) spent a lot of money on outlets in these large cities in order to reach potential voters in remote areas of the state. There were stories of voters in Washington, D.C., going to the polls to vote for Rockefeller because they had seen his ads on TV so often.

Then there are states that have many media markets within their own boundaries. California clearly is the leader in media markets because there are so many large communities to be served in the state, ranging from San Francisco and Sacramento in the northern part of the state to Los Angeles and San Diego in the southern part. And there are many other markets in between. Texas also has many media markets, as do Florida, New York, and North Carolina.

At the other extreme are states with only one major media market that dominates the state. Examples are Colorado, with the Denver media market; Georgia, with Atlanta; and Massachusetts, with Boston. In fact, the Boston media market spreads well into Rhode Island, southern New Hampshire, and southwestern Maine, making it difficult for residents there to get a clear understanding of what is happening in their own states. One New Hampshire state legislator worried that "most citizens in the lower one-third of the state get their news from Boston TV, so we have a very distorted view by many citizens of what is happening in state government."[6] When one such market or major city dominates the state, there is little chance for those in the remainder of the state to voice their own particular interests. A rural-urban or rural-suburban rift in the state's media coverage is the rule.

The states also vary greatly in terms of the number of newspapers published and television and radio stations broadcasting. In 2001, there was an average of 29 newspapers per state, ranging from 92 in California to 2 in Delaware.[7] In 2003, there was an average of 21 television stations per state, with Texas and Delaware at the high and low ends of the range.[8] In 1997,

there was an average of 206 radio stations per state, with Texas and Delaware again at the opposite ends of the range.[9] Much of the variation noted here is tied to the size of the state in terms of land area and population. But some of the variation is related to population diversity, with some newspapers and radio stations targeting specific populations.

How the Media Work in the States

There are several patterns in the way the media cover state politics and state government. They are tied to state politics, to policymaking and administration in the states, and to the legislature.

During political campaigns, when candidates are vying to be nominated and elected, the media are involved selectively. Being involved can mean several things. The media cover some of the campaigns on a day-to-day or week-to-week basis, especially those campaigns with the greatest appeal in terms of what the media feel will sell papers or draw listeners and viewers.

Over the last decade, there has been a perceptible decline in the coverage given to politics and government in the newspapers. For example, the political reporters in one large southeastern city were directed to cover only the presidential, congressional, gubernatorial, state legislative, and maybe one or two other contests. This meant the readers in that newspaper's market did not read anything about the other contests they would be voting on unless there was a scandal or major news event attending one of those races. There weren't, so, when voting, the voters had to fall back on party identification, knowledge of the incumbent's name, or skip voting in that race entirely. Why cutbacks on political coverage? It is a bottom-line decision; publishers and editors feel politics does not interest their readers anymore, so they move to what they feel makes readers buy and read their papers.

The media are also the major vehicle for political messages—the paid fifteen- or thirty-second campaign ads that we see on TV and hear on the radio and the printed advertisements we see in newspapers. In fact, a major new approach in getting messages to the voters is use of drive-time radio, when potential voters are trapped in their cars and have to listen to what is coming at them from the car radio.

Some of the media become part of campaigns when they conduct public opinion polls, which delineate the important issues in the race and show which candidate is leading the "horse race." The media also become part of campaigns when they sponsor debates between the candidates and endorse candidates through editorials. A new role some newspapers have adopted is that of a monitor or critic of political campaign ads, especially television ads. Here, the papers have a reporter present the text of the political ad (often negative in tone and style), then match that with the facts of the situation. Then there may be an analysis of the differences.

For their part, candidates and their campaign organizations develop ways to obtain "unpaid media"—getting candidates and their names on TV or in print to increase their name recognition. Knowing when the major TV stations must have their tapes "in the can" for the nightly news can determine when a candidate makes an appearance or holds a press conference. Of course, any candidate is fearful of the "free media" coverage that comes with scandal or with missteps on his or her part.

A recent trend in some states and communities is for the media to practice what is called "civic" or "public" journalism. Here the media become part of the process of politics rather than just a reporter or critic of the process. The media actively try to set the political agenda rather than let the candidates do so. This is a controversial step, and nowhere is the controversy more heated than within the journalism profession itself.[10]

The second pattern in media coverage of state government is having the media become a part of the calculus by which decisions are made and actions are taken in politics and government. The best example of this is the pervasive influence that the *Manchester Union Leader* has on New Hampshire government and politics. This newspaper has run very conservative editorials on the front page for all to see. An observer of the state wrote in the 1960s that "[m]any state officials said they feared personal and vindictive editorial reprisal on the front page if they took exception to one of the paper's policies."[11] These officials felt "the paper has created an emotionally charged, reactionary atmosphere where new ideas are frequently not only rejected but fail to appear in print for public discussion."[12] In the 1980s, a political scientist observed that this paper "still profoundly shaped politics in the state,"[13] and in the 1990s, one state legislator grumbled that "political bias [is] demonstrated consistently in [its] stories as well as editorials."[14] Sometimes such an atmosphere or situation can be created in more subtle ways than in editorial attacks on the front page, but they exist nonetheless.

Other media organizations have acted in a more responsible manner over the years. These organizations have worked with those in government and politics to help their readers understand what is happening. For years, the *Louisville Courier-Journal* did this for Kentucky and for parts of adjoining states.[15] As one newsman argued, "Publishers have a responsibility to the public to do more. Call it public service, if you will . . . but the press has the responsibility to enlighten and serve."[16]

The third pattern to media coverage and activity in the states is tied to state legislative sessions. There is an adage that when the legislature is in town, no one is safe. In the past, when the legislature was in town, so was the media of the state. Not only did the capital press and media corps regulars cover general legislative activity, but specific newspapers and TV stations sent reporters to cover the representatives from their city or county. But times are changing, and using that same "bottom-line" thinking, media executives have cut back media coverage of the state legislative sessions considerably. For example, in 1998 no major state TV station had a reporter assigned to cover the California legislature, even though that body makes decisions about what the ninth-largest government in the world will be doing in the future.

When the media operated under the "cover-the-legislature-at-all-costs" rule, coverage of other state government activities, programs, and individuals was often neglected. Why? It was "easier to cover the legislature. . . . Stories [were] easy to get. Legislators [sought] out reporters, doling out juicy quotes and swapping hot rumors." Plus, editors wanted their reporters to be there. "When reporters [weren't] there, editors want[ed] to know why not."[17] Now that is changing; editors are much less likely to want their reporters there.

There have also been some changes in the nature of the capital press corps. There tend to be fewer gray beards and more younger reporters than in the past. The tradeoff seems to be youth, vigor, and inexperience versus age and experience; hence the coverage may not be as good as in the past. In one major state capital, when the reporter covering state government for the city's newspaper moved on to a new assignment and his position was open to be filled, no one applied for it, as they could see where the management's priorities were—not in covering state government.

There also are estimates that the average number of Associated Press reporters covering state government in the fifty state capitals has dropped from three to two.

A major factor influencing how state governments and politics are covered by the media is the location and size of the state capital. In some states, the capital city is not the largest

city; instead, it seems to be a "compromise" city between two large urban centers. Examples of this include Springfield, Illinois, located about two-thirds of the way from Chicago toward St. Louis, Missouri; Jefferson City, Missouri, located midway between St. Louis and Kansas City; and Trenton, New Jersey, located closer to the Philadelphia metropolitan area than to the New York area.

Some state capitals are near the geographic center of the state, such as Little Rock, Arkansas; Des Moines, Iowa; Oklahoma City, Oklahoma; and Columbia, South Carolina. However, several capitals are in what seem to be out-of-the-way locations, including Sacramento, California; Annapolis, Maryland; Albany, New York; and Carson City, Nevada. Still other states put their capital in the largest city, where most of the action takes place. Some examples of such capitals are Denver, Colorado; Atlanta, Georgia; Boston, Massachusetts; and Providence, Rhode Island.

When the state capital is in an out-of-the-way location, the media may find it more difficult to cover events, since the government may be the only game in town. When there is not much action—or when the legislature adjourns—many in the press return to their home cities, leaving state government uncovered. When the state capital is located in the state's largest and most active city, there may be better coverage of state government, but that may be drowned out by the coverage of all the other activities in the city.

The National Media and the States

How do the national media treat what goes on in the states? One quick answer is that the national media do not cover the states unless a disaster occurs. Media specialist Doris Graber calls the national media's coverage of state issues "flashlight coverage."[18] She argues that there are basically two types of news in the eyes of the national media: high priority news and low priority news. The former is news that "has been judged in the past as intrinsically interesting to the audience by the usual news criteria. . . . [It is news that is] exciting, current, close to home, about familiar people, and audiences are likely to deem it relevant to their life." On the other side of the coin is low priority news, which "has been judged intrinsically uninteresting although it may be important." [19]

Graber argues that state news traditionally has been in the low priority news category, with only an occasional "entertainment or convenience item" receiving "a brief spotlight" in the news. However, when state news can be tied to high priority news, such as national elections, coverage increases. [20]

Graber also argues that media coverage of state and local government has more holes than substance, which means "state and local issues get . . . short shrift in journalism." The media seek to "serve 'markets' rather than the political entities into which the nation has been divided." [21] Her prognosis for change is not good, "given the deep historical roots of our current media system." [22] Now, with the bottom-line trends leading to less coverage than before, her prognosis looks even worse.

Working with the Press

There is another side to the media-government relationship: how those who serve in state government react to the role of the media. All governors, some state agencies, and a growing number of legislatures have established press offices to work with—and even cater to—the media and its needs. This means each governor has a press secretary or communications director. Recently, state legislators have realized the need for a media liaison who works either for a party caucus or the party leadership. Most agencies in state government have offices that work with the press.

However, elected officials at the local level usually do not have the luxury of a press office to assist them. A mayor may have one, but those serving on elected boards and commissions are unlikely to have that help. This often puts these officials directly on the firing line with the media, with no one there to help them prepare what to say and how to say it.

For press offices, working with the media on a daily basis usually entails distributing press releases and answering queries. But press offices are also responsible for making sure that their bosses handle themselves properly with the media corps. At a New Governors Seminar sponsored by the National Governors' Association, newly elected governors were given the following advice on dealing with the media:

• Good press relations cannot save a poor administration, but poor press relations can destroy a good one.

• Never screw up on a slow news day.

• If you don't correct an error immediately, in the future you'll be forced to live with it as fact.

• Never argue with a person who buys ink by the barrel.

• When you hold a press conference and are going to face the lions, have some red meat to throw them or they'll chew on you. It should be something of substance, as long as the governor isn't the Christian.

• Never make policy at press conferences. [23]

At the 1990 New Governors Seminar, incumbent governors advised the newly elected governors to select their press secretary/communications directors quickly, as the position is a critical one. And in selecting that individual, "the main objective is to have someone who has the respect of the media and knows what is happening, and does not lie or misrepresent the Governor." [24]

Part IV provides some perspectives on the media in the states. Ferrel Guillory of *North*

Carolina DataNet offers a new perspective on how to look at the media in the states. Kathleen Murphy of stateline.org presents some of the unforgettable moments that statehouse reporters have seen. Robert Keogh of *Common-Wealth* reports on how a panel of editorial page chiefs in Massachusetts felt the candidates in that state's 2002 governor's race should operate. Finally, Craig Donovan and Scott McHugh of the *New Jersey Reporter* explore how new technology might change how that state might become a major TV media market.

Notes

1. Thad L. Beyle and G. Patrick Lynch, "The Media and State Politics." Paper presented at the annual meeting of the Midwest Political Science Association, Chicago, April 1991.

2. William T. Gormley Jr., "Coverage of State Government in the Mass Media," *State Government* 52:2 (Spring 1979): 46–47.

3. Ibid., 47.

4. V. O. Key Jr., *Public Opinion and American Democracy* (New York: Alfred Knopf, 1961), 381.

5. Terry Sanford, *Storm over the States* (New York: McGraw-Hill, 1967), 51.

6. Response by a New Hampshire state legislator to a 1990 survey question sent by the editor.

7. Bureau of the Census, *Statistical Abstract of the United States, 2002* (Washington, D.C.: Government Printing Office, 2002), 700–701

8. "Television Stations," newsdirectory.com, March 31, 2003.

9. Bureau of the Census, *Statistical Abstract of the United States,* 1999 (Washington, D.C.: Government Printing Office, 1999), 581.

10. Christopher Conte, "Angels in the Newsroom," *Governing* (August 1996): 20–24.

11. Sanford, 50.

12. Ibid.

13. Richard F. Winters, "The New Hampshire Gubernatorial Election and Transition" in *Gubernatorial Transitions: 1982 Election,* ed. Thad Beyle (Durham, N.C.: Duke University Press, 1985), 304.

14. Response by a New Hampshire state legislator to a 1990 survey question sent by the editor.

15. Sanford, 51.

16. Quoted in ibid., 52.

17. Jack Betts, "When the Legislature's in Session, Does Other News Take a Back Seat?" *North Carolina Insight* 12:1 (December 1989): 63.

18. Doris A. Graber, "Flashlight Coverage: State News on National Broadcasts," *American Politics Quarterly* 17:3 (July 1989): 278.

19. Ibid., 288.

20. Ibid., 288–289.

21. Doris Graber, "Swiss Cheese Journalism," *State Government News* 36:7 (July 1993): 19.

22. Ibid., 21.

23. Thad L. Beyle and Robert Huefner, "Quips and Quotes from Old Governors to New," *Public Administration Review* 43:3 (May/June 1983): 268.

24. Thad Beyle, "Organizing the Transition Team," *Management Note* (Washington, D.C.: Office of State Services, National Governors' Association, 1990), 15.

Campaigns Are Different, Media Are Plural

by Ferrel Guillory

Cable news talk shows, journalism reviews and other national magazines regularly critique press and broadcast coverage of campaigns. But they almost invariably focus on national campaigns and the big media of TV networks and major daily newspapers.

And yet, as the 2000 governor's race in North Carolina demonstrated anew, significant differences exist in how national and state campaigns are conducted—and covered. Within the state, anyone attempting to analyze the relationship between media and politics must take into account important variances among newspapers, television and radio. The accompanying chart seeks to provide an outline of key differences.

In 2000, as in 1996, North Carolina served as a site for new initiatives in the media's treatment of campaigns. Here is a look back at the media-politics landscape:

Television

Capitol Broadcasting Co. in Raleigh took the lead in adopting the so-called 5/30 standard for campaign coverage—that is, devoting five minutes a night of candidate-centered discourse for 30 days prior to the election.

Jim Goodmon, chief executive of Capitol, agreed to provide the time on his company's flagship WRAL-TV as well as its smaller stations in Raleigh, Wilmington and Charlotte.

The 5/30 standard was advocated nationwide by the Alliance for Better Campaigns, a Washington-based organization funded by the Pew Charitable Trusts. The UNC Program on Southern Politics, Media and Public Life served as the "state partner" in North Carolina and focused its efforts on seeking to persuade TV stations to meet the standard, teaching journalists how to improve campaign reporting and monitoring their coverage.

Before the May primaries, Capitol Broadcasting produced three "messages" of one minute, forty-five seconds each from the three Republican and two Democratic candidates for governor. It broadcast these messages daily on WRAL at the end of the noon, 6 p.m. and 11 p.m. news programs. Under the ground rules established by the broadcasting company,

---

Ferrel Guillory is director of the Southern Politics, Media and Public Life program at the University of North Carolina, Chapel Hill. This article is reprinted from *North Carolina DataNet* 27 (February 2001): 4–5.

Key Differences Between State and National Campaigns and Coverage

National	State
Campaigns	
Candidates on the trail	No campaign trail
Institutionalized debates	Discretionary debates
TV ads targeted to states	TV ads dominate
Newspapers	
Pack journalism	No pack
In-depth polls	Shallow polls
Day-by-day journalism	Civic journalism
Broadcasting	
Shift from air to cable	"Wasteland" revisited
Experienced reporters	Few political reporters
Too many talking heads	Not enough talking heads
Late-night comedy	No laughs
Talk radio	Talk radio, and audience-specific commercials

attacks on opponents were prohibited. Candidates were asked to address issues identified by the broadcaster as well as an issue of their own choice.

In the general election, Capitol Broadcasting revised and extended its candidates' messages project. In addition to including candidates for governor, the company also offered messages from candidates for lieutenant governor and attorney general.

For several days in October, Capitol's stations ran opposing candidates' messages back-to-back. This proved more powerful than the one-candidate-at-a-time offering in the spring. In the fall, viewers could see and hear the candidates for governor, lieutenant governor and attorney general speaking, at more length than a sound-bite, one right after the other.

WBTV, the station in Charlotte owned by Jefferson-Pilot, did not give candidates a block of time for "messages." Rather, WBTV produced a daily news report on campaign developments for its 6:30 p.m. newscast, with a reporter and producer assigned to the project, which focused not only on the governor's race but also on congressional primaries in Charlotte-area districts.

Unlike most local TV stations in this state, WBTV has an experienced political reporter, Mike Cozza, who provided much of the coverage. It also has an investigative team that looked at campaign contributions.

Our spot-check monitoring of WBTV throughout the campaign season showed that the station produced some of the strongest daily political journalism of the campaign.

Radio

Talk radio remains part of the political fabric—more so on the national than the state

The Name of the Rag

Politicians and the press have always taken jabs at each other, but animosities reached a new level in Kentucky when a county official snatched a newspaper's name right from its masthead.

It seems the *Mountain Citizen,* an Eastern Kentucky weekly, has been hounding John Triplett, a member of the Martin County Water Board who also used to serve as the board's chairman. In critical stories with headlines such as "Stinking Water Woes," the newspaper accused Triplett of mismanagement and blamed the board for the brown water that sometimes flows from county taps.

Triplett fought back in a most unusual way. He did some digging and found that the *Mountain Citizen* had neglected to file its annual incorporation paperwork with the state. That meant the paper's name was essentially up for grabs—and Triplett grabbed it. All he needed to do was pay a $40 fee. A judge in May agreed that the name belonged to Triplett, and when the paper continued to publish under its old name, the owner, publisher and editor each got hit with $500 fines for contempt of court.

Was revenge the only motive? Triplett won't say, though he's done little to put down rumors that he wants to start a rival newspaper of his own. *Mountain Citizen* editor Gary Ball thinks Triplett just wanted to shut the paper up. "This is just good old boy mountain politics," he says.

Source: Christopher Swope, "The Name of the Rag," *Governing* (September 2002): 17.

---

level, but still a factor in some North Carolina communities. For conservatives in particular, talk radio serves as an outlet for expression and for motivation.

In campaigns, radio serves another function—the targeting of messages to selected audiences. For campaigns, radio time is far less expensive than TV time. And, because radio is so fragmented and because most stations cater to a certain demographic group rather than to a general audience, campaigns buy commercial time on stations as a way of directing messages—whether a get-out-the-vote motivation or an attack on an opponent—to a segment of voters.

Newspapers

Press coverage still bears the imprint of what is known as civic journalism. That is, the state's major newspapers work from the guiding concept that their coverage should be more voter-centered than candidate-centered, that

they should be less tied to the candidates' agendas and to the "horse race," and more devoted to helping citizens make up their minds on how to vote.

News organizations formed the Your Voice, Your Vote consortium, as they had in 1996. It included seven newspapers, as well as six commercial TV stations and WUNC public radio, which conducted joint polls on voters' opinions and joint interviews with the candidates. In addition, major newspapers continued with the regime of "ad watches," in which candidates' TV commercials—though not typically radio commercials—are examined for tone and factual accuracy.

Newspapers, of course, provide coverage beyond the YVYV packages and the ad watches. Still, newspaper coverage is driven far less by day-to-day campaign dynamics, more by the newspapers' own decisions and agendas. Still, there was considerable commentary about the decisions of both Democratic Gov.

Mike Easley and his Republican opponent, Richard Vinroot, to minimize daily campaigning and to devote much more time to raising money to pay for TV commercials.

A kind of circular dynamic seemed to have taken hold. Journalists acknowledge that they are much less likely than in the past to show up for candidates' press conferences and to report on stump speeches. Candidates and their strategists, in turn, ask themselves why spend time giving civic club luncheon speeches that reach only a few, mostly committed, voters when there will be no media coverage and when they can reach many more voters through TV ads.

At least two results grow out of this media-political landscape. One is that the governor's race had few "markers," but they emerged as more crucial because they represented moments at which candidates had to speak at length—to the examination of voters and each other. Those markers included the YVYV candidate-interviews and the two TV debates. The second is that, in the absence of day-to-day campaigning and coverage as in the presidential election, TV commercials have become even more dominant in North Carolina's gubernatorial and senatorial elections.

A footnote: The *Charlotte Observer* went a significant step beyond other newspapers in offering Easley and Vinroot space to expound their views at length. In a newspaper equivalent of WRAL-TV's candidates' messages, the *Observer* invited the Democratic and Republican nominees to write several hundred words on key issues, and the newspapers ran side-by-side articles on five days, including three on big-circulation Sundays.

Statehouse Reporters Recall Unforgettable Moments

by Kathleen Murphy

Lunching with serial killers, digging through trash and getting sued are all in a day's work for the cadre of reporters covering statehouse beats.

There are about 510 full-time statehouse reporters across the country, according to a 2002 study by the Project on the State of the American Newspaper.

Newsroom budget cuts have reduced the number of reporters covering state capitols in recent years. That means fewer reporters are covering stories about the state actions that affect everyone's lives, from land use decisions to drinking laws.

During legislative sessions, they're often chained to their desks, but several reporters told Stateline.org that most of their memorable moments happened far away from the computer.

David Ammons of the Associated Press, who has covered the Washington statehouse for 32 years, said he met serial killer Ted Bundy on the campaign trail in the 1972 governor's race and lunched with him occasionally after Bundy was hired on the state GOP staff. Florida executed Bundy in the electric chair in 1989.

"I remember telling people that this charismatic young man was going places," Ammons said. "Little did I know it was going to be the execution chamber."

Ammons's memories have included being the Associated Press's lead writer about the volcanic eruption of Mt. Saint Helens, writing the story of Dan "D. B." Cooper—the skyjacker who bailed out over Southwest Washington with $200,000—and covering the state's ever-growing initiative process, whereby citizens can place state legislative measures on the ballot. Ammons calls the process, "the shadow legislature."

Ammons said he also loves the intellectual challenge of his work and has tried hard to unravel the complexity of government so that all his readers can understand it.

"I'm crazy about the whole chess game of it," Ammons said. "It's quite a fascinating ringside seat we get here. I think I was born nosy so this gives me entree to ask uppity questions of the governor whenever I want to know something. I try to ask the questions the average Joe Sixpack would."

Kathleen Murphy is a staff writer at stateline.org. This article was reprinted from stateline.org (March 17, 2003).

Being a statehouse reporter is not always a glamorous job and at times puts dedicated journalists to the test.

Jon Craig, a reporter for the *Columbus Dispatch*, said he dug around in a public recycling bin in Albany in order to fish out documents for an investigative series on the New York State Legislature when he was working for a Syracuse paper. A custodian had tipped him off about the documents.

Later, when he did a Medicaid story for the *Akron Beacon Journal*, Craig was sentenced to jail for refusing to name confidential sources.

"My wife warned me to take a toothbrush with me that day, but I never imagined I'd get sentenced. My first thought was, 'How do I get transferred to a safer jail?' " Craig said.

Craig didn't end up spending any time in jail. The sentence was suspended, and the newspaper won the court cases on appeal.

Having a colorful governor to cover made Minnesota reporters' workdays unpredictable.

Laura McCallum, capitol bureau chief for Minnesota Public Radio, said covering former Gov. Jesse Ventura always led to something quotable and strange. Escorted to the governor's mansion for an interview, McCallum waited to get time with Ventura after his workout.

"He came out in a tie-dyed tank top and biking shorts," McCallum said. "No other governor would do something like that."

Kevin Corcoran, reporter for the *Indianapolis Star*, said the job of statehouse reporter often means playing detective.

"Sometimes the trickiest thing is putting the whole puzzle together," Corcoran said.

Corcoran and a colleague, Michele McNeil-Solida, studied legislation passed one-bill-at-a-time over a period of years that proved Indiana lawmakers had been trying to create a post-retirement health insurance benefit for themselves. After their story appeared last year, the measure stopped dead in its tracks.

In another gum-shoe episode, Corcoran combed through law books to determine that legislation supposedly aimed at keeping cigarettes away from kids was a Trojan horse designed to weaken tobacco laws.

"Those are the most challenging things, just reading what they are doing and figuring out what it really means versus what they say on the floor," Corcoran said. "That's the challenge that I enjoy, frankly, about what I do."

Nancy Cook Lauer, capitol bureau chief for the *Tallahassee Democrat*, said one of her most physically challenging assignments was accompanying mullet fishermen who were showing how a gill net ban adversely affected their livelihood. It was a cold day, and her photographer fell overboard.

"It was very, very cold and very, very wet. They kept us out there and wouldn't let us come back in," Lauer said. "A good story came out of it, though."

In Their Opinion

by Robert Keough

Political campaigns have their rituals, one of which is a round of meetings with newspaper editorial boards. Before the summer is out, the various candidates for governor will make their pitches for the coveted endorsements of every local paper in the Commonwealth. But how much more fruitful might these conversations be if the talk went the other way: the editorial writers telling the candidates what's most important to them, and their readers?

After all, editorial-page editors, especially those in regional and community newspapers outside the Boston metropolis, occupy a unique journalistic niche. It's their job not only to influence public and official opinion through editorials but also to weather the occasional uprising of readers. (Somebody has to read all those letters to the editor before they go in the paper.) Who better to gauge public sentiment and set a political agenda than the region's editorial chiefs?

With this in mind, *CommonWealth* gathered up a fair sampling of opinion-page gurus representing newspapers east of the Quabbin Reservoir for a picking of brains, if not necessarily a meeting of minds. Our panel: James Campanini, editorial-page editor of the *Lowell Sun;* Christine Dunphy, editorial writer for the

Worcester Telegram & Gazette; JoAnn Fitzpatrick, editorial-page editor of *The Patriot Ledger* of Quincy; Richard Holmes, opinion editor of *MetroWest Daily News;* and Melvin Miller, publisher and editor of the *Bay State Banner,* the weekly newspaper serving the African-American community in the Boston area.

Over lunch at a regionally central location—the Olive Garden restaurant in Framingham's Shopper's World mall—these professional opinion-mongers came up with no small number of forceful assertions. But if there was a consensus among these independent minds, it came down to this: The recession-induced state budget crunch and the tax hikes that have been imposed to solve it have not yet lit a prairie fire of public outrage against politics-as-usual in Massachusetts. But the gubernatorial candidates would be wise to pay attention to three key issues: out-of-control housing costs; education for young people and adult immigrants; and government integrity.

Robert Keough is an editor at *CommonWealth*. This article is reprinted from *CommonWealth* (summer 2002): 72–73.

71

With New Technology, New Jersey *Should* Be A Major TV Media Market

by Craig P. Donovan and Scott McHugh

To lifelong residents of the Garden State, it is almost an unquestioned fact of life that New Jerseyans hear and see less about what is going on in their state than do citizens in virtually any other state in the nation.

Decisions by the federal government in the early part of the last century placed first the major radio stations and then the network television stations not within our borders, but across the rivers in New York City to the north and Philadelphia to the south, and there they have remained.

Those decisions have a major negative effect on New Jersey's self-image, cohesion as a state, governance and the cost and conduct of political campaigns. New Jersey is a major state that ranks ninth in population and second in per-capita income, but it isn't even a minor news or TV advertising market.

Today, for the millions of New Jerseyans who turn on their television sets and watch "local" news before and after work, the network affiliates and the independent stations provide an endless stream of information about just about everything but New Jersey. It is little wonder that in a recent survey of northern New Jersey college freshmen, more of them could correctly identify the Mayor of New York City and the Governor of New York State than the Governor of New Jersey.

When analyzing media in America, the nation is broken down into Designated Market Areas (DMAs). The all-important Nielsen company ratings that are used to count the number and types of people who are watching a show and thus measure the success or failure of programs, both local and national, are based not on the 50 states, but rather on the 210 DMAs that divide up the nation.

New Jersey's 21 counties are divided into the country's largest- and fourth-largest DMAs, New York and Philadelphia. If New Jersey's 21 counties were a separate and distinct DMA, New Jersey would be the fourth-largest Designated Market Area in the nation, ranking behind only Los Angeles, New York City and Chicago, and ahead of eastern Pennsylvania/Philadelphia, the San Francisco/Oakland/

Craig P. Donovan serves as vice president for policy and research for the Public Policy Center of New Jersey, which publishes *New Jersey Reporter*. Scott McHugh is an assistant professor in the Department of Communications at Kean University. This article is reprinted from *New Jersey Reporter* (January–February 2003): 45–49. Reprinted with permission of the Public Policy Center of New Jersey.

San Jose area, and such other major markets as eastern Massachusetts/Boston, Washington D.C., Dallas, Detroit, and Houston.

If two New Jersey DMAs were created, North Jersey would rank no worse than eighth, still ahead of Philadelphia, and South Jersey would still be a top-50 market.

Despite increases in news programming from cable-only stations and the Internet, local television news is still the primary source of news concerning public affairs. Most viewers still turn to the major networks and the local news on broadcast television, and for many citizens, television is the primary and often only source of news in their daily lives. Almost every home in the state has at least one television.

Once upon a time, the roofs of New Jersey were festooned with television antennas that proclaimed them a part of the "modern age." Today, the TV antenna is going the way of the phonograph. More than four out of five of all New Jersey homes today get their TV through cable and/or satellite technology, and that number is growing.

Not only has the ability of cable and satellite providers to produce or deliver programs to a small demographic audience led to channels focusing on animals, sports, travel, and cooking, but cable and satellite companies are also required by the Federal "Must Carry" laws to deliver broadcast channels over their systems on the basic tier of cable/satellite channel packages, thus greatly increasing the reach of all the various stations in New York and Philadelphia into and across the length and breadth of New Jersey.

Viewers in North Jersey receive their news information from the New York City market and those in South Jersey from the Philadelphia stations. Those who are "lucky" enough to live in Central New Jersey often receive both New York and Philadelphia signals and can choose which "not New Jersey" news they get to hear about.

There are other options. New Jersey Network, the state-owned public television station, has been broadcasting statewide since 1969. The two largest cable companies, Rainbow Media (a subsidiary of Cablevision) and Comcast, have developed regional news channels—News 12-New Jersey and CN8—to compete with the broadcast networks for the New Jersey audience. But the total viewership for these three stations is only a fraction of that of the major commercial stations outside our borders. What most viewers want is their state and local news interspersed as an integral part of an overall broadcast of international, national, state and local news and features, sports, entertainment and weather—what the citizens of almost every other state or city of any size elsewhere in the country take for granted.

The impact of this lack of New Jersey-based news programming on network television affects not only what we know about what is happening in the state, but also governs what happens as we try to determine who we choose to elect to lead us.

A joint study recently conducted by the Eagleton Institute of Politics at Rutgers University and the Washington, D.C.-based Alliance for Better Campaigns looked at how the New York City based stations handled the Fall 2001 elections. The study focused on two major races—for Governor of New Jersey and for Mayor of New York City—and included all local evening newscasts on New York City's network affiliated stations for the 30 days before the Nov. 4, 2001 election.

The study also sought to monitor the extent to which local television stations complied with the recommendation that stations provide five minutes of "candidate-centered discourse" per night for the month preceding elections. The recommendation, known as the "5/30 standard," came from a commission comprising leaders from the broadcast industry and public interest groups that met in 1998.

So what did New Jerseyans get to watch? While New Jersey gubernatorial candidates placed 40 percent of all the campaign ads that aired on the WABC, WCBS and WNBC television stations in New York City, only 17 percent of the stations' election news stories focused on the New Jersey governor's race. More than four out of five stories from the New York City stations looked at their Mayor's race.

"It is not just the lack of attention paid to New Jersey that is of concern," said Ingrid Reed, director of the Eagleton Institute's New Jersey Project, "The amount of political advertising time during evening newscasts (442 minutes) was nearly equal to the amount of time devoted to election news coverage (489 minutes). And, only two-and-a-half of the more than eight hours of campaign news programming (30 percent) focused on the candidates and their issues, while the other 5.5 hours were devoted to 'horse race' and campaign strategy stories. We need to provide more and better coverage of New Jersey candidates in New Jersey races to the people of New Jersey.

Time and technology have combined to provide New Jersey with a potential solution to this informational dilemma. In the original days of over-the-air broadcasting of television programs, the indiscriminate wide net cast by the powerful television station transmitters meant that all viewers everywhere had to see the same thing at the same time. [But no more.]

For the more than four out of five viewers in New Jersey who watch their TV shows through cable or satellite sources, it is possible to provide these viewers with separate and distinct content based on where they are watching. Take a New Jersey viewer today who might have cable and satellite in his house. If you were to climb up on your roof and connect up an old TV aerial, turn on one of your favorite programs, then flip back and forth between the antenna, the cable, and the satellite versions, you would at once notice that the show was a few seconds ahead or behind depending on which source you were watching and, more important, you would see different commercials through each source.

If the cable and satellite companies can use their technology to tailor the advertisements we see based on where we live and which source we use for our signals, the same could be done for the shows themselves, especially for the news shows.

Imagine a system under which any New York City or Philadelphia commercial station that wanted to have its news programming aired in New Jersey would have to create a separate New Jersey-based news program.

Thus, whenever a news show was being shown over cable or satellite from, say, FOX5 or WCBS in New York, people in New York City would see and hear say about the New York's fish market, an accident in Long Island, Governor Pataki, and the weather in Central Park. At same time, a different group of reporters based in New Jersey would be reporting about redevelopment in Atlantic City, a new stadium to be built in the Meadowlands, Governor McGreevey's latest press conference, and the weather from the shore in the south to the mountains in the north. Ditto Philadelphia.

This targeted, zoned, split news coverage would not reach every single New Jersey resident, of course, because those residents who only get their news (and entertainment and ads) from signals carried over the air waves on those rooftop aerials would continue to get the broadcast New York City or Philadelphia news shows. But New Jersey news would reach most New Jersey citizens.

This is important because "historically, neither television nor the newspapers cross state boundaries very well," said Robert Cole, director of the journalism program at The College of New Jersey and the dean of the state's journalism professors. "I'm sure today they [the cable and satellite companies] can do incredible things if they wanted to but I'm awfully cynical about them ever choosing to do so. People here would much rather have news that is based on New Jersey than New York or Philadelphia, and it would be very good for the state."

Creating separate news broadcasts, while not inexpensive, is not all that dissimilar from the zoning that newspapers such as the *Philadelphia Inquirer* do in publishing a separate South Jersey section. Both New York and Philadelphia station or send reporters into New Jersey every day. Furthermore, it is quite conceivable that one news team working for ABC could prepare New Jersey news reports that would service both the New York and Philadelphia ABC station's New Jersey viewers, and the same with CBS and NBC.

The creation of such separate news broadcasts, in and of themselves, would be a major campaign finance reform, in that they would enable candidates to purchase advertising only aimed at New Jersey viewers, rather than being forced to buy air time to reach all of New York City, its suburbs and western Connecticut in one market or all of Philadelphia, southeastern Pennsylvania and Delaware in the other.

Campaigns for U.S. Senate that cost $10 million to $15 million now could cut that price-tag in half, lessening the pressure on candidates to spend most of their time raising money. Furthermore, New Jersey campaigns for Congress, County Executive or even the state Legislature could then afford to reach voters through network television ads, as they do now in virtually every other state.

It is conceivable that one network station might seek a ratings boost by providing a separate New Jersey broadcast. But it is more likely that neither the cable or satellite companies nor the New York City or Philadelphia television

stations are going to embrace the opportunity to increase their news production costs just because it is the right thing to do.

"Giving a fully New Jersey focus to the overall news and especially the election coverage would be great for New Jersey," said Reed. "But, we shouldn't be naïve. Broadcasters don't think creatively about how to get or provide the news to us nor how to best meet the needs of those who watch their shows."

However, broadcast privileges are franchises regulated and granted by the Federal Communications Commission, and Congress certainly has the power to direct such a reform.

Opposition to such legislation would likely come not only from the stations and networks, but from the National Association of Broadcasters (NAB) as well. The FCC recently has been reducing or eliminating, not expanding, most television regulations now in existence and the NAB and other media outlets would immediately challenge virtually any new regulations that would pass Congress.

That does not mean that New Jersey's congressional delegation should not try to push legislation to make New Jersey a major media market of its own. It is difficult to function as a strong and independent state when you are only allowed to see yourself as a small satellite to another, outside entity. Seeing, hearing, talking, and thinking about ourselves as New Jersey, and not as a suburb or after thought to New York or Philadelphia, as wonderful as they are, is critical not just to our children's public affairs or geography knowledge, but to our own ability to live up to the sleeping potential that is an independent, autonomous, unified New Jersey.

It is time for New Jersey to cease being, in the words of Ben Franklin, "a barrel tapped at both ends."

V. STATE LEGISLATURES

In theory, state legislatures fulfill the representative democracy function in state government. Each legislator represents a particular district with particular interests. Legislators then meet in the state capital to meld the interests of the districts they represent with the interests of the state as a whole. The results of this tugging and hauling are the state budget, state policies, and occasionally a constitutional amendment.

In practice, however, state governments operate somewhat less democratically. Not everyone can afford to run for a seat in the state legislature, nor can many afford the time and loss of income that a legislator faces while serving in the legislature. So there tends to be a bias in just who serves based purely on economics: those who can afford to serve do, those who cannot don't. The resulting shortfall deprives a legislature of well-rounded representation of all the people of the state.

Further, subject-area specialists both within and outside the legislatures have an inordinate amount of power over legislators. This power relationship is concentrated toward those legislators who chair or are on money committees: finance or revenue, and appropriations. Because of their heavy workload, individual legislators increasingly must rely on these experts—their peers and lobbyists—for guidance on how to vote. Thus, in the basic operating processes of the legislature, some individuals, both inside and outside the legislature, wield more power than others.

Finally, once the legislation has been signed into law, the governor and the administrators of state agencies and programs are largely on their own to interpret and implement the laws. The courts often become important in helping define what a legislature really meant in passing certain legislation when conflicts arise. Or they can determine that the legislature was wrong in what it decided and declare a legislative act unconstitutional or void. In effect, the state legislature is only the starting point for action in the states. Once legislators have made their decisions, it is up to others to interpret, carry out, and resolve the issues created by legislation.

Legislative Reforms

The original reapportionment decisions, starting with *Baker v. Carr* in 1962, coincided with a general revival of state government during the mid- to late 1960s. The revival came at a time when the states sorely needed a new, more positive image. Numerous publications described the apparent failures, unrepresentativeness, and corruption of state governments.[1] It took national legislation such as the Civil Rights Act of 1964 and the Voting Rights Act of 1965 and U.S. Supreme Court decisions to force state governments to fulfill their responsibilities to those they represented.

In the 1970s and 1980s, state after state passed laws that drastically reformed state legislatures and improved their public image. Some of the most important of these reforms included providing offices for legislators, creating greater staff capability for the legislature and for individual legislators, installing newer technology to assist and monitor legislative action, removing some restrictions on schedules and sessions while tightening deadlines for action, moving to longer annual sessions, and providing for longer terms.

In the past decade, more changes have been afoot as voters in many states have made their state legislatures the target of the initiative process. Reform now is aimed at restricting rather than enhancing legislatures. In many states, the term limit movement has taken direct aim at the state legislatures. The 1990 term limits initiative in California "also cut the legislature's operating budget by 38 percent. Layoffs of staff began soon after, and California's staff has been cut substantially."[2]

Why are voters targeting their legislatures? One reason might be the continuing decline in public esteem of state elected officials. A recent analysis of state polls asking citizens about the performance of their state legislatures found more indicating the legislature was doing a fair or poor job than indicating it was doing an excellent job.[3]

Another reason for a decline in citizens' views of how well legislatures operate is the increasing number of states in which scandals have been found. The roster of states with such problems continues to grow.[4] A December 1996 Gallup Poll asked a nationwide sample of adults how they "would rate the honesty and ethical standards" in a variety of fields. State office holders ranked fourth from the bottom of a list of twenty-six fields, with only 13 percent of the respondents rating them very high or high—just ahead of car and insurance salespeople and advertising professionals.[5] Alan Ehrenhalt suggests that the trend toward negative campaigning may also be a factor. The negativity of campaign rhetoric often leaves voters with the feeling that they are selecting the lesser of two evils when they make their decision.[6]

But some observers argue that a major cause for the decline in public support has a budgetary policy base to it. In the 1980s, the economy grew and state revenues outpaced state expenditures. It was easy to make decisions with an ever-increasing pot of money available. New or additional taxes were not needed to provide more for citizens. Beginning in the late 1980s and continuing into the 1990s, however, the states and their elected leaders began facing hard times as the economy faltered nationally and, in some states, catastrophically. The decision calculus changed dramatically as legislators and governors were forced to raise taxes even as they cut back on state services.[7] This cutting mood was furthered with the results of the 1994 elections, when so many new legislators were elected—many with explicit promises to cut back state government and its programs.

Then, most states began seeing healthier revenues in a robust economy, and state legislators along with governors were able to chart new programs and paths in such areas as welfare reform. But now, in the early twenty-first century, the economic tide has turned once again and many states are facing shortfalls in revenues greater than those of a decade earlier. Trying to redress these shortfalls again places the legislators and other state leaders in a hard position. Do they just cut back on programs—if so, which programs? Or do they consider raising taxes or other types of revenues? However, raising taxes at the state level while the president and Congress are cutting federal taxes adds a difficult twist to the debate at the state level.

Separation of Powers

State legislatures do not operate in a vacuum. In most instances they are uneasy partners with other actors in state government. Other parts of state government, not just the legislatures, were reformed in response to the "indictment" of the states in the 1960s. Gubernatorial powers were strengthened to make governors the chief executives of the states in fact, rather than just in theory. However, these reforms did little to reduce the natural conflict between the executive and legislative branches that is built into state constitutions.

The U.S. Constitution and state constitutions share a fundamental principle: separation of powers. Consider, for example, this article from the Colorado Constitution that clearly separates legislative, executive, and judicial authority:

Article III. Distribution of Powers. The powers of the government of this state are divided into three distinct departments, the legislative, executive and judicial, and no person or collection of persons charged with the exercise of powers properly belonging to one of these departments shall exercise any power properly belonging to either of the others, except as in this constitution expressly directed or permitted.

Executive Branch Appointments. Appointments are perhaps the area of greatest tension between the executive and legislative branches of state government. Legislatures often have a constitutionally mandated power to confirm gubernatorial appointments. They can cause the governor problems with this authority by refusing to confirm appointments.

In some states, legislatures have the statutory or constitutional authority to make appointments to boards and commissions; they even can appoint their own members to these positions. Only four states strictly ban legislators from serving on boards and commissions. Eleven states allow legislators to serve on advisory bodies only. This "legislative intrusion" into the executive branch has been challenged successfully in Kentucky, Mississippi, and North Carolina.

Legislative Veto. A second area of tension lies in the increasing use of the legislative veto—a procedure permitting state legislatures (and the U.S. Congress) "to review proposed executive branch regulations or actions and to block or modify those with which they disagree."[8] In lieu of legislative veto legislation, some states have enacted laws regarding review of administrative rule-making procedures.

In the early 1980s there was a rapid rise in the use of the legislative veto—up to forty-one states by mid-1982. However, the tide then turned against this legislative bid to gain increased control over the executive branch. Courts, both state and federal, invalidated the legislative veto as an unconstitutional violation of the separation of powers principle.[9] And voters in several states rejected their legislature's use of a legislative veto.[10] In the 1990s, two state high courts—Idaho and Wisconsin—have reopened this power for their legislatures, albeit with some restrictions.[11] In 1997, the Missouri state Supreme Court ruled that state's legislative veto unconstitutional, as the law permitting this veto "allowed the legislature unconstitutionally to interfere with the functions of the executive branch . . . and it allowed the legislature to circumvent the constitution's bill passage and presentment requirements" through the use of the legislative veto process.[12]

The State Budget

With all of the action focused on the state budget, it is no surprise that power politics is also involved. In some states, governors and legislative leaders are locked in a struggle over who will control the state's finances. Because of uncertainty over projecting the next year's revenues, the need to cut back on expenditures, or even whether or not to raise taxes, budgets are being adopted much later than in the past—some well into the budget year. Governors want increased power and flexibility over budget making, while legislators find themselves forced to make difficult decisions with little time for deliberation.

Further, when governors and legislatures argue over the budget, delays in providing funds for programs and local governments occur. This leads to the embarrassing situation of the governor and legislature fighting budget battles in broad daylight with a seeming "inability to make even the most basic decisions on time."[13]

Part V explores different aspects of state legislatures. Alan Greenblatt of *Governing* looks at the problems that state legislatures are having getting their work done. Michael Jonas of *CommonWealth* presents the problems or ills that are afflicting the Massachusetts legislature. Ellen Perlman of *Governing* explores how well state legislators understand and use technology projects. Finally, Ronald Weber of *Spectrum: The Journal of State Government* reviews the status of the redistricting efforts that state legislatures go through following the most recent U.S. Censuses.

Notes

1. See, for example, Frank Trippett, *The States—United They Fell* (New York: World Publishing, 1967).

2. Alan Rosenthal, "The Legislative Institution—In Transition and at Risk," in *The State of the States,* 2d ed., ed. Carl E. Van Horn (Washington, D.C.: CQ Press, 1993), 127.

3. Karl T. Kurtz, "The Public Standing of the Legislature," National Conference of State Legislatures, August 1991.

4. To learn more about this problem, see "Evaluating State Legislatures," *State Policy Reports* 9:4 (January 1991): 8–13; Rob Gurwitt, "Deadly Stings and Wounded Legislatures," *Governing* 4:9 (June 1991): 26–31; and Jeffrey L. Katz, "Sipping from the Cup of Corruption," *Governing* 5:2 (November 1991): 27–28.

5. Leslie McAnemy, "Honesty and Ethics," *The Polling Report,* January 13, 1997, 8.

6. Alan Ehrenhalt, "An Embattled Institution," *Governing* 5:4 (January 1992): 28.

7. Rosenthal, "The Legislative Institution," and Thad Beyle, *Governors and Hard Times* (Washington, D.C.: CQ Press, 1992).

8. Walter J. Oleszek, *Congressional Procedures and the Policy Process,* 3d ed. (Washington, D.C.: CQ Press, 1988), 297.

9. The U.S. Supreme Court case was *Immigration and Naturalization Service v. Jagdish Rai Chadha* (1983).

10. New Jersey in 1985, Alaska and Michigan in 1986, Nevada in 1988.

11. "Idaho Court Says Legislature May Veto Administrative Rules," *State Legislatures* 16:6 (July 1990): 14; and "Wisconsin Finds No Separation of Power Violation in Statute Authorizing Legislative Committee to Suspend Administrative Rule," *State Constitutional Law Bulletin* 5:6 (March 1992): 1–2.

12. *Missouri Coalition v. Joint Committee on Administration,* 948 S.W.2d 125 (Mo. banc 1997) as reported in Jerry Brekke, "Supreme Court of Missouri Legislative Veto Unconstitutional," *Comparative State Politics* 19:1 (February 1998): 32–34.

13. Linda Wagar, "Power Play," *State Government News* 35:7 (July 1992): 9.

Why Are We Meeting Like This?

by Alan Greenblatt

Smart lawyers, it is often said, don't ask questions in court unless they already know the answers. And smart governors try not to call legislatures into special session unless they have the script written ahead of time. "If a governor calls a special session without knowing what the outcome's going to be," says Mississippi House Speaker Tim Ford, "it's chaos for everybody."

Chaos is exactly what Ford and his ally, Governor Ronnie Musgrove, are trying to avoid this month. Musgrove has called a special session to address the issue of medical lawsuits. Mississippi has seen several big-dollar malpractice awards, making it harder for physicians to get insurance. Doctors need the coverage to work in hospitals, and that has created a situation that is reaching crisis proportions. Unfortunately, many physicians don't think Musgrove's proposal to form a new risk pool will solve the problem, and the trial lawyers' lobby is fighting any attempt to cap damages. So this will not be an easy event to script or control.

Still, the administration is trying. Because it's such a contentious issue, Musgrove announced his special session plans back in May, giving Ford and other legislative leaders weeks to hold numerous hearings, make conference calls to anxious members and do all the other outreach necessary to work out a deal before everyone convenes in Jackson. "We try to grease it on the House and Senate side beforehand," Ford explains. "It doesn't always work, but 95 percent of the time, it does work."

Maybe the success rate is that high in Mississippi, but it's been otherwise this year in much of the country. In Wisconsin, where the legislature isn't even supposed to meet in even-numbered years, a witch's brew of budget shortfalls and divided party control have made a long-running joke out of a special session that's been lingering since January. Republican Governor Scott McCallum pushed a plan to abolish revenue sharing with localities—an idea the GOP-controlled House embraced to some degree but the Democratic Senate rejected outright. "It's the session that doesn't end," says Dan Thompson, executive director of the League of Wisconsin Municipalities, "but not a lot is happening while it's not ending." Legislators did manage to get together on a bill to address chronic wasting disease in deer.

Alan Greenblatt is a staff writer for *Governing*. This article is reprinted from *Governing* (August 2002): 40, 42.

Republican Governor Jeb Bush of Florida had a similarly frustrating experience, even though both legislative chambers were in the hands of his own party. Bush spent months trying to reach agreement on budget, education and insurance regulation issues, and in the end, talked angrily about the difficulty of dealing with the "children" who run the legislature.

Wisconsin and Florida stretched out the frustration; more often, special sessions that self-destruct do so rather quickly. Kentucky, for example, concluded its regular session this year without passing a budget, and Governor Paul Patton called lawmakers back into special session a week later. Patton had hoped to work out a deal with legislative leaders, but he was unable to do so, and the House and Senate met for 10 days, arguing over the issue of public financing for gubernatorial candidates. Patton and most of his fellow Democrats wanted it; Republicans felt it would put them at a disadvantage in future campaigns.

The argument soon produced a stalemate, and nothing was accomplished on the budget at all. ("They read newspapers. They snacked. They milled around," the *Lexington Herald-Leader* reported.) And the state entered its fiscal year July 1 without a budget having been enacted into law. Patton announced he could fund operations according to the House-passed blueprint, inviting lawsuits, and the state's bond rating was lowered.

Deadlock arrived even faster in Iowa, where Democratic Governor Tom Vilsack called his legislature back just after the regular session in May, hoping to restore funding for education and health. The Republican majority snickered and adjourned after a single day without debating any bills. "We just came in and went home," says state House Majority Leader Christopher Rants. Vilsack then sat down with legislators and unhappily signed a package of budget cuts he'd accepted in meetings with legislators before a second special session met, also in May.

But there are more humiliating fates a governor can suffer: After New Mexico Governor Gary Johnson vetoed two budgets this spring, the legislature decided to bypass him and call itself into "extraordinary" session for the first time in state history. It met for one afternoon, overrode the governor and went home. Johnson complained that he had been steamrolled, but there wasn't much he could do.

If you think there have been a lot of special legislative sessions this year, you're right. Just two years ago, 12 states held them. Last year, there were 46; by June of this year, there had already been 25. Quite a few of these actually were short, non-controversial and little-noticed—it's the sessions that erupt in anger or sputter away in futility that attract most of the attention.

But the increase in overall numbers is no mystery. Special sessions follow budget problems, and practically every state can boast of those problems this year. Meanwhile, the states are coping with redistricting, an exercise frequently distracting enough to delay the passage of other crucial legislation. (Redistricting "just tied everything all to pieces," according to one lobbyist in Kentucky.)

The connection between redistricting and special sessions is easy to document. At the start of every decade, as states grapple with the need to redraw their district lines, the number of these sessions spikes up. There were 58 special sessions in 1981, for example, and 52 in 1991.

But some states seem to have grown addicted to the extra sessions regardless of the political and economic climate. Republican Mike Foster has been governor of Louisiana for seven years, and has called a special session every year. One reason is that the state constitution doesn't allow legislators to offer non-budget bills during general sessions in even-numbered years. As a result, legislators want the special sessions for their pet non-budget

How a Bill Becomes State Law

This graphic shows the most typical way in which proposed legislation is enacted into law in the states. Bills must be passed by both houses of the state legislature in identical form before they can be sent to the governor to be signed or vetoed. Of course, the legislative process differs slightly from state to state.

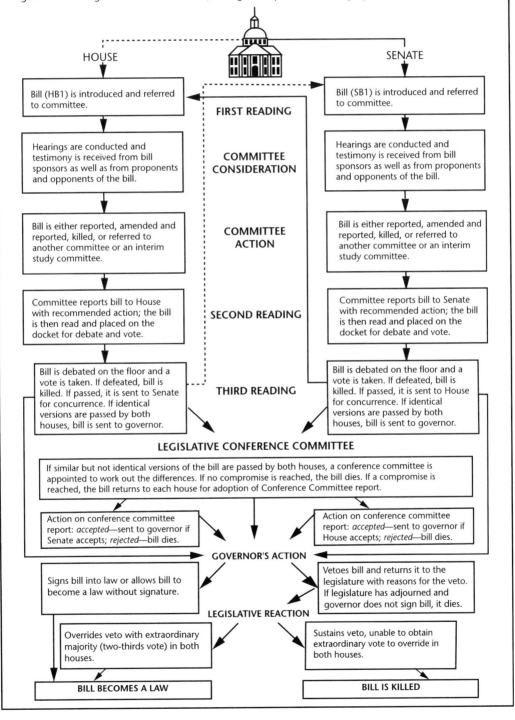

HOUSE

SENATE

Bill (HB1) is introduced and referred to committee.

FIRST READING

Bill (SB1) is introduced and referred to committee.

Hearings are conducted and testimony is received from bill sponsors as well as from proponents and opponents of the bill.

COMMITTEE CONSIDERATION

Hearings are conducted and testimony is received from bill sponsors as well as from proponents and opponents of the bill.

Bill is either reported, amended and reported, killed, or referred to another committee or an interim study committee.

COMMITTEE ACTION

Bill is either reported, amended and reported, killed, or referred to another committee or an interim study committee.

Committee reports bill to House with recommended action; the bill is then read and placed on the docket for debate and vote.

SECOND READING

Committee reports bill to Senate with recommended action; the bill is then read and placed on the docket for debate and vote.

Bill is debated on the floor and a vote is taken. If defeated, bill is killed. If passed, it is sent to Senate for concurrence. If identical versions are passed by both houses, bill is sent to governor.

THIRD READING

Bill is debated on the floor and a vote is taken. If defeated, bill is killed. If passed, it is sent to House for concurrence. If identical versions are passed by both houses, bill is sent to governor.

LEGISLATIVE CONFERENCE COMMITTEE

If similar but not identical versions of the bill are passed by both houses, a conference committee is appointed to work out the differences. If no compromise is reached, the bill dies. If a compromise is reached, the bill returns to each house for adoption of Conference Committee report.

Action on conference committee report: *accepted*—sent to governor if Senate accepts; *rejected*—bill dies.

Action on conference committee report: *accepted*—sent to governor if House accepts; *rejected*—bill dies.

GOVERNOR'S ACTION

Signs bill into law or allows bill to become a law without signature.

Vetoes bill and returns it to the legislature with reasons for the veto. If legislature has adjourned and governor does not sign bill, it dies.

LEGISLATIVE REACTION

Overrides veto with extraordinary majority (two-thirds vote) in both houses.

Sustains veto, unable to obtain extraordinary vote to override in both houses.

BILL BECOMES A LAW

BILL IS KILLED

items, and lobby the governor to include the items on the special session calendar. The legislative leadership tries to hold the line, warning of undesired consequences. "The more you open up the agenda," says Jerry Luke LeBlanc, chairman of the Louisiana House Appropriations Committee, "the more potential there is for some controversies and some battles to erupt." LeBlanc and other legislators have put a ballot initiative before voters this fall to allow legislators to introduce a handful of non-fiscal bills in the off-year, so they can cut down on special session clutter.

Texas used to have a bad case of special session addiction. Despite its size and governmental complexity, the Lone Star state still officially meets just once every other year, and during the 1980s, it never seemed to be able to get its work done without scheduling at least one special session in the off-year. More recently, though, the state seems to have broken that habit; it hasn't held a special session since 1992. Governor Rick Perry resisted calls to hold a session on medical malpractice this year, largely because he couldn't get a deal worked out in advance. "This is a complex issue," says Perry spokeswoman Kathy Walt, "and one that the governor believes is best addressed in a full session of the legislature."

If a survey of the 50 governors were taken, Perry's would probably be the majority view. But there have always been some who see it the opposite way, viewing a special session as an opportunity to tackle a big problem at a time when legislators' full attention can be focused on that one issue alone. West Virginia's Cecil Underwood, who served in the 1990s, was determined to overhaul the state's antiquated tax system, and to convene a special session to get the job done. "When you get into a regular session," explains Robin Capeheart, who was Underwood's finance secretary, "you've got so

many things floating around. With something as serious and broad as reforming tax structure, we didn't want to get in a situation where the need for horse trading would get in the way of a major structural proposal." Ultimately, something else got in the way: Underwood was defeated for reelection in 2000.

But West Virginia continues to stand apart from most other states in handling many of its pressing issues in special legislative sessions. There has been one every other month over the past two years, dealing with flood cleanups, medical malpractice, nursing homes and numerous other crucial and time-sensitive subjects.

Over the years, West Virginia's leaders have learned the same lesson as their counterparts elsewhere: It's better to script things in advance. Rank-and-file members are courted, says Keith Burdette, legislative director for Governor Bob Wise, but for the most part, they are presented with a limited menu of options and expected to sign off on the deals that have been worked out.

It's not impossible for the unscripted approach to succeed: Indiana legislators surprised themselves and most of the state this year by reaching bipartisan agreement on a new tax code in the final hours of a special session, long after they seemed destined to break up in failure. The outcome represented a triumph for both the Republican Senate and Democratic House, whose leaders were determined to prove they could work together.

But results like those are the improbable exceptions. Governors and legislative leaders nearly always end up happier when they follow the textbook and avoid high drama. The event may be a little dull—a legislative Kabuki play, with all the real action having taken place offstage—but when it comes to special sessions, spontaneity is rarely an ingredient of success.

Beacon Ill

by Michael Jonas

It's a steamy afternoon in late July, and you might expect the temperature to be rising even higher beneath the golden dome of the Massachusetts State House. The state Senate is getting ready to vote on the biggest tax increase in state history, a $1.2 billion tax package designed to plug a gaping hole in the state budget. When Senate Minority Leader Brian Lees rises to speak on the matter, everyone knows what's coming.

"Unbelievable," thunders the Republican leader, one of the Legislature's acknowledged kings of the floor-debate stemwinder. "The out and out arrogance of some members of the chamber. You are going to be so, so sorry when this comes home to roost," he says, tearing into those supporting the tax increase.

Despite Lees's effort to turn up the heat of the debate and inject some fear into his Democratic colleagues, Senate President Thomas Birmingham, sitting in the presiding officer's chair, looks more bored than worried. With Democrats holding 34 of the 40 seats in the Senate, and 134 of 160 seats in the House, Lees and his tiny band of GOP compatriots—along with Jane Swift, a lame-duck acting governor from a nearly invisible minority party—hardly amount to a speed bump on the road to Demo-cratic victory on this issue. Or any other, for that matter.

After 12 years of Republican control of the governor's office, the clout of the Democrat-dominated Legislature has never been greater. A steady waning of executive branch authority that began halfway through Bill Weld's first term as governor—helped along by the virtual disappearance of Republicans from the Legislature—has created a political vacuum that Democratic lawmakers have been happy to fill. But the storyline of legislative ascendancy comes with an ironic twist: While the Legislature's power has never been greater, the role of individual legislators has perhaps never been more diminished.

"I'd say this is the worst I've seen in my 25 years as a lobbyist," says Barbara Anderson, the longtime executive director of Citizens for Limited Taxation. "In the past you could talk to people" outside of leadership who could make a difference. "Now there's no one to talk to." It's not that there's "no level playing field," she says. "There's no playing field at all. They're just following the leadership."

Michael Jonas is an associate editor at *CommonWealth*. This article is reprinted from *CommonWealth* (fall 2002): 38–43.

When Anderson and others refer to "the leadership," everyone knows they don't mean some inner circle of Beacon Hill honchos, but simply the two men who have been the force and face of legislative might for more than six years. Since their parallel rise to power in 1996, House Speaker Thomas Finneran and Senate President Thomas Birmingham have come to dominate Massachusetts government to a degree that is striking even in a state known for its powerful legislative leaders. Rank-and-file members, in turn, have been largely reduced to bit players—"extras on the state's political stage, members of the chorus backing up the two Toms," as a *MetroWest Daily News* editorial called them last winter.

But the curtain is coming down on this act of state government starring the "two Toms." Birmingham is on his way out the door, having decided to give up his post in order to run for governor. The jockeying to succeed him is in full swing, and there are signs of a hankering among senators to play a larger role in the new regime.

And Finneran's role, while still getting top billing, seems to be changing. Though very much in charge in the House, he has had to contend recently with flashpoints of trouble. A would-be challenge to his rule last December seemed to fade as fast as it appeared. But the rumble of discontent has lingered, and Finneran, who can be as nimble as he is blunt, seemed to alter his style this spring, winning over many of his most persistent House critics in the process of engineering unprecedented support for a politically unpalatable menu of tax hikes and spending cuts.

Meanwhile, regardless of who wins the governor's race, the corner office will be home to the first chief executive since Weld who has won the post outright, rather than inherited it. That could mean the return of a stronger executive branch counterweight to legislative power, but it hardly ensures it.

Do these changes add up to a new day of democracy and power sharing dawning on Beacon Hill? Or spell new life for a Legislature that, for all its amassed power, is regularly derided as out of touch and out of kilter? Probably not. But there are plenty of reasons to hope they do.

The House That Two Toms Built

If the Legislature has become a body stuck in torpor, Finneran and Birmingham, in many respects, are unlikely figures to have presided over such a decline. The two leaders harbor a breadth and depth of intellectual capacity uncommon among State House pols, and they are each eloquent spokesmen for coherent—though often conflicting—visions of state government. Finneran is a furrowed-brow skeptic of unchecked state spending who has elevated his own ceremonial profile by delivering an annual "Speaker's address to the Commonwealth," an event symbolic of many observers' assessment that he is more the governor than the governor is. Meanwhile, Birmingham, a Rhodes scholar whose progressive politics are delivered with an Oxford vocabulary and a Chelsea chip on the shoulder, has made a compelling case for state government as the great equalizer in a society where the cards are often dealt unfairly.

The two leaders bring to their posts the type of brainpower and passion that one would wish for in every legislator, and certainly every legislative leader. But the Legislature they lead, in a bicameral division of labor, has degenerated on their shared watch in both form and substance.

Nowhere has this been more evident than in the annual state budget debate, which has turned into a recurrent—and deeply personal—confrontation between the two legislative chieftains and their respective public philosophies. This clash played itself out on a level of public spectacle in 1999, when the two leaders spent r8

summer and fall on the balcony outside Birmingham's State House office, personally hashing out a $21 billion state spending plan, which they delivered five months late. The following year, an all-night April budget session in the House morphed into something resembling a booze-soaked frat party, with phantom votes being cast for lawmakers who were not present, while other representatives reportedly dozed off in their offices. The true scandal of what became known as the "Animal House" budget was not so much that legislators' judgment may have been clouded by their late-night imbibition, but that their state of mind hardly mattered as they rubber-stamped spending decisions already made by House leaders.

A year ago, budget talks again dragged on for months beyond the July start of the new fiscal year, with a spending plan dropped on lawmakers the day before Thanksgiving, giving them only hours to digest the 500-page document before casting an up-or-down vote. Finally, after agreeing last summer to more than $1 billion in tax increases and tax-cut reversals, Finneran's House and Birmingham's Senate could not settle on a common spending blueprint, leaving it to [Gov.] Swift—a lame-duck acting governor whose vetoes the Legislature could have overridden at will—to make the final $300 million in cuts.

And these fiscal follies are by no means the only symptoms of advanced legislative dysfunction:

• Legislative committees and their chairmen—once powerful centers of authority and expertise—have seen much of their clout vanish as Speaker and Senate president exercise near-total discretion over whether bills reach the floor.

• Budget riders, or "outside sections" to the annual state spending plan, have become the prime vehicle for the most important legislative initiatives, bypassing committee hearings, public testimony, and the due delibera-

tion that educates lawmakers and the public alike on pending proposals. Criticized by the Swift administration and good-government watchdogs for excessive use of this legislative end-around, lawmakers cut down the volume of outside sections in the last two budgets. But these budget riders remain the legislative fast track for major leadership initiatives ranging from a revampaing of the state's special education law to recent changes in Medicaid eligibility that could cut benefits to 50,000 people.

• With leadership-backed proposals sprung on them without warning, lawmakers say they sometimes don't know what they're voting on. At the hearing called in September to sort out, after the fact, the consequences of a Legislature-approved cut in prescription reimbursement rates that had chain and independent pharmacies threatening to pull out of the state Medicaid program, representatives and senators alike testified they had been in the dark when they cast their votes. "It's clear to me that we had no idea what we were doing," said state Rep. Daniel Bosley of North Adams. "Many of us were not fully informed about the some of things we were doing to balance the budget," echoed Sen. Susan Fargo of Lincoln, a member of the budget-writing Ways and Means Committee.

• Even the obligation to conduct routine business in a timely manner is regularly ignored. A longstanding rule requiring joint House-Senate committees to hold hearings on and report out all bills in the first six months of the Legislature's two-year session is now repeatedly extended not only for particular bills, which might need further review, but all bills. In the 2001–2002 sitting of the Legislature, the bill-reporting deadline was pushed past the end of formal sessions on July 31.

• Indeed, for this two-year session of the Legislature, the two houses never did get around to adopting rules that govern their joint operation, a matter of legislative protocol usually disposed of in the opening days.

None of these failings and foibles is by itself a scandal. But taken together, they form a disturbing pattern of legislative malaise. "It's all slight changes here and there that are not noteworthy singly," says John McDonough, a former Boston state representative. "Collectively, they have added up to a diminishing of the role of committees, of rank-and-file members, and the public."

And as the role of individual legislators has diminished, so has interest in running for these posts. This year's legislative races feature among the fewest number of contested seats in the 24 years since the House was reduced in size from 240 to 160 members. In just 49 seats in the House and only 12 of 40 Senate seats will there be two major-party candidates on the ballot in November.

Of course, this lack of electoral competition is also a direct consequence of the continuing decline of the Massachusetts Republican Party. What had looked like a budding Republican revival at the time of Weld's election as governor in 1990, when the GOP won enough Senate seats to sustain a gubernatorial veto, proved to be little more than a flash in the political pan. Within two years, Democrats won back enough Senate seats to knock the legislative prop out from under Republican executive authority.

As the Democratic ranks have continued to swell, what's been lost is not only Republican leverage but also sufficient opposition, loyal or not, to maintain even a semblance of debate. In the House, where four GOP members are not seeking re-election this fall, state Rep. Bradley Jones, the assistant minority leader, says his biggest concern is that Republican ranks, which now stand at just 22, could fall below 20, the number needed to force a roll call vote. During House debates these days, says Jones, "We have to worry about people leaving to go the bathroom."

The Mouse That Didn't Roar

Without the push and pull of vigorous two-party competition, the axis of tension in the House, such as it is, has been between legislative leadership and disenchanted members. For the most part, it hasn't been much of a match. Indeed, the political muscles of House backbenchers have so atrophied that they can't even mount a decent revolt.

Although his dominating presence made him a lightning rod for criticism outside the building almost since the day he took power in 1996, within the House Finneran faced little challenge beyond the grumblings of a small band of diehard liberals he once dismissed as "cranks." That is, until last winter. Fresh from the Thanksgiving eve budget debacle, a group of House members that had been meeting to discuss their growing discontent with Finneran's rule went so far as to raise the idea of a Beacon Hill palace coup.

The Boston Globe caught wind of the confabs in mid-December and made them front-page news, with the paper reporting breathlessly of a challenge to Finneran "that could include a motion to oust him from office." But the would-be revolt proved to be more a belch of rank-and-file indigestion than the mustering of a well-ordered militia. "I think mini-rebellion overstates the case," says Rep. Jay Kaufman, a Lexington Democrat who was part of the group. "What there was was a collection of frustrated and angry people, but no clear direction or leadership."

There clearly was no stomach—or plan— for a confrontation along the lines of the mid-1980s overthrow of Speaker Thomas McGee, in which House dissidents (including rank-and-filer Tom Finneran) used a coming election cycle to recruit candidates pledged to a leadership change. Indeed, the House dissidents tapped an unlikely general to lead an anti-Finneran charge: Rep. Daniel Bosley, a 16-year House veteran who serves as House chairman of the joint Government Regulations Committee. And Bosley says now that a full-blown leadership challenge was never in the cards.

"We didn't start a little cabal to overthrow the Speaker," says Bosley, suggesting that the conspirators' main objective was changing House rules to open up the legislative process. But with no specific demands even put forward, the revolt-that-wasn't seemed to suffer from the same rank-and-file listlessness that keeps Finneran unquestionably the man in charge.

"I could not have envisioned something as staggeringly weak," says long-time liberal activist Jim Braude, a veteran of many Beacon Hill battles.

As weak as it was, the abortive revolt revealed that a measure of discontent had spread beyond liberals alienated by Finneran's politics to members more in the House mainstream.

Members like Charley Murphy, who would be nobody's idea of a bomb-throwing House rebel. A 36-year-old ex-Marine who represents the blue-collar Boston suburb of Burlington, Murphy is a centrist Democrat whose views on fiscal matters aren't out of step with those of the Speaker himself. But after two terms as a loyal foot soldier, following the leadership lead on everything from procedural votes to budget decisions, Murphy simply grew weary of what he calls the "go along to get along" mindset that permeates the House.

Murphy says he's had four different committee chairmen tell him, when he's asked about particular bills, that they're waiting for word from Finneran on whether to move the legislation forward. "So now, that's a chairman of a committee," says Murphy. "I mean, do you think people on that committee are going to feel like, hey, let's dig in, roll up our sleeves and get some work done?"

In January, Murphy took his criticisms public, co-authoring an op-ed column in the *Globe* with fellow representative Barry Finegold, an Andover Democrat. "The House has ceded its authority to leadership to such an extent that debate is rare and the participation of the membership in substantive policy making is more so," wrote the two lawmakers. "We have allowed this to happen. It must stop."

If the spread of disenchantment has Finneran shaking in his boots, he hides it well. Asked his reaction to the Bosley-led uprising and Murphy's op-ed chafing, Finneran pauses for a moment before answering. When he does, he sounds less like a chastened autocrat than a parent whose teenager has committed some foolish stunt. "Disappointed," says Finneran. "Disappointed would be the word."

But the Speaker's father-still-knows-best demeanor masks a willingness to shift course in the face of a strong headwind. Following last year's budget mess and the aborted coup attempt, Finneran's Monday morning meetings with his top lieutenants involved some uncharacteristic introspection—and some blunt talk. "It did come to a head," says Rep. Kevin Fitzgerald, a member of Finneran's leadership team. "People were critical of him. I think we all came to the realization that we could do a better job."

That realization could not have come at a better time.

Legislators Who Get IT

by Ellen Perlman

As recently as last year, the Arizona Senate was using a 1980s-era roll-call system that showed lawmakers' names and a bar that turned green or red, depending on whether their vote was yea or nay. When it worked, the system was adequate, if antiquated. The problem was, it often didn't work—forcing senators back to voice votes tabulated on pieces of paper. Repairing the system meant flying people out from Washington, D.C., since there was only one company left in the country that knew how to maintain it. Since the upkeep was more expensive than the purchase of a new system, a decision was made to rip out all the old equipment and start fresh.

With the installation of a fully computerized video system that has a large screen that drops down from the ceiling, senators got a personal look at the benefits of upgraded technology. The state-of-the-art system not only turns voting legislators' names green or red—or yellow if they haven't voted yet—it also provides a screen where they can show presentations to enhance their remarks in debate.

Since most lawmakers are not well versed in information technology issues, any firsthand experience with and lessons on the benefits of technology are sorely needed in legislatures.

"Sometimes it's difficult for legislators to see the potential of technology," says Arizona state Senator Dean Martin, who is the founder of a digital media development company and one of the few lawmakers there with a technology background. "They balk over a million-dollar expenditure when it would result in a $10 million savings over 10 years in man hours or overhead."

Martin figures that if technology is integrated into legislators' way of life and their job duties, they will be more likely to understand what executive-branch agencies are asking for when they seek funding for technology projects. Right now, the level of understanding of even basic technology varies widely among legislators. "There are people who don't know how to turn on a computer and are afraid of e-mail," Martin says. "They have assistants who print out e-mails for them and respond to them. If you have a legislature that's been doing things the same way for 100 years, they may not be as willing to have other agencies upgrade."

Ellen Perlman is a staff writer for *Governing*. This article is reprinted from *Governing* (May 2002): 26, 28, 30.

Getting legislatures to understand the technology needs of executive-branch agencies has been a tough assignment for chief information officers and department heads. Legislators often have great interest in technology from an economic development point of view; that is, the business of attracting technology companies to a region or laying fiber for more sophisticated use of technology around the state. And there's been no shortage of ideological stands taken on technology issues, such as stopping Internet pornography and using filtering software in schools.

But when it comes to understanding and overseeing the complex technology projects that run state governments and their agencies, legislators often are at a loss or just not interested. "Legislators don't get it," Ohio CIO Gregory Jackson told vendors who sell hardware and software to state and local governments, at a recent technology conference. He called on the private sector to help educate local legislators on technology issues.

Few legislators would argue with the assessment that although they hold the purse strings for millions of dollars in technology spending, most of them don't stay on top of technology issues very well. In some cases, legislatures are getting better at it. They've had to. Embarrassing, expensive and highly public failures of large IT projects have forced the issue into the spotlight. "There have been some bad stories of cost overruns," says Minnesota state Senator Steve Kelley. "Projects have been either poorly conceived or poorly executed. Legislators have had to pay attention to those issues."

Yet getting legislatures to routinely focus on state IT projects is an ongoing process, one that gets interrupted with every election cycle. Some states have done better than others at making room for legislators at the IT table, and keeping them there. Washington State formalized a structure that brings the legislative

branch into the loop with the executive and judicial branches early on, as IT projects are being discussed. A little more than half of the states have created technology boards or councils with legislators as members, and some develop policy and formulate spending guidelines for statewide IT projects. Thirty-one states have set up House, Senate or joint IT committees to focus on technology.

Some states benefit from a convergence of factors that leads to effective technology policies and practices. In Utah, the stars have aligned with a savvy and technology-oriented governor, Mike Leavitt, and a number of individual legislators who happen to have technology know-how and interest. State legislators sit on an IT commission with executive branch and private-sector members. And legislators all have laptops that they use for constituent e-mail and to read and review amendments and bills, so they have a basic comfort level with technology.

If legislators aren't at ease with technology or aren't interested enough to spend time on it, they can't just pick up and start talking about it. "It takes awhile to understand what's going on," says Mary Winkley, who worked as a legislative analyst in California, after a stint as a technology staffer to state Senator Debra Bowen, who chairs the Energy, Utilities and Communication-New Technology Subcommittee.

That's why the role of the executive branch is so crucial. "It has really been up to the administration to get folks in position to understand the cost savings, and go to legislators with proposals," says Arizona's Martin. CIOs and department heads who do the legislative hand-holding, educating lawmakers and building relationships with them, have a leg up when it comes time to request funding for a big project. "You have to constantly give the big picture," says Susan Patrick, strategic communications manager of the Government Information Technology Agency in Arizona, an executive-branch agency that does oversight, planning and coordination of IT projects and is headed by the state's CIO, a member of the governor's Cabinet.

Patrick and others from GITA not only present information formally at the beginning of a session, but also during the summer when study committees are meeting and at informal meetings throughout the year. Patrick recalls speaking with a rural economic development committee made up mostly of rural legislators who felt they had little interest in technology. Once she talked to them about steps the state was taking to bring broadband capacity to rural areas for telemedicine and distance learning, "they had much more interest in technology—versus rural issues—than they realized they did."

When Iowa legislators have questions about the value of IT projects being proposed, they can refer to the state's return-on-investment program, a methodology for evaluating the benefits of IT projects. The program summarizes, analyzes, prioritizes and explains the specifics and the worth of all the technology projects being done across government in any year. Technology projects are ranked and get points based on whether the project will improve customer service, whether there are requirements mandating it, whether it will have a direct impact on Iowa's citizens, whether the project will be for one agency, multiple agencies or the entire state government enterprise.

As to the request for vendors to help educate legislators, Richard Varn, Iowa's CIO, believes there is a useful way and a not-so-useful way for them to do so. When it comes to their own economic well being, technology companies don't need to be persuaded to approach and educate legislators. They do what it takes to get IT contracts signed. But when it comes to promoting the technology industry in general, Varn notes, vendors are conspicuously absent.

Everyone would benefit from legislators becoming more informed about issues such as telemedicine, distance education, e-government services, digital signatures and identity theft. But vendors do not typically engage in those discussions, Varn says.

Legislators agree that few technology companies seek them out. "A lot of people in the IT industry stick to their knitting," says Minnesota's Kelley. "They're not comfortable breaking out and working with politicians." They do make their way to the executive branch to lobby for contract awards and promote their wares. But in his state, Kelley says, they have not figured out how to make themselves effective at the capital nearly as well as, say, the chamber of commerce. "I partly attribute that to the fitful motivation of folks in the technology industry. Most of them would rather government go away. They'd rather not deal with us at all." Nor have there been many IT-types who run for office, producing instant legislative experts.

How can legislators do their homework and learn what they need to know about technology? California's Bowen says she learned from experts. When she observed agencies in state government that were good at delivering projects on time and on budget, she focused on what they had to say in hearings. Over time, her staff has developed a list of questions to ask others based on that knowledge, such as "How do you know when to pull the plug on a project" and "How can you divide that project into segments so you build on success, rather than take on big projects without knowing how well they'll do?"

The California legislature is certainly more sophisticated than it was in 1994 when it approved a welfare IT project that quickly fell to pieces. The welfare system was supposed to automate the calculation of benefits for welfare recipients and was piloted in a few counties. But an audit determined it wasn't robust enough to handle the entire state's caseload and the project was stopped.

Back then, the budget committee was presented with no deliverables, no benchmarks and no evidence of strategic planning, Bowen says. Very few legislators were thinking about how to achieve service-delivery goals or efficiencies, or eliminate errors. They thought more in terms of how to automate an existing paper trail. Bowen didn't claim to know the ins and outs of IT but was able to turn to the auditor's office and the legislative analyst's office for their expertise. Both have the authority to retain IT consultants.

California now has House and Senate committees and subcommittees on technology. Some officials consider the existence of such committees in state legislatures as vital for overseeing technology matters. Others say technology shouldn't be channeled so narrowly. All agencies should be focusing on technology, even within program areas such as health and social services. Legislators who get a judiciary committee assignment may think they have to deal only with judicial issues but may find themselves voting on whether to modernize data tracking systems in the judiciary.

In any case, technology committees are not generally considered plum assignments. "A lot of legislators like to get into committees that can make major changes or major splashes in the media," says Arizona's Martin. "Technology committees are more oversight of upgrading government. Most people don't give you an award for making the DMV line move 10 percent faster," he says. "But for most people, if a three-hour wait becomes a two-hour wait, it's still an accomplishment."

Minnesota does not have formal technology committees. Instead, the legislature created an ad hoc IT committee as a forum for technology discussions, education and information. "We tried to get everybody together to look at issues that cross functional boundaries," Kelley says. But for the most part, busy legislators failed to show up. "Until a particular committee forces you to make a decision, time-budgeted legislators aren't going to get background on an issue." As a result, there's less of a build-up of IT expertise in the legislature and more reliance on the executive branch or staff.

As term limits sweep out the old guard in some states, opportunities open up for younger legislators to step in. In theory, at least, the thirty-somethings that come into office would seem likely to push legislatures up to speed on technology issues. "To the extent there are term limits and younger members of the legislature, the use of technology will become matter of fact," says state Representative Ed Jennings, a member of the Florida House Committee on Information Technology.

But even though these young professionals have been using technology most of their adult lives, that doesn't guarantee they have the know-how to oversee complex, enterprise-wide technology projects that change the way government does its business. "People come in who know technology better, but they don't stay long enough to know the business processes of government," says Iowa's Varn.

When legislatures are not knowledgeable in technology, it leaves a lop-sided arrangement in government. "In the absence of participation by the legislature, the executive branch has no checks or balances," says Winkley. "The legislature is missing how important technology is for making executive branch programs successful."

Emerging Trends in State Legislative Redistricting

Ronald E. Weber

In this article I will assess preliminarily how the states are doing in redrawing state legislative district lines for the elections of 2002 now that the 2000 Census of Population data are in the hands of state legislatures. Whereas the redistricting round of the 1990s can be described as the round of racial and ethnic predominance, the 2000 round will be characterized as the rejuvenation of partisanship. A line of U.S. Supreme Court cases beginning with *Shaw v. Reno* in the 1990s made it clear that state legislatures could not draw districts predominantly based on race or ethnicity but would have to use other factors in drawing revised lines during this decade. These other factors might correlate highly with race or ethnicity and, since political partisanship of voters correlates highly with the racial and ethnic makeup of populations, the 2000 decade is likely to be the round of partisan gerrymandering.

The Supreme Court cases of the 1990s ultimately sanctioned the use of partisanship as a predominant factor in redistricting, even though the Court in *Miller v. Johnson* in 1995 argued for the use of a set of race-neutral, objective criteria such as compactness, contiguity, respect for political subdivisions, and respect for communities of interest. The controlling case is *Easley v. Cromartie,* where the Court upheld North Carolina's use of partisanship when it redrew its unconstitutional Congressional districting plan, despite the plaintiffs' contention that the plan relied predominantly on race. This decision sanctioned the unbridled use of partisanship as the predominant factor in redistricting in the current decade.

Partisanship Unbridled?

Legislative redistricting is among the most partisan of policy activities undertaken by state legislatures. In essence, the legislature takes the position that political districting is a matter of preserving self-interest: the spoils of politics belong to the strongest, and district line-drawing can be manipulated to improve the political position of the party which controls each chamber. A large number of states operate under the norm that each chamber is the primary arbiter of the lines for its chamber

Ronald E. Weber is Wilder Crane Professor of Government at the University of Wisconsin, Milwaukee. This article is reprinted from *Spectrum* (winter 2002): 13–15. Copyright 2002 The Council of State Governments. Reprinted with permission from *Spectrum.*

so that the House defers to the wishes of the Senate and vice versa. Furthermore, many state legislators take the position that it is not the governor's job to intrude on the turf of the legislature when it comes to drawing districting lines for the state senate or house. Of course, some districting schemes require a degree of cooperation between the two chambers, such as "nesting" house districts within state senate districts. This cooperation gets a little dicey when the Democrats control one chamber and the Republicans control the other, as is the current situation in Illinois and Wisconsin.

How each political party seeks to advance its political interests varies. The issue is to determine the best way to waste the vote of the partisans of the other party. To do so requires a great deal of information about past turnout patterns and levels of political support given by party followers. For example, Democrats are well aware that Republican supporters typically turn out at higher levels than Democratic followers. Democrats thus can "waste" Republican votes by using election history information to identify areas with proven records of Republican voting patterns along with higher than average levels of voter turnout. This has created the cul-de-sac theory of districting where Democrats concentrate all the neighborhoods with gated communities and cul-de-sac street patterns in Republican districts. This approach was refined in Texas redistricting in the 1990s and was followed again this decade as the Texas Legislature worked unsuccessfully on state legislative districts.

Republicans, on the other hand, find the use of racial and ethnic data most useful in locating potential Democratic voters. Here the approach is to pack potentially as many African-American or Hispanic minority voters into legislative districts so as to minimize the number of seats that the Democratic Party can win, while then spreading Republican supporters over the remaining districts. This approach

was used effectively in the 1990s in Ohio where the Republican-dominated apportionment board drew state legislative districts by concentrating African-American populations at the highest possible levels in Democratic districts. Thus, the Republicans minimized the number of Democratic-leaning districts and produced a decade of Republican control of both chambers in Ohio. The Ohio Republicans also spent the decade fending off legal challenges by the Democrats to this approach of wasting minority Democratic voters (see the *Quilter v. Voinovich* cases of the 1990s). Since this approach was validated largely by the federal courts in the 1990s, state legislatures learned it might be legal to "waste" minority votes to achieve political gerrymandering. With the exception of Ohio, the state Democratic parties of the 1990s were more interested in cooperating with minority office holders who wanted potentially safe electoral districts than in fighting Republican efforts to pack minority populations in Democrat districts. But this all changed in the early rounds of the 2000 redistrictings.

During the 1990s, a number of political scientists explored the question of what level of minority population is necessary to equalize the opportunity of minority voters to elect candidates of choice to Congressional and state legislative office. Invariably, this research determined that a combination of cohesive minority group support along with white or "Anglo" voters would enable Democratic candidates to win Congressional or state legislative office. And with regularity, the researchers determined that the appropriate minority population percentage was less than 50 percent and usually closer to 40 percent. This research gave ammunition to Democrats who argued that anything above those minority percentage levels constituted "packing" of minority populations and thus would minimize the opportunity of Democratic voters to elect Democrats. My work for plaintiff interests in the *Shaw*-type of cases in the 1990s demonstrated that Democratic candidates could count on various levels of white or "Anglo" cross-over votes and that these votes had to be taken into account in determining whether plans were narrowly tailored to advance compelling state interests. Thus, the Democrats learned that they had been mistaken in the 1990s to attempt to maximize minority populations in state legislative districts as the minority office-holders often argued should be the case. Of course, the Republican sweep in the 1994 elections, particularly in the South, brought home to the Democratic Party the consequences of minority population maximization as the Republicans scored big gains in state legislative elections.

In this round of state legislative redistricting, the Democrats have reversed their approach because of the lessons learned during the 1990s. Now the lines of the partisan battle are quite clear. Democrats want an optimum percentage of minority populations in state legislative districts. Their goal is neither to waste too many Democratic votes nor to have so few Democrats so that the districts might not elect Democrats. Thus, this optimum percentage must be determined in each state before beginning the state legislative districting. Most instructive on this point is the *Page* federal court case from New Jersey. In this case, the Democratic-inclined chair of the New Jersey Apportionment Commission had drawn a nested set of state senate and house districts in which the minority populations were apportioned to permit more minority and Democratic senators to be elected than under the previous districts. New Jersey Republicans and the NAACP both challenged this approach in federal court. The three-judge panel ruled that the New Jersey Apportionment Commission had made the right decision not to pack minority populations (or Democratic voters) as the New Jersey Republicans had wanted. Thus, in

the first federal court decision of the 2000 decade, the Democratic Party approach to state legislative districting was upheld.

Is Retrogression a Problem Anymore?

In states covered wholly or in part under Section V of the U.S. Voting Rights Act of 1965 (as amended in 1982), the state legislature must keep in mind the opportunity of minority voters to elect candidates of choice when redrawing state legislative district lines. The legal standard under the *Reno v. Bossier Parish School Board* U.S. Supreme Court case is that the minority group must not be deprived of the opportunity to elect candidates of choice when the previous plan permitted the group's voters to elect candidates of choice. This interpretation means that the percentage of the minority group population in a proposed district can be reduced only if the reduction does not make the group's voters unable to elect their preferred candidate. The exact parameters of the Section V standard of retrogression is determined by the Voting Section of the U.S. Department of Justice (DOJ) unless the state elects to seek pre-clearance from the U.S. District Court of the District of Columbia. There is only limited evidence on DOJ interpretation of the retrogression standard as only a few states have received pre-clearance letters or letters of objection. To date, the Alaska and Virginia state senate and house plans have received DOJ pre-clearance as has the Texas State Senate plan. However, the DOJ objected to the Texas State House plan. The DOJ voting section objected to reducing the number of districts in which minority Hispanic voters would have had the opportunity to elect their candidate of choice. The voting section used a rough proxy measure of citizen voting age population— Spanish Surnamed Voter Registration—to assess the Hispanic voter opportunity to elect and found a net reduction of three potential Hispanic House districts. It is clear from this rejection letter that the voting section will determine whether a plan is retrogressive by simply counting the number of opportunities in the current plan and comparing them against the proposed plan. Any net reduction in opportunities will result in an objection. The problems which led to the voting section objection were then remedied by a three-judge panel of the U.S. federal court which heard a challenge by minority group interests to the new Texas State Senate and House districts drawn by the state Legislative Redistricting Board. As of this writing, the legislatures of Georgia, Louisiana, and South Carolina have completed their redistrictings and are in the process of preparing Section V submissions. Georgia and the Louisiana House have decided to bypass the administrative process for pre-clearance offered by the voting section and instead will seek pre-clearance from the District Court of the District of Columbia.

Emerging Trends in the 2000 Redistricting Round

Although a number of states have not begun legislative consideration of plans to redraw their state legislative districts, enough states have completed their redistricting to enable me to summarize some trends of the decade. I believe my observations will be confirmed as the remaining states complete drawing their new districts.

Whereas the plans of the 1990s increased the representation of racial and ethnic minority interests within state legislatures, I do not anticipate similar gains in this redistricting round. There are several reasons for reaching this conclusion. First, in the states covered wholly or in part by Section V of the U.S. Voting Rights Act, the concept of retrogression will limit further gains in minority representation. And it is clear that some of the covered states are choosing to have their plans reviewed by the District Court of the District of Colum-

bia instead of the DOJ voting section, because they feel they will get a more favorable hearing in court than from the DOJ voting section. The anticipated result of such efforts will be a preservation of the status quo in racial or ethnic representation in those states. Second, the main plaintiffs in Section 2 litigation against state legislative plans will come from Latino interests, not African-American interests. The burden of proof for Latino interests will be difficult because high percentages of non-citizen population have to be taken into account in assessing Latino plaintiff claims. The experience in the two challenges already brought to the Texas senate and house plans illustrates how difficult it will be for Latino interests to gain additional districts that were not created by the state legislative plans. Third, in states with significant numbers of both African-American and Latino populations, the continuing desire for African-American and Latino interests to gain separate places at the table of representation will necessarily limit the number of occasions which might exist to create combined majority-minority districts. Since these two groups seem to vote together in general elections, those who wish to create combined majority-minority districts must demonstrate that the two groups also support the same candidates in primary elections. Here the evidence is very mixed in the parts of the country where these conditions exist. Thus, it is highly likely that there will be few gains in racial and ethnic diversity in the state legislatures of the 2000s.

If this round will show less consciousness of race and ethnicity in districting, does this mean that the states will end the practice of constructing non-compact and bizarrely shaped legislative districts? I see no evidence that the plans adopted so far are any less bizarre in shape than the plans that are being replaced. This round, however, the bizarrely shaped districts seem to have more to do with partisan considerations than with racial and ethnic considerations. The technology of redistricting now makes it very easy to construct districts based on the partisan predispositions of the voters and a number of states have invested in the technology to enable them to do so. Since the courts now typically hold that an absence of geographic compactness may be evidence of impermissible race consciousness in districting, the states simply have to respond that they followed partisan preferences when drawing bizarrely shaped districts, not racial factors. The legal challenge of the 2000 round for the federal courts will be to determine whether the claim of justifiability decided in *Davis v. Bandemer* has any real meaning in the context of the technological advances of this decade. I expect a number of legal challenges to be brought this decade to challenge the widespread practice of partisan gerrymandering while drawing state legislative redistricting plans. One challenge has been filed in Nebraska and I anticipate that others will be filed as states complete their map drawing.

Finally, there will be a number of cases heard by the courts as some states reach partisan impasses in the creation of plans. Complicating the dispute resolution process is the understanding now that the federal courts must first defer to the state courts if the parties wish to be in state court (see *Growe v. Emiston*). This need to litigate in state court is likely to delay the final resolution of the disputes at a time when the states are racing to meet candidate qualification deadlines for the 2002 primary and general elections. Again I point to the experience within the state of Texas, where the state court process yielded no state plans at all and the final resolution had to be handled by a three-judge panel of the federal court. The U.S. Congress granted an exceptional priority to statewide districting controversies that allows them to be heard by three-judge panels with expedited appeal to the U.S. Supreme Court. The Congress understood the need to resolve these districting cases quickly so the election process would not be disrupted. The doctrine of the *Growe* decision clearly undermines the need to resolve these disputes quickly. To date, state legislative districting plans have been or are being reviewed by federal courts in Alabama, Minnesota and Oregon, in addition to the previously mentioned cases in New Jersey and Texas. Overall, I expect the same amount of litigation this round about redistricting plans this decade as during the 1990s, but, in the final analysis, I expect challenges to be less successful as the state legislatures more effectively justify the decisions they have made in redrawing district lines.

VI. GOVERNORS AND THE EXECUTIVE BRANCH

As the head of state politics and government and the elected representative of the people, governors must perform a wide variety of duties. They greet visitors, travel to other states and even other countries to lure new businesses to their states, rush to the scenes of disasters to demonstrate concern, prepare annual and biennial agendas for government activity, and, on occasion, discuss important issues with the president. From state to state the record varies on how well these and other gubernatorial responsibilities are fulfilled. Some governors are reelected to another term, others are excluded from service, others are elected to higher office, and some just retire.

Since its weak beginnings after the overthrow of colonial rule, the American governorship has grown in power and influence. The extensive reforms of the past four decades are becoming evident throughout the executive branches of the fifty states. As Larry Sabato reported two decades ago, "Within the last 20 years, there has been a virtual explosion of reform in state government. In most of the states, as a result, the governor is now truly the master of his own house, not just the father figure."[1] Many of the powers that were restricted have been expanded, and governors now have new powers at their command, such as the ability to reach the people directly through the media and to serve as the key state official in the intergovernmental system of grants and programs.

Like any office or position, the caliber of the individuals who seek and then serve as governors varies considerably. Most states have been able to say "goodbye to good-time Charlie" and hello to "a thoroughly trained, well regarded, and capable new breed of state chief executive."[2] This does not mean that all governors have spotless records. In 1988, Evan Mecham (R-Ariz., 1987–1988) was impeached by the state House, convicted by the state Senate, and removed from office. In April 1993,

Guy Hunt (R-Ala., 1987–1993) was convicted "of diverting $200,000 in inaugural funds for personal use" and was automatically removed from office.[3] In October 1993, David Walters (D-Okla., 1991–1995), in a plea bargain, pleaded guilty to a misdemeanor charge of violating a state campaign finance law in his 1990 election, and thereby avoided being tried on more serious felony charges.[4] In 1996, Jim Guy Tucker (D-Ark., 1992–1996) announced that he would resign after being convicted on twenty-four counts of felonious conspiracy to commit bank fraud in connection with the Whitewater investigation. And in 1997, Arizonans saw their second governor in nine years forced to leave office, as Fife Symington (R, 1991–1997) resigned after being found guilty of fraud during his pregubernatorial career as a real-estate developer.[5]

Over the past decade it was not clear whether the governors were better or not. But one thing was very clear: the governors of every state were facing fiscal situations that have some resemblance to a roller-coaster ride—with many ups and downs. At the beginning of the decade these problems were tied to the recession, as economies faltered, state revenues fell, and programs had to be cut back while taxes had to be raised to keep the budget balanced.[6] Then, toward the end of the decade, most states were raising more revenues than they were spending—they had budget surpluses—and the call was to cut taxes. Now, at the beginning of the twenty-first century, almost every state is facing serious fiscal problems again. Some states cut taxes too much, most see their economies slowing down, and all are feeling the demands for spending more in a variety of ways.

But with the shift in program and fiscal responsibility from the federal government to the states, governors and other state leaders have been put into the spotlight. They are the leaders who now must address much of the domestic side of our policy agenda, and some fear they may yet be faced with additional, and as yet unknown, responsibilities devolving from the federal government, including homeland security responsibilities. They are already feeling the impacts of a faltering national economy, so any shifts in responsibilities would be hard to cope with now. Yet they must respond to potential or actual shocks to their states as exemplified in the terrorist attacks in the Northeast.

Governors and the State Ambition Ladder

An interesting aspect of the governorship is its place on the "ambition ladder" that eager politicians climb to attain higher and higher levels of success. Clearly, the governorship is the top political office in the states, though there have been instances where the true political leader was a U.S. senator. For example, in Louisiana in the 1930s Huey Long moved his power base from the governor's chair to the U.S. Senate, and in Virginia U.S. senator Harry Byrd ran the famous "Byrd Machine" for several decades earlier in this century.[7] On the whole, though, few offices hold as much promise of political power as does the governorship.

Governors may be all the more powerful if their party also controls the state legislature, though if it holds too many legislative seats, ideological and personal splits in the party can arise and diminish the governor's ability to control. However, as noted earlier, more states have a political power split than a political power concentration that could enhance the governor's position.

With both potential and actual political power available, it is no surprise that the governorship is a coveted position at the apex of most states' political ambition ladders. Certain pregubernatorial positions are particularly valuable while climbing the ladder: state legislative office, other statewide elective office,

law enforcement work, and local elective office. More recently, some of those holding congressional or U.S. senatorial office are shifting toward the governorship, as are some individuals who have had no previous elective position at all.

Moving up from a local position, usually as mayor of a large city, has not been built into this ladder. For example, in the 210 gubernatorial elections conducted between 1987 and 2002, just 7 of the 39 large-city mayors running achieved the governorship.[8] As Richard Benedetto pointed out, prior to the 2002 elections, "history is not on their side." He cites these examples: no mayor of Philadelphia had been elected governor since 1908; no mayor of Chicago had been elected governor of Illinois since 1913; no mayor of Boston had become governor of Massachusetts since 1935; and no New York City mayor had been elected statewide since the city was incorporated in 1898![9] But, the Philadelphia jinx was broken in the 2002 gubernatorial election.

But what is the next step after the governorship? Is it a higher elective office? Four of our five most recent presidents were governors—Jimmy Carter (D-Ga., 1971–1975), Ronald Reagan (R-Calif., 1967–1975), Bill Clinton (D-Ark., 1979–1981, 1983–1992), and George W. Bush (R-Texas, 1995–2000). Reagan indicated that "being governor was the best training school for this job [of being president]."[10] In 2003, there were eleven former governors serving as U.S. senators and one serving as a U.S. representative.

Most former governors enter the private sector, usually to develop a lucrative law practice. These governors must give up what former governor Lamar Alexander (R-Tenn., 1979–1987) called "the very best job in the U.S.A."[11] Is there life after being governor? The National Governors' Association (NGA) asked some former governors what had happened to them since leaving office. Yes, there was life, but the quality of that new life can be determined only by the individual. By planning early for the transition, the NGA suggests, the governors "can also help ease their own adjustment to the 'good life.'"[12]

Campaigning for Governor

Being elected governor is not as easy as it once was. One reason is the new style of campaigning that has led candidates to create their own organizations instead of relying solely on their political party. Opinion polls, political consultants, advertisements tailored to specific audiences in the major media markets, direct mailings, telephone banks, and air travel are extremely expensive, and full-time fund-raisers often are needed to help gubernatorial candidates wage winning campaigns. Without the party to alert the faithful and bring in the straight-ticket votes, candidates must create what Sabato calls their own "instant organization" or "party substitute."[13]

This way of building a campaign organization is obviously expensive, and indeed the cost of running for governor has escalated greatly in recent years. But to be competitive, a candidate must raise considerable funds for his or her campaign. For those with private wealth, or access to wealth, this hurdle can be overcome more easily than for those without such resources. For the latter group, conducting a campaign for the governorship requires continuous fund raising, or the campaign will be impaired.

But the 1998 Jesse Ventura (Reform Party) campaign for governor of Minnesota may be a signal of an entirely new approach to campaigning for governor or any other office. Using the Internet and a Web site as his virtual organization and coordinating vehicle, he did not have to rely on a person-to-person physical campaign as most all campaigns do.[14] And the cost of his campaign was only $626,000, compared to the near $6 million his two major party

opponents spent.[15] None of this seemed to hinder his campaign, as he won.

Gubernatorial races are also more competitive than in the past. Awareness of the importance of state government and of the key role of the governor in state politics has increased interest in seeking the office. But with the cost of running a statewide campaign rising over the past few decades, some of those with an interest cannot afford to fulfill that interest. For example, the amount of money spent by all candidates in the fifty-four gubernatorial races held between 1977 and 1980 was $468 million in equivalent 2002 dollars. In the fifty-two most recent races held between 1999 and 2002, the total amount spent by all candidates was $1,024 million—more than doubling the cost of these elections![16]

Finally, there has been a decline in the number of opportunities to be elected governor. Only New Hampshire and Vermont restrict their governors to two-year terms, and only Virginia limits its governor to a single term. In addition, the power of incumbency gives a sitting governor a considerable advantage in any reelection campaign. The result is that fewer new governors are being elected in the states. Between 1870 and 1879 there was an average of 4.2 new governors elected in each state. In the 1990 through 1999 elections, the average was only 1.4 new governors elected per state.[17] Interestingly, between 1999 and 2002 there were thirty-three new governors elected in fifty-two gubernatorial elections, and in the upcoming 2003 elections, there will be at least two new governors elected. The years around the turn of this century have proven to be a time of change for those who sit in the fifty governors' chairs.

One Among Many

The governor is not the only official in the executive branch of state government who is elected statewide. In 2000 there were 305 separately elected executive branch officials in the states including attorneys general, auditors, lieutenant governors, secretaries of state, treasurers, and several other executive offices.[18] In a few states there were also boards made up of separately elected officials. The legislatures appoint some state officials, mainly in the postaudit function, and the lieutenant governors in a few states have some appointive power. This means that governors have little or no power over some parts of state government, except their own power of persuasion or the power they can create through the budget.

Fragmentation of executive branch leadership complicates the politics between the actors involved. Over the past two decades the governors and the lieutenant governors of several states were pitted against each other over the issue of who is in charge of state government when the governor is out of state. Can the lieutenant governor make appointments to office or the bench (patronage)? Call a special session of the legislature? Issue pardons? And who receives the governor's salary while he or she is absent? In some situations these fights can be over issues such as what to do with a budget surplus or how to regulate a certain industry. Fights often break out between the governor and other separately elected officials, such as the state attorney general or state auditor. Some of these disputes flare into larger battles that end up causing parts of state government to grind to a halt until they are resolved.

Executive branch fragmentation has other consequences. Perhaps most importantly, it restricts what governors can accomplish in high priority areas such as education. A gubernatorial candidate may pledge to improve primary and secondary education, but, once elected, have difficulty fulfilling this goal because other elected officials with responsibility in the education policy area may have different views on what should be done.

Recent federal court decisions have begun to restrict a chief executive's ability to remove or fire government employees, an action often needed to open up positions for appointing the executive's own team. After a series of cases restricting the power of patronage, the U.S. Supreme Court took direct aim at the gubernatorial power of patronage.[19]

In 1990, the Supreme Court decided narrowly in *Rutan et al. v. Republican Party of Illinois* that state and local government violates an individual's "First Amendment rights when they refuse to hire, promote or transfer . . . [an employee] on the basis of their political affiliation or party activity."[20] This case, which focused on the patronage process of the Illinois governor's office, highlights a basic tension in these situations. The tension is between the right of employees to be protected for their political beliefs and the need of an executive to put into place individuals who will seek to achieve the goals for which that executive was elected.

The most significant restriction on a governor's ability to be governor is the relationship that he or she has with state legislators. There are many types of advice and counsel that governors give each other on this relationship; consider these comments by incumbents to newly elected governors in 1982:

Don't necessarily judge your success by your legislative score card. . . . Avoid threatening to veto a bill. You just relieve the legislature of responsibility for sound legislation. . . . A governor successful in managing the selection of legislative leadership gains a Pyrrhic victory. . . . It's too easy to dismiss one or two legislators because there are so many. You do so at your own peril. . . . Legislators will complain about your spending too much time with the staff, but what they really mean is you don't spend enough time with them. . . . If someone urges your support on a bill by saying it's a "merely" bill, sew your pockets shut; there are no "merely" bills. . . . Legislators will learn that press coverage comes from opposition to the governor.[21]

Part VI provides a close-up view of the governorship as we enter the twenty-first century. Alan Ehrenhalt of *Governing* profiles former Illinois governor George Ryan and the problems he had while in office. Ehrenhalt also takes a look at West Virginia Governor Bob Wise, who is trying to change the economic course of his state. Finally, Alan Greenblatt of *Governing* profiles the superactivist attorney general of New York, Eliot Spitzer.

Notes

1. Larry Sabato, *Goodbye to Good-Time Charlie: The American Governorship Transformed,* 2d ed. (Washington, D.C.: CQ Press, 1983), 57.

2. Ibid., xi.

3. "Alabama Gov. Hunt Guilty: Office Now Folsom's," *Congressional Quarterly Weekly Report,* April 24, 1993, 1035.

4. "Oklahoma: Walters Pleads Guilty to Misdemeanor," *The Hotline,* October 22, 1993, 15.

5. Alan Greenblatt, "Symington Convicted of Fraud; Hull Takes Over as Governor," *Congressional Quarterly Weekly Report,* September 6, 1997, 2094–2095.

6. For an in-depth discussion of the fiscal problems facing governors in ten states, see Thad L. Beyle, ed., *Governors and Hard Times* (Washington, D.C.: CQ Press, 1992).

7. V. O. Key Jr., *Southern Politics in State and Nation* (New York: Knopf, 1949), 19–35, 156–182.

8. Tony Knowles of Anchorage, Alaska (1994), Mike Johanns of Lincoln, Nebraska (1998), George Voinovich of Cleveland, Ohio (1990), James Mc-Greevey of Woodbridge, New Jersey (2001), Linda Lingle of Maui County, Hawaii (2002), Ed Rendell of Philadelphia, Pennsylvania (2002), and Phil Bredesen of Nashville, Tennessee (2002). Anchorage is the largest city in Alaska, Lincoln is the second largest city in Nebraska as is Cleveland in Ohio, Woodbridge is the fifth largest city in New Jersey, Maui County is the third largest county in Hawaii, Philadelphia is the largest city in Pennsylvania, and Nashville is the second largest city in Tennessee. We should also note that Jesse Ventura, the former mayor of Brooklyn Park (60,000+ residents), was elected governor of Minnesota (1998), but he is

not counted among the "big city mayors" for this count.

9. Richard Benedetto, "Statewide-Election Jinx Hits Big-City Mayors," *USA Today,* March 12, 2002, A-10.

10. "Inquiry: Being Governor Is Best Training for Presidency," *USA Today,* September 11, 1987, 11A.

11. Lamar Alexander, *Steps Along the Way: A Governor's Scrapbook* (Nashville: Thomas Nelson, 1986), 9.

12. "Is There Life after Being Governor? Yes, A Good One," *Governors' Weekly Bulletin,* August 8, 1986, 1–2.

13. Larry Sabato, "Gubernatorial Politics and the New Campaign Technology," *State Government* 53 (Summer 1980): 149.

14. David Beiler, "The Body Politic Registers a Protest," *Campaigns & Elections* (February 1999): 34–43.

15. Public Disclosure Board, State of Minnesota, March 2000.

16. To see how much money candidates have spent in gubernatorial elections over the past quarter century, visit this website: www.unc.edu/~beyle. For the most recent elections in each state, see Thad Beyle, "Governors: Elections, Powers and Priorities," in *The Book of the States 2003* (Lexington, Ky.: The Council of State Governments, 2003), forthcoming.

17. Thad Beyle, "The Governors," in Virginia Gray and Russell Hansen, eds. *Politics in the American States: A Comparative Analysis,* 8th ed. (Washington, D.C.: CQ Press, 2003), forthcoming.

18. Kendra A. Hovey and Harold A. Hovey, *CQ's State Fact Finder 2003* (Washington D.C.: CQ Press, 2003), 96–115.

19. The cases involving local governments were *Elrod v. Burns* (1976), *Branti v. Finkel* (1980), and *Connick v. Myers* (1983).

20. Cheri Collis, "Cleaning Up the Spoils System," *State Government News* 33:9 (September 1990): 6.

21. Thad L. Beyle and Robert Huefner, "Quips and Quotes from Old Governors to New," *Public Administration Review* 43:3 (May–June 1983): 268–269.

Tragic Official of the Year

by Alan Ehrenhalt

Every year, this magazine honors people who have accomplished impressive things in state or local government. This year, there are 11 of them; as always, one is a governor. I'm not supposed to say who it is yet—that gets announced next month—but I can disclose the name of one governor who didn't get a moment's consideration: George H. Ryan of Illinois.

Ryan is leaving office after one term as a pariah, shunned even by his old colleagues and friends. Fellow Republicans run commercials denouncing him. The GOP gubernatorial nominee says Ryan "ran the worst administration in the history of Illinois." When it came time for the annual Governor's Day at the Illinois State Fair this summer, the sponsors changed the name to Republican Day to avoid embarrassment. Nevertheless, hardly anyone came.

Humiliation of this sort would be somewhat unusual punishment even for a governor who had done everything wrong—squandered the treasury, picked fights with the legislature, misbehaved horribly in his personal life. But Ryan has done none of those things. In fact, many who denounce him in public admit in private that he has been competent, effective and often courageous.

He will leave office in disgrace next year not because of anything he did as governor, but because of crimes committed by other people long before he became governor. Is that fair?

I'm afraid so.

To understand what's happened to Ryan, it might be helpful to take a short detour into the recesses of my home state's politics. In Illinois, the Secretary of State is not merely an election referee or document collector, as in many other states. He is the czar of motor vehicles and driver registration. When you want a driver's license, you go to a branch office of the Secretary of State. And it has been common knowledge for decades, all over Illinois, that you may need to pay a bribe to get one.

When I went for my first road test there, in 1966, I was counseled by my driving instructor not to worry if I failed—I might have an examiner who wouldn't pass anyone without money changing hands. As it happened, I never found out; I failed the test because I couldn't make a U-turn.

But it's clear that lots of people were being hassled, and there was no way to separate this

Alan Ehrenhalt is executive editor of *Governing*. This article is reprinted from *Governing* (October 2002): 6, 9.

petty corruption from the Secretary of State. Huge pictures of him hung all over every office. On the license itself, the signature of the Secretary appeared in type larger than the name of the motorist. For years, when I rented a car out of state, I was sure the agent would think my name was Paul Powell.

Nor was there much doubt that some of the money that bought licenses ended up in the Secretary of State's pocket. When Powell died, in 1970, $150,000 in cash was found in shoeboxes in his apartment, leading Adlai Stevenson III to deliver his famous eulogy: "This is a man whose shoeboxes will be hard to fill."

So when Ryan took over as Secretary of State in 1991, he was moving into an office with deeply rooted problems. He may not have made them worse, but he didn't do anything to clean them up, either. "Corruption was there when I was there, probably going to be there in the future," the governor once reflected. "It's part of the culture."

The way the culture worked under Ryan has been made clear in the federal probe called Operation Safe Roads, which began in 1998. The employees in the motor vehicle offices were required to contribute substantial sums annually to the Republican Party, including the Secretary of State's campaign fund. Some of the branch managers have said they were pressured to buy as much as $20,000 worth of tickets to fund-raisers in a single year—a requirement they could not meet with their own money. So they took bribes for licenses, and paid their party dues with the proceeds.

It's quite possible, as has been argued, that some crooked employees were pocketing most of the bribes, and used the party contributions mainly as an excuse. But prosecutors have also said that $170,000 clearly identified as bribe money ultimately reached Ryan's campaign fund.

The governor has always insisted he was unaware of this connection, and that anybody

taking bribes in his department was doing it freelance. No evidence has emerged contradicting him, and there has been no move to indict him.

Still, even if you believe him, it's not much of a defense. This wasn't isolated corruption, it was a massive department-wide shakedown scheme, and he was a direct beneficiary of it. Any public official who didn't know this was going on can be justly accused of gross negligence.

Even so, it's unlikely the scandal would have brought Ryan down had it not been for a catastrophe on a Wisconsin highway in 1994. A metal taillight assembly fell off a long-haul truck and crashed into a passenger van, killing six children. It turned out the truck driver, who was from Illinois, had been warned about the problem but couldn't understand the warning because he spoke no English, even though English literacy is required in Illinois for a commercial truck license. The driver had paid a bribe to skip the language test.

The tragedy didn't become a scandal until 1998, when the details were reported by a Chicago television station. Ryan was in the middle of his gubernatorial campaign at the time. He questioned the evidence, insisted that any bribery in his department was an aberration, and won easily. Only afterward, as prosecutors unearthed seemingly endless stories of corruption in the Secretary of State's office, indicted 57 people and obtained 46 guilty pleas, did the governor find himself hopelessly enmeshed in the scandal, no matter how hard he tried to position himself above it.

The ethical indictment against George Ryan is pretty compelling. The record of his achievements is also compelling.

In January 2000, when he proclaimed that the capital punishment process was unacceptably flawed and placed a moratorium on it, he was moving into uncharted territory. Less than three years later, bills to reform the process have been introduced in 19 states, and while executions continue to take place, the fairness of the law is a national issue in a way it wasn't before. "There will be changes," U.S. Senator Russell Feingold of Wisconsin has said, "and when the history is written, the most important name will be George Ryan."

When Ryan traveled to Cuba in 1999, carrying $1 million worth of medical supplies and declaring it was time for the embargo against Fidel Castro's regime to end, he was taking a step bound to cause him trouble in his own party, and one that promised few political benefits. But he did it anyway, and since then, numerous other elected officials have been willing to take the same step.

Those are largely symbolic issues. Ryan's Illinois First building program is not symbolic. It is a $12 billion investment in infrastructure that no previous administration was able to enact, despite nearly universal agreement that it was needed. A few months after its passage, Ryan reached agreement with Richard M. Daley, Chicago's Democratic mayor, to end an airport-siting dispute that had lasted a decade. "I've worked with many governors," Daley said afterward, "and I tell you very honestly and frankly: This governor gets things done."

Critics point to the numerous pork-barrel concessions that Ryan made to get Illinois First passed, but the smartest thing for him to do politically would have been to sponsor a tax cut. Instead, he raised cigarette and liquor taxes to raise money for capital construction. "In decades to come," says political scientist Paul Green, of Roosevelt University, "a lot of Illinois citizens will benefit from those projects. It took a lot of courage for him to do it."

Such is the case for Ryan's defense, cited regularly by a small but vocal band of loyalists, perhaps most prominent among them the Chicago novelist Scott Turow, who is a Democrat. "What I see," Turow wrote recently, "is the scandalizing of a man who in his time in the governor's office has been good government incarnate."

The whole affair inevitably brings up one of the oldest and most troubling questions in politics: We want to have leaders who are capable and clean. If we can't have both at once, where do we draw the line?

It is a question almost certainly being asked in Providence, Rhode Island, where Mayor Buddy Cianci, who masterminded a dramatic urban comeback, is about to go to prison for taking bribes in exchange for city jobs and contracts. He didn't exactly commit a victimless crime—some job applicants no doubt lost out because they didn't pay off Cianci. I suppose justice has been done in this case. But who ends up better off with Cianci's demise? I can't think of anybody.

And I might make the same argument about George Ryan—his disgrace ultimately benefits no one—if it weren't for the literal human suffering that the corruption in his department ultimately caused. The crimes in the Illinois Secretary of State's Office were not trivial or harmless in any respect. They were matters of life and death. There are many commodities in government that shouldn't be for sale, but only a few whose sale is morally repellent under almost any circumstance. An election is one of them. The safety of children on the highway is another. George Ryan is a man of proven moral sensitivity. This is something he should have understood.

That's why people in Illinois find it so difficult to forgive him, and why the whole case is so unusual and so troubling. "This is almost Shakespearean," says Green. "He is in many ways a tragic figure."

Moving Mountains

by Alan Ehrenhalt

Two or three times a week, Governor Bob Wise leaves his office in the West Virginia Capitol, walks across the Capitol grounds to the Economic Development Department, sits down at a table and starts making phone calls to corporate CEOs, one after another. Some are the heads of companies within the state, and Wise is checking to see if they have any problems he can help with. But most of the calls are to CEOs in other states and other countries. Wise tells them he has heard they are looking around for a business location and wants them to know what West Virginia can offer them— cheap utilities, lots of water, a stable workforce, and perhaps most important, a newly enacted array of tax breaks. Before he hangs up, he gives them his private e-mail address and private phone number.

All in all, Wise figures, he probably spends a third of his time lobbying to bring in new companies or hold on to the ones already there. That amount of time may not be remarkable for the governor of a poor state, but it seems remarkable for Bob Wise.

This is the same man who entered politics a quarter-century ago as a grassroots activist demanding that the state's coal companies pay higher taxes. It is the same man who led a con-

sumer rebellion against telephone companies and proclaimed that his congressional office was simply "a large community organizing effort." Throughout his career, nobody has doubted Bob Wise's political ability or prowess as a salesman. What they never expected was that he would perfect those skills as a master seducer of CEOs.

Wise hasn't exactly mellowed—he's as intense as ever, and he still evokes populist themes to audiences that want to hear them. He thinks timber and coal companies all but starved the state in the old days. "We gave our profits away," he likes to argue. But Wise is a consensus politician now, and if there's a consensus on anything in West Virginia, it's that the state needs new industry—and needs it in a hurry. "The world has changed," he says. "I've changed. My critics and I understand economic development better than we once did."

The phone calls that Wise makes, the tax incentives he boasts about and the recruitment bonuses he offers are part of what is called "A

Alan Ehrenhalt is executive editor of *Governing*. This article is reprinted from *Governing* (December 2002): 36, 38–39.

Vision Shared," a high-profile development program that has become the preoccupation not only of the Wise administration but of every interest group and political faction in the state.

In many of its approaches, Vision Shared isn't much different from what other states do to recruit business. What makes it something new in West Virginia is the "shared" part—Wise's conviction that the state can rise from economic stagnation only with business and labor collaborating in a way that has been unthinkable in the past.

There is more than a little irony in all this. In recent decades, West Virginia basically has had two kinds of governors: pro-business Republicans and wealthy Democrats with strong personal ties to the corporate elite. All were determined to promote economic development; none lifted the state very far. The idea that an anti-corporate agitator from the 1970s might succeed where they failed is intriguing.

And yet it may work. There is a Nixon-going-to-China quality to some of Wise's policies: Building on 20 years of cozy alliance with the state's major Democratic interest groups—unions, teachers and trial lawyers—Wise is betting that he can coax compromises from them that none of his predecessors could have managed. Even some Republicans believe that. "If I tried something like this," says Vic Sprouse, GOP leader in the state Senate, "the unions and the trial lawyers would go to war against it." As things stand now, they are on board.

Of course, that may be because the really contentious issues remain to be settled: namely, the dysfunctional workers' compensation fund and tax laws geared to the steel-and-coal economy of the 1930s. The package of tax incentives and grant money that Wise pushed through the legislature this year was an impressive accomplishment but one that could be achieved without inflicting serious pain on any major economic interest. The hill gets steeper after this.

"We have to do the easy things first," says Steve Roberts, president of the West Virginia Chamber of Commerce and a convert to Wise's agenda. "Perhaps then we can develop the trust to take on the hard ones."

Grandma's Closets

It's indisputable that there are plenty of hard ones to take on. "I inherited grandma's closets with 60 years of problems," Wise likes to say.

While it is well known that West Virginia has spent the past century in recurring economic difficulty, it's not often appreciated by outsiders how much things have worsened in recent years and how strong a feeling of defeatism hangs over the state as a result.

The recession of the early 1980s, which was severe throughout industrial America, was much worse in West Virginia; in many ways, it has never recovered. State income per capita is barely 70 percent of the national average.

Most crucially, it has been hit by an ever-accelerating exodus of its young people. During the 1990s, the number of West Virginians age 25–34 declined by 12 percent, while those over 75 increased by 13 percent, allowing West Virginia to overtake Florida as the oldest state in the country, with a median age of almost 39 years. Studies have repeatedly shown that young adults don't leave immediately after graduation from college—they try living and working in West Virginia for a few years before growing discouraged about job opportunities and moving away.

It's almost impossible to overstate the importance of this trend to ordinary West Virginians. When pollsters ask them what they consider the state's most pressing issue, most of them mention the population drain. Wise plays to this concern as he promotes economic development across the state. His speeches quote a sentence from the Book of Jeremiah: "There is hope in thine end, saith the Lord, that the children shall come again to their own border."

The New Coal

But if Bible quotations were a solution to this problem, it would have been solved a long time ago. The issue in a nutshell is that West Virginia remains deeply mired in the obsolete economy of heavy industries. All the Rust Belt states have had a similar problem, but over the past 20 years, they have made decent progress at moving beyond it, guiding their economies into the technology-driven present. But in West Virginia, nearly 20 percent of the jobs still are related to coal mining, and coal and utilities together pay 60 percent of the business taxes. There is a healthy mineral severance tax, but instead of being targeted for reinvestment in new businesses, the money is split proportionately among all the counties in the state, a de facto revenue-sharing program that is largely useless from an economic development standpoint.

So the task for Wise and Vision Shared is not merely businesses recruitment but the redirection of the state's economy, its reputation and even its perception of itself. "It's not only image, it's self-image," says Kenny Perdue, secretary-treasurer of the state AFL-CIO and a Vision Shared strategist. "To get people to come back, we've got to convince them that there's been a change."

There has been some. Along the 35-mile corridor from Clarksburg to Morgantown, in the northern part of the state, high-tech enterprises are beginning to emerge, based on the science of biometrics and tied to the FBI's Criminal Justice Information Center and Fingerprint Identification Center, both sited in Clarksburg in the 1990s through the influence of U.S. Senator Robert C. Byrd.

"In five years," Wise says hopefully, "West Virginia will be the Silicon Valley of biometrics." David Satterfield, who runs the Economic Development Department, exudes the same confidence. "We have the new coal," he boasts, "and it's identification sciences, biometrics and computer software development."

He may be right, but if so, the new coal is being mined painfully slowly. There are still only an estimated 450 biotech jobs in the state, far too few to describe the Clarksburg-Morgantown corridor as an economic cluster, let alone the birthplace of a genuine boom. The development office has created more than 40,000 jobs in the years since 1993, but the vast majority of them are in telemarketing and other low-paid service categories.

"We've got to do something," says Senator Sprouse, "unless we want to stay 49th in everything. We've got to do things even if they turn out wrong." His Democratic counterpart, Brooks McCabe, says the same thing. "Right now," he insists, "West Virginia is all about reinventing itself. That's what Vision Shared is trying to do."

Attitude Adjustment

To that end, West Virginia is promoting cooperation in ways it has pointedly avoided in the past. A few weeks after Wise defeated incumbent Governor Cecil Underwood in 2000, the two men jointly endorsed Vision Shared, the first draft of which had appeared in the closing months of Underwood's administration. This year, when Wise proposed a ballot measure permitting tax-increment financing for new state projects, it was with the backing of both political parties, the Chamber of Commerce and the AFL-CIO. Four years earlier, when Underwood tried something similar, the unions derailed it. This time, pacified by a "prevailing wage" clause placing a floor under TIF project wages, labor went along, and on Election Day the measure passed by a wide margin.

Amendment One was a modest accomplishment from a policy standpoint, especially given the fact that more than 40 other states have long had similar laws. But it was a tangible symbol that Vision Shared is about as bipartisan as anything in West Virginia ever gets. "We've got a history of confrontation. It's still in the back of our minds," says the AFL-CIO's Perdue. "But there's an attitude change amongst a lot of people. We have people collaborating that have not collaborated—ever." Dana Waldo, president of the Business Roundtable, echoes that sentiment. "There's too much on the line for us to be fighting," he insists. "When you're looking up from the bottom, you've got to be together."

The coalition held together better than many expected during this year's session of the legislature, in which a long list of archaic tax incentives were repealed and a new series of measures aimed at building a more modern economy were enacted.

The previous generation of tax breaks, policy makers now concede, actually made the economy worse. Among the most notorious was the so-called "Super Tax Credit," instituted in 1985 to reward new business that created more than 50 jobs. It may have been the most complex tax incentive anywhere in America. The computation schedule was 12 pages long, with 16 pages of instructions. "Even CPAs couldn't figure out how to calculate it," says Brian Kastick, the current state Tax Secretary. "That was ridiculous—obviously it was more a hindrance than a help."

But that wasn't the worst part. The law didn't insist on net job creation. A coal or steel company could shut down a plant with 100 workers, open a new one with 50, and claim the money while causing a net loss in employment. In the first four years of Supercredit, coal companies took $35 million in credits while eliminating 1,300 jobs. After a decade, the program had cost the state $180 million. "They really didn't think through what they wanted to do," says Kastick. "The state was desperate. It ended up being abused."

Then there was the Industrial Expansion and Revitalization Credit, a subsidy that dated all the way back to the 1960s. Between 1988 and 1997, it cost the state $207 million. Yet when Kastick's department analyzed its value, it couldn't find any. Companies were permitted to make a single investment in new plant or equipment, and reap a whole sequence of benefits. "There is very little or no correlation," the study concluded, "between the use of the IERC and employment or economic output."

Indeed, that was what Kastick's study concluded about the state's entire network of business tax benefits. "Most of these tax credits are ineffective," it reported, "as tools of economic development."

The most significant achievement of Vision Shared so far has been to wipe out more than a dozen wasteful or useless tax incentives and replace them with ones that make more sense in a 21st-century economy. West Virginia now has strategic research and development tax credits for the design and testing of new product prototypes, from biometrics to polymers; a $25 million venture capital fund to attract new entrepreneurs; and a $10 million "sunny day fund" to help close deals with companies considering a move.

As a result, says Mike Basile, the corporate lawyer who spearheaded much of the lobbying for the package, West Virginia has "one of the most aggressive research and development programs in the nation." On the other hand, Basile is quick to point out, "tax credits are poetry. The other issues are the plumbing."

Plumbing Problems

Most of the state's economic plumbing is in bad shape. The tax incentives may have been repaired, but the tax code itself remains antiquated and inefficient. It essentially assumes that the most important taxable wealth is in fixed capital infrastructure, such as coal mines and steel mills. Companies that have those are taxed at an unrealistically high rate, while service companies with few assets, an ever-growing proportion of the employment base, are taxed very lightly. The tax code for each sector of the economy is riddled with obscure exemptions and penalties. In the words of one corporate official, "we don't even have a tax system. We have bits and pieces." In 1999, the Underwood administration called for a special legislative session to rewrite the tax code, but it was never held.

A thoroughly modernized tax code might be the sort of dramatic accomplishment that could make Vision Shared an undisputed success. As the Business Roundtable's Waldo says, "We've captured the low-hanging fruit. We need one or two big policy hits that show we're serious about change."

Yet to assume that West Virginia can enact major tax reform when almost every other state has failed to do so sounds to some like a dangerous case of overreaching. Moreover, there remains the long-time curse of West Virginia's economic life: workers' compensation.

Workers' comp rates aren't abnormally high in the state. Rather, the problem is that the workers' comp system is $2 billion in debt, largely because of cases stemming from the years when 100,000 West Virginians worked in coal mines. Many of the companies that initially incurred this debt are out of business, but their bills have to be paid by those firms still in existence, even ones with no liability of their own.

A business in West Virginia might spend $35 in workers' comp costs for every $100 in wages it pays out. Comparable obligations in neighboring states can be as much as 75 percent lower. Mike Basile, the governor's Vision Shared strategist, calls ameliorating the workers' comp burden the "true litmus test" of any economic development agenda.

There is no shortage of experts, including some public supporters of Vision Shared, who fear that these fundamental problems will ultimately prove to be more than the current coalition can survive. "My sense is the big things won't be tackled," says Michael Hicks, of Marshall University's Center for Business and Economic Research. Hicks feels it's crucial for the state to have a new tax code, but he doubts there will be one. So does Robin Capeheart, who was Underwood's chief tax adviser. "There are issues on the periphery that you can get diverse interests to agree upon," Capeheart says. "But at some point, protecting interests is going to rise above the level of cooperation."

That pessimism is built on almost all the things that have held back West Virginia in the past—political pettiness, ill-conceived economic reforms, careless stewardship of capital and natural resources. The one real source of optimism is a sense of urgency that even skeptics agree has not been present before.

To many of them, the day of judgment will be the next census. If it shows what the one in 2000 did—an aging population, an exodus of educated talent and a poorly trained workforce—the opportunities for change may evaporate. "If we don't do something now," Waldo warns, "the 2010 census is going to be a disaster."

Bob Wise concurs: "We've got five years to turn the state around." It's enough to transform an old-time populist into a born-again corporate recruiter. And to make him dial the phone a little faster.

Super-Activist

by Alan Greenblatt

In recent years, congressional inaction and U.S. Supreme Court decisions have served to offer states lots of latitude in matters once thought the exclusive province of Washington. Few officeholders, though, have made as much of this moment of opportunity as Eliot Spitzer, New York's attorney general.

Spitzer has become a ubiquitous figure in the major legal fights over social and fiscal policy in our time, including such areas as abortion, labor rules, air pollution, gun control and, perhaps most notably, corporate malfeasance.

Spitzer made his biggest splash this past May, when he announced a settlement with Merrill Lynch, which included a $100 million fine that went to New York and other state treasuries. The deal also called for the brokerage house to abandon the practice of encouraging its analysts to tout the stocks of its investment-banking clients. "Eliot Spitzer did investors everywhere—I mean everywhere—a big service by bringing the issue of analyst conflicts to the fore," says Ashley Baker of the North American Securities Administrators Association.

Now, as regulators in at least 10 states look into the practices of other firms, Spitzer is going after investment-banking clients of Salomon Smith Barney to whom the firm sold hot initial price offering shares in what Spitzer calls "commercial bribery."

Earlier, Spitzer had suffered a backlash in Congress, where some House members wanted to strip his office of authority over securities. But he can now point with pride to recent measures announced by the federal Securities and Exchange Commission requiring that Wall Street research departments be kept at arms' length from investment-banking operations. "It was a lonely endeavor initially," he says, "but we've made a lot of progress."

Spitzer has stirred up many other pots as well, pursuing high-profile cases in the areas of abortion rights and racial profiling. He shamed the U.S. Environmental Protection Agency into taking action against Midwestern power plants he was suing for air-pollution violations. His work in forcing grocers to pay their immigrant workers a minimum wage continues to result in fresh settlements, and his pursuit of auto insurance fraud has led to 50 indictments in recent months.

Alan Greenblatt is a staff writer for *Governing.* This article is reprinted from *Governing* (November 2002): 22.

Driven and smart, Spitzer grew up and lives among New York's wealthy classes and holds degrees from Princeton and Harvard Law School. He first won fame as an assistant district attorney prosecuting members of the Gambino crime family. In the late 1980s, Spitzer helped break the Gambino hold on the city's garment business (he set up a factory of his own rather than rely on moles) then left for private practice soon after. Although he didn't particularly enjoy corporate work, he recounts with pride the time that William Guthrie, a light-heavyweight boxer on whose behalf Spitzer successfully sued for a shot at a title fight, expressed his gratitude from the ring after his victory. It was, he says, a unique way for a client to offer thanks.

Spitzer's high-profile triumphs, coupled with an effective press operation, have carried him a long way politically. After finishing fourth in a field of four in the 1994 Democratic primary for his office, he unseated Republican Dennis Vacco by such a narrow margin in 1998 that Vacco refused to concede for six weeks. (Spitzer borrowed $10 million from his developer father to win that latter race.) Spitzer is now universally considered a lock for reelection this month and a probable candidate for higher office in the future.

His more recent crusades against power plants, investment bankers, auto insurers and grocery chains, he says, have led many of his conservative enemies, who in theory support the idea of power shifting from the federal government to the states, to turn against the creed when those new state powers are wielded by him. He recalls receiving a less than gracious welcome from the Federalist Society when the group invited him to speak. He claims they were less interested in displaying him as a paragon of what federalism can accomplish than "to show the risks of the devolution of power to states when the wrong person, in their opinion, is making the decisions."

VII. STATE AND LOCAL BUREAUCRACIES AND ADMINISTRATION

Departments and agencies within each state carry out the laws passed by the legislature and approved by the governor. These departments vary in size and in responsiveness to executive control. Transportation, human services, corrections, education, and health usually are large departments with sizable budgets and staffs. These "big ticket" agencies perform services quite visible to the public, and governors and legislators alike pay close attention to them. Governors appoint the heads of these agencies with great care, and the legislatures often must confirm the appointments.

Many parts of the state bureaucracy, however, appear to be remarkably immune to the vagaries of legislative and gubernatorial politics. The key to successful bureaucratic politics is to keep a low profile. Governors come and go, legislators come and go, but some agencies keep on doing what they have always done with minimum intrusion from outside. State government encompasses so many agencies and activities that it is virtually impossible for the governor and the legislature to keep track of them all.

Between a Rock and a Hard Place?

State bureaucrats—this is not a derogatory term—often are torn by competing values: economy and efficiency on the one hand and political expediency on the other. In the world of politics, points often are scored for achieving an electorally advantageous goal rather than for saving money or doing a job efficiently.

Another problem is accountability. To whom are state employees accountable? To the governor, the legislature or particular legislators, the interest served by the agency, the public at large, themselves? The numerous lines of accountability give those in the state bureaucracy the opportunity to play one group against another and thereby do what they want.

In recent years important changes have been made that have improved the caliber of the states' work forces. The standards for hiring, promotion, and retention have been raised. Educational requirements are more exacting. In-service training has been upgraded. State employees who report wrongdoing in state government—"whistleblowers"—are better protected against retaliation. And more employees are covered by civil service and merit systems, which has reduced the number of patronage positions. Moreover, minorities now have better opportunities for employment and advancement within state government.

Another related development has been the growing political influence of state employee organizations. State employee groups and state employee labor unions have become stronger in almost all states. Like other interests, they lobby their own concerns and proposals before the governor and the state legislature—and with increasing effectiveness. What do they want for their efforts? Higher wages, better health and retirement benefits, and more recognition of their professional status. When it comes to preparing the budget, the most influential parties often are those who carry out the intent of the budget—namely, state employees.

Finally, we must note the dynamic growth of state governments over the last several decades. Between 1950 and 1990, the number of state government employees increased by 300 percent; only the increases in primary and secondary education employment were greater. While there was a consistent "core" of about forty administrative agencies in most of the states in the late 1950s, this had grown to over seventy-five by the mid-1980s.[1] In the 1990s up to 1996, state and local governments added nearly 1.5 million of the 10 million new jobs in the non-farm economy. While most of this job growth was at the local level, nearly 350,000 of these new jobs were in state governments.[2] This growth continued into the late 1990s. So both the number of people working for state government and the number of agencies in which they work increased greatly.

In the late 1980s and early 1990s, both state and local governments suffered in the nation's economic recession, and decreased tax revenues caused strains in providing needed services. The goals of seeking higher wages, better health and retirement benefits, and recognition of professional status within state bureaucracies gave way to trying to protect programs, agencies, and jobs, and trying to hold the line on the level of salaries and benefits. Hard times cut very sharply into state bureaucracies.

In the aftermath of the 1994 elections there were still more efforts to cut back state programs and state bureaucracies, and thereby the state budget. While the drive for cutbacks in the early 1990s was economic, by mid-decade it had become ideological and political, as the view in many state capitals of what state government should be had changed. Then the situation changed as the economy boomed and state revenues provided surpluses in most every state. With so much cash in the state bank accounts, the goal of many state politicians was to cut back on taxes—a very popular political move.

But the "hard times" experience of the earlier 1990s and some rising fiscal responsibilities tied to the devolution of federal programs to the states in the later 1990s raised caution flags in many state policy makers' eyes. State-level policy makers suddenly needed to increase both the state government work force and state budgets as federal programs devolved down through the system. And as we move into the twenty-first century, the "hard times" of the early 1990s have returned, tied to the economic downturn that has had a negative impact on state revenues. The much-desired and often excessive tax cuts of the 1990s in the states has only exacerbated many states' revenue problems.

Organizational Problems

How are state agencies organized? Some would argue they aren't. Governors trying to "run" state government or citizens trying to find out where to get help often are baffled by the apparent organizational chaos of the many departments and agencies. Periodically, the states reorganize their executive branch departments. This usually is done to improve economy and efficiency, to clear up the lines of accountability so that the governor is the chief executive in fact as well as in theory, or to gain control over some agencies that are perceived as out of control—usually the control of the governor.

Not surprisingly, reorganization often is resisted by the agencies themselves and by groups with vested interests in the way things are. Those who know how the system works prefer the status quo and are extremely reluctant to learn new ways. And when the goal is to give the governor more power and influence, the agencies fight hard: they are far from willing to lose or share their power. Organizational battles are so difficult to mount and win that many governors and legislatures avoid them, believing victory is not worth the political costs.

Republican governors are particularly attracted to setting up economy and efficiency commissions to survey state government programs, organizations, and policies in an effort to find ways to save the taxpayers money. These commissions, which usually are made up of members of the business community and supported by an out-of-state consulting firm specializing in such studies, review a state's budget, governmental organization, and programs. The commission issues a well-publicized final report pointing out waste in state government and indicates three to four hundred suggested changes as to how the state could save millions of dollars.

Some of the suggested changes make sense, and others do not. They usually include some reorganization and consolidation of agencies, turning over some of what the agencies do to the private sector (privatization), eliminating some programs, charging or increasing user fees for some services, or transferring a program to another level of government.[3] One observer concludes that such studies have "been largely discredited" and may be more "a political than an administrative tool." [4] Even reorganizations have been criticized as doing more to spawn confusion "about program goals and work responsibilities" and sparking "political brushfires" that keep "managers from getting back to those basic issues of responsibility and accountability." [5]

Major executive branch reorganization efforts have occurred in twenty-seven states since the 1960s.[6] The goals usually articulated in these efforts were "modernization and streamlining of the executive branch machinery, efficiency, economy, responsiveness, and gubernatorial control."[7] Reorganizations are not apolitical events; they involve a battle for power among the branches of government. Aside from the built-in resistance that state bureaucrats have to such changes, legislators often oppose them as well because reorganizations usually increase the power of the governor over the executive branch at the expense of the legislature.

Rather than seek major reorganization of the bureaucratic structure, state leaders may attempt partial reform when there is a pressing need to consolidate overlapping and confusing jurisdictions, or when they wish to tackle a particular problem facing the state by eliminating organizational barriers. This has been especially important in economic development, in the environmental area, and in the actual administration of state government.

Management and Personnel Changes

Where the states have made the most headway is in adopting new management techniques. Budgets no longer are worked out in the back rooms of statehouses by employees wearing green eyeshades; they are part of a larger policy-management process headed by the governor.[8] Nearly all governors must operate under a balanced budget requirement. If there are any mid-year problems or revenue shortfalls, the governor needs to know about them immediately so he or she can take appropriate remedial action.

Changes in state government administration and personnel have been made, but not without considerable furor. Controversies over affirmative action (Should minorities have a leg up in hiring and promotions?) and comparable worth (Should men and women be paid equally for dissimilar jobs of similar skill levels?) bedevil state legislators and administrators. Politically, it makes sense to open up jobs for women and minorities; they are becoming more active in politics and their support often is needed to win elections. According to one observer of the state government scene: "We're going to have to move beyond the good ol' boy network to include in the profoundest way the good ol' girls and the good ol' minorities."[9]

A recent study of state government agency heads suggests that women in state government are circumventing the so-called "glass ceiling" or administrative lid rather than trying to break through it. They are doing this by moving into expanded state government activities, such as consumer affairs and arts agencies, by involvement in governmental and political activism, and by reaching parity with men in terms of education, experience, and professionalism. "The administrative ballpark or ball game [has been] substantially enlarged. The park's gotten bigger."[10] However, this does not mean that there are not some very strong and capable women heading major, mainline agencies across the states.

There have also been some major changes in making state governments more accessible to the people they serve. This has mainly come about through the Internet and state government efforts to develop web sites that allow users to find the information they are looking for. This information runs from being able to download and print various forms needed for utilizing government programs to paying taxes. Each agency is accessible via the state's web site and has information about the agency's mission, programs, and personnel. There is usually a way set up to contact agency personnel by email. The starting point in this process is the state's web site: www.state.al.us.[11]

Ethics

How government officials, elected or appointed, behave while in office is increasingly a topic of concern at the state level. We generally recognize a corrupt act—or do we? Handing cash to a public official to influence a decision would seem to be a corrupt act. But what about a public utility political action committee that contributes funds to incumbent legislators' campaigns so that legislators might look more favorably on revising the utility rate structure? Is that a corrupt act? Or is that politics?

Like beauty, corruption and ethical misbehavior often are in the eye of the beholder. Some states are trying to clarify this issue by establishing codes of ethics, a set of ethical standards, and ethics commissions. Several states have established inspectors-general offices to probe into allegations of wrongdoing in state government. In some instances, the inspectors general have the authority to "identify programs or departments that *might be vulnerable* to corruption. . . . [12] Some observers suggest that these steps, along with measures to open up electoral and governmental processes and to develop accountability measures, "have . . . been at least as significant as the other reforms" occurring in the states over the past few decades.[13]

How widespread are ethics and corruption problems in the states? Again, the question really is, just what is an ethical problem? One point worth considering is that, given the size of our state governments, the number of people working in them, and the amount of money involved in their ongoing budgets, there is amazingly little corruption. What we see are the flashy, individual cases in which a governor has made an ethical error, a legislator has accepted money for a vote, or a state government employee has taken money for favorable treatment. These cases of state government "bad news" dominate the media; the good news—that no corruption occurred today, or yesterday, or last week—does not make the evening news.

Part VII explores some of these and other controversies concerning state bureaucracies. Alan Greenblatt of *Governing* presents a portrait of California's state budget director, a man operating under a $3[8] billion shortfall. Norma Riccucci and Judith Saidel of *Spectrum: The Journal of State Government* take a look at the progress that women state agency heads have made in recent years. Anya Sostek of *Governing* examines the problems that states are having with sports agents and their response to scandals. Christopher Swope of *Governing* discusses the problems that local governments are having trying to make public buildings and infrastructure safe in this day of seeking more homeland security.

Notes

1. Deil S. Wright, Jae-Won Yoo, and Jennifer Cohen, "The Evolving Profile of State Administrators," *Journal of State Government* 64:1 (January–March 1991): 30-31.

2. "State and Local Government Is a Major Source of New Jobs in the 1990s," *Government Employment Report* 1 (August 1997): 1.

3. Tim Funk, "Efficiency Study Commissions: Is an Old Idea a Bad Idea?" *North Carolina Insight* 11:4 (August 1989): 42–43, 46–50.

4. James K. Conant, "Reorganization and the Bottom Line," *Public Administration Review* 46:1 (January/February 1986): 48.

5. Les Garner, "Managing Change through Organization Structure," *Journal of State Government* 60:4 (July/August 1987): 194.

6. Keon S. Chi, "State Executive Branch Reorganization: Options for the Future," *State Trends Forecasts* 1:1 (December 1992): 13. South Carolina, which reorganized in the early 1990s, was added to this list.

7. James K. Conant, "In the Shadow of Wilson and Brownlow: Executive Branch Reorganization in the States, 1965 to 1987," *Public Administration Review* 48:5 (September/October 1988): 895.

8. See James J. Gosling, "Patterns of Stability and Change in Gubernatorial Policy Agendas," *State and Local Government Review* 23:1 (Winter 1991): 3–12; and Robert D. Lee Jr., "Developments in State Budgeting: Trends of Two Decades," *Public Administration Review* 51:3 (May/June 1991): 254–262.

9. Comment by Jesse L. White Jr., former executive director of the Southern Growth Policies Board and a public policy consultant, in "On the Record," *Governing* 4:8 (May 1991): 18.

10. Study by Deil S. Wright and Angela M. Bullard, reported in Liz Lucas, "Women Winning State Posts," *Chapel Hill* (North Carolina) *News,* May 7, 1993, 7, 12.

11. This particular web site is for Alabama. For the web site of other states, insert the state's Zip Code abbreviation where "al" for Alabama is in the example.

12. Cheri Collis, "State Inspectors General: The Watchdog over State Agencies," *State Government News* 33:4 (April 1990): 13.

13. Fran Burke and George C. S. Benson, "Written Rules: State Ethics Codes, Commissions, and Conflicts," *Journal of State Government* 62:5 (September/October 1989): 198.

Pray for Peace

by Alan Greenblatt

When California Governor Gray Davis telephoned Steve Peace in December to offer him the post of state finance director, Peace was shopping with his wife in the underwear section at Nordstrom. After accepting the job, Peace told reporters he and Davis had discussed government restructuring "between the bras and panties."

Such a remark is characteristic of Peace, known during his 20 years in Sacramento for language that is blunt, provocative and sometimes inappropriate. The gamble that Davis took in hiring Peace to manage California's $35 billion budget shortfall, though, is not the former state senator's loose language. It's the likelihood that he will toss out ideas far wilder than anything Davis is comfortable with.

Peace—long ago the producer of the schlock classic film *Attack of the Killer Tomatoes*—is unafraid to put forth a thousand ideas in the hopes that one will be brilliant, and the other 999 won't be held against him. In that sense, his approach puts him totally at odds with the cautious Davis. But in the past, enough of Peace's ideas have stuck to convince Davis he is the right man to deal with the huge state money gap.

Most state finance directors are scrupulously loyal to the governor, and go to extra-ordinary lengths to reflect the thinking in the executive office. Peace, by contrast, has already floated trial balloons that haven't sounded like they were carefully vetted. Davis, for example, wants to raise vehicle license fees, which are shared with localities. Peace, who favors an increased property tax on businesses, recently derided the license fees as the "crack cocaine of local government."

If examples of Peace's impolitic remarks abound, so do stories about his ambitions as a public policy thinker. During the recession of the early 1990s, Peace seemed omnipresent in discussions of budget fixes, although he lacked much of a formal role in the process. In 1993, he drafted a complete overhaul of California's workers' compensation law. Peace's legislative career was marred, however, by his role in the state's electricity deregulation debacle. When the bill deregulating the power system came through the Senate, Peace pushed for a more consumer-friendly approach than the one that prevailed. However, his chairmanship of the conference committee that drafted the final

Alan Greenblatt is a staff writer for *Governing*. This article is reprinted from *Governing* (March 2003): 64.

A Powerful California Commission Survives a Demise

California's Coastal Commission was down—but now it is not necessarily out. Despite state and federal court rulings that deemed the agency unconstitutional, the California legislature is reviving it.

The commission's structure was at the heart of the constitutional issue. Eight of its 12 commissioners, who regulate construction and preservation along the coastline, were appointed by the legislature. Because they serve no fixed term but instead remain in office at the will of the legislature, the courts—both the California Supreme Court in December and a federal appellate court in January—ruled that the commission violated the separation of powers doctrine.

The decision put in doubt the commission's ability to continue regulating development along California's 1,100-mile coastline. California Governor Gray Davis, eager to have the commission in action to do battle with the Bush administration over offshore drilling, called a special session to remedy the problem. State lawmakers passed a bill to provide members appointed by the legislature to fixed four-year terms. The state attorney general is confident a fixed term will satisfy the court's concerns.

The debate over the court rulings and the legislative action widened into more general criticism of the commission, which its critics say has overstepped its original bounds. The commission was established to help local governments adopt coastal plans but has gotten involved in decisions over development of much of the state's 1.5 million acres of coastal property.

However controversial the commission may be, the legislature's fixed-term solution will either remedy the problem outright or at least win a fresh hearing in court.

Source: Alan Greenblatt, "A Powerful Commission Survives a Demise," *Governing* (March 2003): 55.

version probably doomed any aspirations for higher office. In any case, term limits had already ended his legislative career at the time Davis reached him in the lingerie department.

Peace now faces the challenge of selling Davis' package of massive spending cuts and tax increases to dubious former colleagues. Democrats control both chambers of the legislature, but they can't do much by themselves. Budgets require at least a two-thirds majority, and there are no Republicans who favor any tax increase.

Even so, a tax increase may be inevitable. Peace, who shares with Davis a desire to restructure California's tax system completely, predicts any tax increase will be coupled with a strict cap on spending in order to secure GOP votes. Getting to that combination will take more skillful massaging of the legislature than Davis has previously mastered.

That's just where Peace may prove most helpful. Davis' strategy in previous years has been to get budgets passed by buying off a few Republican votes with money for local projects. That stopped working when things turned ugly last year, and it is unlikely to work this time. "The governor's office has been very weak in understanding how to get to the endgame," says Fred Silva, of the Public Policy Institute of California. "Steve Peace is probably the most knowledgeable about how to get there."

Women State Agency Heads and Their Leadership

by Norma M. Riccucci and Judith R. Saidel

According to a recent study conducted by the Center for Women in Government, the percentage of women state agency heads increased very slowly, but steadily, between 1997 and 1999. Women department heads in the 50 states held just over 25 percent of chief executive agency leadership positions in 1999. If this trend continues, the cohort of top-ranking gubernatorial appointees will include more women leaders willing to challenge, perhaps subtly, the way political systems usually operate. The possibility thereby increases that, in those states where the proportion of women agency heads is close to or exceeds the national average, at least some of "the way things have always have been done" in state government may be about to change.

Most women appointed by governors to direct the affairs of government agencies articulate remarkably similar ideas about their leadership. Regardless of geographic region, party of the governor who appointed them, organization mission, tenure in office, their own professional background and race or ethnicity, women at the helm of state agencies frequently describe their leadership in terms of two major themes—connection and systems change.

Top-ranking women appointees define themselves as connectors to a wide range of internal and external policy actors and constituencies and/or as systems change agents. In addition, they often use the language of connection to explain departmental actions undertaken to implement their top priorities. It is particularly interesting that most women state agency heads describe their leadership strategy as playing by the rules, while simultaneously bucking the system.

In an exploratory study conducted in the spring, summer and fall of 1998, we interviewed 24 women heads of departments or agencies in eight states: California, Delaware, Georgia, Illinois, Indiana, Maryland, New York and Vermont. These states were a purposive sample selected for variation in size of state,

Norma M. Riccucci is a professor of public administration and policy at the University of Albany, State University of New York. Judith R. Saidel is executive director of the Center for Women in Government at the University of Albany, State University of New York. This article is reprinted from *Spectrum* (winter 2002):18–19. Copyright 2002 The Council of State Governments. Reprinted with permission from *Spectrum.*

geographic location, party of governor and political culture as measured by a composite index of state policies on a number of issues. We also identified states with a concentration of women gubernatorial appointees.

Forging Connections

Illustrating a strategy of "playing by the rules," women department heads consistently define their leadership in terms of forging connections with policy players inside and outside government. Some agency leaders emphasize their determination to make personal contact with all agency staff. They schedule time for open access to the director, interact with individual employees frequently and informally, and circulate through field offices to facilitate face-to-face connections with employees.

Other women leaders describe efforts to strengthen linkages with external actors. They invest in expanding ties between government agencies, as well as between community groups, their own agency, and other government entities.

Partnerships with communities and community organizations figure prominently in the strategizing of women policy leaders. In comments about actions undertaken to implement her priorities, one commissioner highlighted the formation of a new working group representing communities and major state agencies involved in providing children's services. Another pointed to a new invitational group of community leaders from industry, academia, planning groups, and others to whom she said, "We are going to work with you to develop our state's strategy. We're going to jointly do this." Later she noted the participants' observation that they had never before heard of an approach like this by her agency.

Interestingly, a number of bureaucratic leaders spoke explicitly about building firmer and more far-reaching connections with the public. This finding is consistent with other research on gender-related leadership strategies in which women are reported to encourage a larger circle of people to participate in the policy process by engaging citizens in governmental decision-making. One director stated that communicating with the public, outreach, and letting the citizens know what the agency does are top priorities. Efforts to build connections often went beyond the notion of informing the public to a more inclusive strategy of directly involving the public in the work of state government.

Partnerships with the private sector, a policy approach frequently undertaken over the last two decades, were also part of the connection strategies of several women agency heads. In several instances, however, a distinctive element of the strategy was the explicit targeting of a previously overlooked constituency in the business community.

Changing Systems

Even as women at the helm of large public agencies play by the rules, working hard to forge connections with key collaborators, they do not shy away from bucking the systems within which they operate. Some agency heads define their leadership in terms of internal organizational systems change; others explicitly challenge the structure, processes and participants in larger policy systems. A representative comment by one department head illustrates the point. In response to the question, "When you say 'bucking the system,' who are you pushing against?" she said, "Whoever is in my way. Sometimes it's the state statute; sometimes it's the legislature; sometimes it's the budget agency; sometimes it's the governor's office; sometimes it's the agency."

In terms of changing internal agency systems, several of the women leaders talked about changing the culture of their organizations in order to better meet the established goals. One talked explicitly of changing bureaucratic cultures. A major personal priority of hers was, "To prepare the agency for the challenges of succeeding in a more complex and less bureaucratic world. I call it in my initiatives, 'creating a bias for action.' It means that the department can no longer do everything with checks and balances. It must become proactive; it must set its own agenda to some degree and not be merely a responder to the legislature; and it must change the way it makes decisions in order to facilitate that."

Other foci of internal organizational change revolves around human resources, state budgeting and information systems. In terms of human resources, several of the women we interviewed talked about the importance of racial and gender diversity not only within the ranks of state government, but also in the management and executive teams that work closely with them. A representative comment was that it makes good sense from a management and leadership standpoint.

Focusing their energies on changing the internal systems of their agencies is only one part of the leadership strategy for the women appointees we interviewed. Another centers on broader changes to the systems within which they operate. For example, several women discussed their attempt to bring about change within policy delivery and regulatory systems. Others discussed their efforts to change the overall system of state government. One female policy-maker, serving her eighth year at the helm of a state agency, explained: "we had to change the way the public sector operates."

Conclusion

This exploratory study on the way in which women gubernatorial appointees define their leadership suggests that top-ranking women think similarly about how they run their agencies and departments. On the one hand, they demonstrate leadership strategies that rely on playing by the rules. And yet, at the same time, they buck the system and attempt to bring about change to the operations and systems that affect their ability to lead their organizations. This snapshot of the way in which women lead state agencies provides insight into the overall performance of state governments. It also suggests that women identify themselves as change agents in the states, the increasingly important focus of policy-making authority in this steady era of devolution.

According to a recent study conducted by the Center for Women in Government, the percentage of women state agency heads increased slowly, but steadily, between 1997 and 1999. Women department heads in the 50 states held just over 25 percent of chief executive agency leadership positions in 1999. If this trend continues, the cohort of top-ranking gubernatorial appointees will include more women leaders willing to challenge, perhaps subtly, the way political systems usually operate. The possibility thereby increases that, in those states where the proportion of women agency heads is close to or exceeds the national average, at least some of "the way things have always been done" in state government may be about to change.

Jock Trap

by Anya Sostek

State Representative Gerald Allen still vividly remembers the August afternoon seven years ago when the glory of his beloved University of Alabama football team was irrevocably sullied. As he sat in a country restaurant and watched in disbelief, the National Collegiate Athletic Association announced that it was putting his alma mater on probation—taking away the Crimson Tide's scholarships and changing eight victories into losses. The reason for the punishment: a star cornerback had played for the school for a full season after receiving money from a sports agent.

When the probation was handed out, Alabama had won 12 national championships without a single blemish on its record. To Allen, who grew up near the campus in Tuscaloosa and also watched his son play football there, it seemed impossible that one sports agent could cause such a storied program to crumble. "I thought, something is wrong with this picture," he says. "Something is missing here."

As a freshman legislator in 1995, Allen became one of the first to study laws about sports agents, requesting legislation from all of the states with laws on the books. He discovered that during the 1980s, Alabama and a few other states had passed laws regulating sports agents in response to their growing influence following the start of free agency. But enforcement of such laws was sporadic at best.

Today, states are well on their way to stopping unscrupulous sports agents, and making life significantly easier for legitimate agents. The solution comes in the form of the Uniform Athlete Agents Act, which sets the same requirements for agents across the country. With essentially no opposition, 14 states have currently adopted the law and legislation is pending in an additional eight states.

Although agents' primary role is to negotiate contracts and endorsement deals, they also will do everything from coordinating volunteer opportunities to teaching young players "life skills" to get them from college to professional life. Under NCAA rules, agents are allowed to talk to athletes at any time, as long as there is no agreement for future representation. The second an athlete agrees to be represented, or accepts a gift of any kind, that athlete is no longer eligible to play college sports.

If an athlete plays, and is later shown to be retroactively ineligible—as was the case in

Anya Sostek is an associate editor for *Governing*. This article is reprinted from *Governing* (June 2002): 42, 44.

Alabama—the school can be sanctioned with a costly punishment. In 1996, for example, Marcus Camby led the University of Massachusetts basketball team to the Final Four. When it was later revealed that Camby had accepted clothes, cars and stereo equipment from agents, the school had to return $151,000 to the NCAA. "It's not just that a private university can lose its own money," says Ted Curtis, a sports attorney and a professor of sports administration at Lynn University in Boca Raton, Florida. "When you start dealing with state universities, that's when the legislature gets involved."

After a spate of similar scandals in the mid-1990s, the NCAA and state governments did indeed get involved. The NCAA asked the National Conference of Commissioners on Uniform State Laws, the organization that developed the Uniform Commercial Code and Uniform Probate Code, for help in forming a uniform code for a sports agent law.

Initially reluctant to deal with sports agents because it had traditionally worked only in the areas of commerce and family law, NCCUSL eventually decided that it would take up the issue. The group held three years of hearings to develop a model law, including testimony by athletes, university conferences and agents. In 2000, NCCUSL voted to accept the Uniform Athlete Agents Act in its annual meeting, and last year, Utah became the first state to adopt the law.

The idea behind the law is that states working together can succeed where states working independently have failed. Under the previous system, about half of the states had no law on the books at all. In other states, agent legislation ranged from a simple criminal designation in Michigan to a hefty fee and a competency exam in Florida. "It's not that the states hadn't done anything," says Michael Kerr, deputy executive director of NCCUSL, "it's that they had done completely different things."

What's more, few states enforced any of their agent laws, whether they required registration, notification or criminal penalties. And it was lucky for agents that the states didn't pay much attention, because they frequently travel the country looking for the next hot prospect to sign. Keeping up with numerous state laws would have amounted to a recurring nightmare. "In one state, they had to keep records for three years, in other states, four or five years. In some states, an athlete had 15 days to rescind a contract, others had 10 or 12," Curtis says. "Agents had no idea how to do their jobs."

Through reciprocal registration, the Athlete Agents Act eliminates much of that hassle. An agent registers in one state by filling out a standard form and paying a set fee, which varies from $20 in Arizona to $100 in Mississippi. Once agents follow the law and register in one state, they need only to fill out a simple form and pay a nominal fee in all other states that have adopted the act. That way, each state has to do less paperwork and agents can easily follow the law without having to worry when they cross state lines to do their business. Registration information, such as criminal records, past clients and educational experience, also then becomes available to the public. The hope is that the wealth of consumer information will be the first step in weeding out unscrupulous agents.

For the corrupt agents that do still get hired, the law also provides concrete enforcement measures. Under the Uniform Athlete Agents Act, an agent is not allowed to give false information or promises, give anything of value to a student before a contract is signed or initiate contact with a student before the agent has registered with the state. If an agent disobeys, the law gives states subpoena power to obtain any necessary documents and spells out penalties for infractions. Most states that have already passed the law chose to punish violators with some class of felony. Punishments range from a $2,500 fine in Arizona to up to two years in prison and a $10,000 fine in Mississippi.

The act also deals with specific player contracts. It stipulates that a contract must include a specific warning to athletes, notifying them that by signing a contract with an agent, they will lose their NCAA eligibility. The contract also lets both the student and the agent know that they must notify the college within 72 hours that an agreement has been reached and that the student has the right to cancel the agreement within 14 days. If the student or agent does not notify the school, the school has the right to sue them for monetary damages.

Thus far, passage of the law has been remarkably smooth. "It isn't the kind of thing where everybody will agree that every part is perfect," Curtis says. "But NCCUSL did a good job of trying to please everybody."

In addition to simplifying their legal paperwork, the law provides agents with an opportunity to combat the common perception of their profession as wily and exploitative. "It's a great act for legitimate agents," says Roy Kessel, a sports agent and president of Chicago's SportsLoop company. "The old system made it so difficult that even some of the most high profile and legitimate agents didn't comply. This way, if you're not complying, you're not trying to comply."

For schools and states, the law is a tool to help prevent embarrassing and costly scandals. More than half of the states have either introduced or approved the law, and Kerr expects that the rest of the states will pass it in the next three or four years. In states where the act has been debated but not enacted, passage has stalled because of financial or administrative hurdles—not a quarrel with the bill on policy grounds.

The lone act of policy opposition to the measure came last year in New Mexico, when Governor Gary Johnson vetoed the bill after it passed overwhelmingly in both houses. Johnson's veto message to the Speaker of the House stated that "while I am generally supportive of uniform laws as a means to provide certainty in the courts, I am troubled that New Mexico would become one of the few states in this country to enact these provisions. In addition, the regulation of agents for student athletes is best left to governing organizations such as the National Collegiate Athletic Association."

States that already have sports agent laws, especially those that have passed laws recently, may prove to be equally unenthusiastic. In Ohio, for example, legislators finally passed an agent law in 2001, and are not eager to scrap it for a brand-new one. Although the spirit of the Ohio law is the same as the Uniform Athlete Agents Act, some of the punishments and restrictions are different, causing problems for agents who expect all state laws to be consistent.

Also, some states may oppose one controversial provision in the uniform act: that schools can sue students for monetary damages if students do not notify them that they have retained an agent. The American Bar Association initially raised concern about that provision, before approving the act as a whole. So far, however, legislators have not identified that issue as a stumbling block.

Most of the states that have enacted the measure are not traditional stomping grounds for sports agents, so registration has not yet gained much momentum. That's likely to change in July, when the law goes into effect in Florida, where many agents are headquartered. It also remains to be seen whether states will enforce the uniform agent law, given that they have not traditionally enforced such laws in the past. Because of the simplicity of the law and the endorsements by players' associations and the NCAA, Kerr is confident that this time the law will stick. "For the first time, to some degree, it will be the sports agents themselves who will drive the enforcement," he says. "Once they have a finite idea of what the law will look like, they will be more likely to follow the rules."

Cloaked in Security

by Christopher Swope

Visit New York's City Hall Park on a warm, sunny day, and you're almost certain to see a bride and groom in formal attire being photographed there. After taking vows at the Municipal Building, newlyweds can't resist crossing the street into the leafy park and posing in front of the granite fountain, with its graceful jets of arcing water and elegant bronze candelabras. Amidst the marital bliss, nobody realizes this fountain serves a double purpose. Not only is it a nice spot for pictures, it's also a blockade for truck bombs.

New York installed the fountain three years ago during a complete renovation of the grounds around City Hall. Then-mayor Rudolph Giuliani ordered the redesign as part of a strategy to protect City Hall from terrorist attacks. This was before terrorists destroyed the World Trade Center only a few blocks away. But it came after truck bombs had killed hundreds in two American embassies in east Africa. The city's landscape architects labored to make new security features as invisible as possible. So the fountain blends gracefully with gardens of colorful blooms—and also obstructs a lane where a truck could pick up speed and ram into the front of City Hall. Security cameras hide in the tree canopy. And a new Victorian-style steel fence that rings the grounds is specially hardened to stop a vehicle in its tracks.

At their unveiling, these security features were lambasted by local critics. However, in the wake of 9/11, the ingenuity and subtlety used in City Hall Park is especially noteworthy. Take a five-minute walk north from there, and you'll see a very different approach to security. That's where the New York County Supreme Court sits in a new kind of concrete jungle. Jersey barriers—those ubiquitous and utilitarian barricades along highways—are lined up on the sidewalks. Not only are the barriers ugly and out of place in an urban streetscape but they also send the public a frightening message: You aren't safe here.

The two government complexes are just two blocks from each other in Lower Manhattan, but they are worlds apart in their attitudes toward security. One says finesse. The other says fortress. Unfortunately, since the terrorist attacks, the fortress mentality seems to be winning out in cities across the country. Many of

Christopher Swope is a staff writer for *Governing*. This article is reprinted from *Governing* (January 2003): 36–39.

our icons of democracy—city halls, state-houses, courthouses and federal buildings—have been made to look like military facilities. Nowhere is the problem worse than in Washington, D.C., where hundreds of Jersey barriers are deployed around town, and giant sewer pipes still guard the lawn of the U.S. Capitol.

"We cannot barricade our public buildings and deaden the streets and sidewalks of our cities," insists Mayor Joseph Riley of Charleston, South Carolina, a leading proponent among his peers for good urban design. Indeed, City Hall Park demonstrates that safety and beauty can be compatible if both are weighed in equal measure. It is a lesson that a growing number of planners, architects and landscape specialists are solidifying into a "security design" movement. As they draw blueprints for new public buildings and spaces, they are incorporating security features right into the landscape—much the way architects have learned to build wheelchair ramps seamlessly into their plans. At the same time, they are crafting creative ways to shield older structures without constructing mini-Maginot Lines around them.

Subtle security changes are being made inside public buildings as well. Designers are using new kinds of blast-proof glass so they can continue the trend toward transparency in public architecture. They utilize redundant support structures to guard against a pancake-type building collapse. Increasingly, public buildings are designed to accommodate metal detectors if they are deemed necessary and have key-card security systems that limit access within buildings.

Looking to the Bench

Yet trade-offs are inevitable. There is a natural tension between security and democracy. Government buildings are supposed to be open and free. How do you keep the bad guys away while welcoming everyone else in? Sure, outdoor fences can be made to look classy. Likewise, anyone used to air travel likely won't object to passing through a metal detector in the lobby of a city hall or statehouse. But do these measures send forbidding signals? Architect David Hart thinks so. He is overseeing the design for Utah's capitol campus expansion, complete with two new office buildings and a restoration of the 1915 capitol building. "You could go so far toward the secure side that you make buildings impenetrable for the public," Hart says. "If we close them and screen everyone, then we're treating the public, whose houses they are, as intruders."

There are other sensitive and emotional questions: Would terrorists realistically strike a city hall? Are smaller cities safer than big ones? Obscurity might inspire confidence if not for two words: Oklahoma City. And what sorts of hideous acts should we be designing for, anyway? Experts say truck or car bombs are the likeliest terrorist threat. But what about shoulder-launched missiles? Anthrax attacks? "You have to ask yourself what are the likely threats," Hart says. "There's no way I can reinforce the dome of our capitol to withstand an airplane attack. We just have to pray that nobody does that."

City and state officials are finding, however, that there are creative, inexpensive and largely hidden defense measures they can take. Consider Chicago's Daley Plaza, the central square known for its giant Picasso sculpture. After 9/11, city officials worried that a bomb-laden vehicle could accelerate across the plaza and blow up the adjacent municipal skyscraper. It turned out that parts of a security solution were already in place, in the form of 2,000-pound limestone benches scattered about the plaza. The benches were simply rearranged around the plaza's perimeter. On warm afternoons, you'll still find people lounging on the benches eating lunch or reading a newspaper. Unwittingly, they are also sitting on a car-bomb barrier.

Benches are one part of the security strategy as Austin, Texas, builds a new city hall. As it happened, Austin broke ground on the new building just before 9/11. After the attacks, the city hired a security consultant, weighed its risks and decided to edit the blueprints. There were already plans for the front of the building to have some benches cut into limestone boulders. More were added. Plans for a passenger drop-off area close to the building were eliminated. The lobby was also altered to allow for the installation of metal detectors and package screening. "We thought a lot about security," says Ron Davis, Austin's city hall project manager. "But if security were the top priority, we'd have to scrap the design we had. We really felt we should incorporate security to the degree we can but not make it the overriding concern."

In California, state lawmakers feel the terrorist threat more acutely than in other parts of the country. In January 2001, a man with a history of mental illness plowed an 18-wheel truck into the south side of the state capitol building in Sacramento, killing himself and causing $16 million worth of damage. After the incident, legislators debated putting up a fence around the building, but they rejected it for fear the public would find it off-putting. Instead, they opted for a $2.7 million plan to place 600 protective planters around the building and metal detectors at the doors. "There was a great deal of consternation among members over this," says Tony Beard, the chief sergeant-at-arms for the California Senate. "But the reality is somebody tried to kill us. There's no way to deal with this without in some way, shape or form limiting access to the capitol."

Security Creep

In the weeks following the 9/11 attacks, a visitor to Washington, D.C., may well have mistaken the nation's capital for a war zone. If federal agencies, museums and monuments hadn't already cordoned themselves in with Jersey barriers after the 1995 Oklahoma City bombing or the 1998 embassy bombings, they reasoned this was the time to place an order. The wall-it-off impulse was understandable. But it went beyond reason.

The unfolding story of how the capital cleans up its concrete mess matters far outside the Beltway. For one thing, the choices Washington makes will likely set a tone for cities, states and counties facing their own security design issues. But more directly, every major city has its own microcosm of downtown D.C., in the form of federal buildings and courthouses. As Richard Friedman sees it, Washington's problems are just like any other city's—only magnified a hundred times. Friedman is a Boston developer and a Clinton appointee to the National Capital Planning Commission, which oversees planning for federal land in D.C., including its monumental core. Some agencies—the FBI or State Department perhaps—clearly require significant security measures, he says. Others tend to give in to what he calls "security creep." Building managers, each sharing the same worst nightmare, begin one-upping each other. Every building takes its own approach, and nobody's minding the overall blow to the city's urbanism. "Most often, the people making security decisions don't report to an urban planner," Friedman says. "If you want a beautiful home, you wouldn't hire the Secret Service to design it."

Friedman chairs a planning task force that even before 9/11 was looking at how to resolve these issues. In an October 2002 report, the task force issued some suggestions. Most were specific to streets and buildings in Washington. But the underlying principles are applicable anywhere, at least when it comes to preventing vehicle-borne attacks. It's important to create standoff distance around sensitive buildings: "Every foot counts," Friedman says. But rather than throw up concrete barriers or cold rows of bollards, cities should instead rely on the everyday elements of their urban streetscape. Street lights, benches, newsstands, parking meters, garbage cans, signs and bus shelters can all be hardened and anchored to stop (or at least slow down) large vehicles. "The best security item in our kit of parts is a tree," Friedman says. "Maybe it means you plant large caliper trees rather than saplings. That's expensive. But bollards cost $5,000 each. You can buy a pretty big tree for $5,000."

For now, many federal buildings, both in Washington and in other cities, seem willing to trade their Jersey barriers for an only slightly less obnoxious measure: concrete planters. Often topped with wilting pansies, these generally look exactly like the Band-Aid they are. Responding to complaints nationwide, the U.S. General Services Administration—essentially the federal government's landlord—has held design charettes with city planners and architects in Boston, Chicago, New York and other cities to come up with more attractive and permanent options. But funding is tight and landscape-design options are limited, especially with older buildings packed tightly into dense downtowns. "The Jersey barriers are no-no's," admits Ed Feiner, GSA's chief architect. "They're a temporary measure, and we're trying to replace them as quickly as possible as the money becomes available."

While some cities grumble that GSA is de-militarizing too slowly, the feds do get high marks on security design in their newest buildings. Since the Oklahoma City bombing, newly commissioned federal buildings now must meet a lengthy set of security criteria, depending on the tenant's "threat assessment." Setbacks, the use of blast-proof glass and redundant building supports are prescribed. Loading docks, garages and mailrooms are designed to absorb explosions. Air intakes guard against the release of biological or chemical agents into ventilation systems. Cameras, key cards and alarms are suggested for monitoring movement in sensitive parts of the buildings.

This list may sound like a formula for a bunker. Yet the remarkable thing is that architects, following the security guidelines, have been producing highly acclaimed buildings. Critics are raving about new federal courthouses in Las Vegas and Islip, New York, as well as designs for a replacement for the Murrah Building in Oklahoma City. States and cities are taking notice, according to Kristina Feller, a director with KMD Architects in San Francisco, a firm that gets a lot of state, local and federal commissions. "One thing we've seen post 9/11 is that state and local governments are more aware of the federal security guidelines," Feller says. "They're using them as an a la carte menu to pick and choose what security measures are most appropriate for their communities."

The Big Picture

Ultimately, every statehouse, city hall and county courthouse requires a security strategy tailored to its location and the amount of risk occupants are willing to live with. But where government buildings are clustered, it makes sense to think through design issues on a broader scale. This is what Utah is doing with its state capitol complex. "Rather than just protecting the state capitol and then protecting the other state buildings, we're looking at the overall campus," says architect David Hart.

To be sure, they weren't always thinking this way. After 9/11, Utah slapped concrete barriers and orange traffic barrels around its capitol just as lots of other states did. Last year's Olympics, however, forced state officials to deal with the situation: A city under siege was not the image Salt Lake City wanted projected to the world. For starters, they replaced the Jersey barriers with planters. Thinking longer term, however, Hart incorporated security into every aspect of the 20-year campus master plan.

Landscaping is a big part of the plan. Planners went back to the Olmsted brothers' original design for the grounds, including an oval walkway that rings the whole site. In the new vision, this path will form a border between a secure zone and a nonsecure zone. Strategically placed benches and cherry trees will line the walkway to deter cars and trucks from making a charge toward any of the buildings. Chances are, they won't get that far anyway. A landscaped berm will line the street-side edge of the 43-acre site.

Building design will also play a role in security. Part of the capitol restoration, as well as construction of the new state office buildings, involves erecting a granite "podium" around each of the buildings to act as a blast shield. Inside the capitol, plans are to accommodate metal detectors for the occasional presidential visit or other sensitive events. But they will be stationed at side entrances, so that most of the time when the public comes through the main entrance into the rotunda, they won't see any visible security at all. "Our hope is that if someone comes in to do mischief and cases the place, he'll find it's not easy to pull off and go somewhere else," Hart says. "For us, the driving issue is still the concept of being open. We want to make sure that everyone is safe. But we also want to make sure the public has full access to its capitol."

Admittedly, public access was less of a consideration at New York's City Hall. This is still quite controversial. Ask any New Yorker lounging by the fountain what he thinks about City Hall Park, and he'll tell you it's beautiful—especially compared with the broken benches and scrubby grass there before. Still, you'll hear the same complaint over and over: The fence turns people away from City Hall. Just getting to the steps, a traditional soapbox for political dissent, now requires passing through a security checkpoint.

When the park opened in October 1999, the newspapers trashed it. *New York Times*

architecture critic Herbert Muschamp called the design "paranoid-schitzoid urbanism at its creepy best." Columnist Jimmy Breslin likened the fence and guard booths to a penitentiary. Most of the insults were hurled at Mayor Giuliani, who allowed City Hall access only to people who had official business inside the building. Public gatherings were capped at 50 people (although Giuliani famously made exceptions for celebrations whenever the Yankees won the World Series). A federal judge loosened those rules some, but even with a new mayor, Michael Bloomberg, in office, the steps still are pretty empty most of the time.

Len Hopper, a city landscape architect who was involved with the project and is past president of the American Society of Landscape Architects, notes that nothing in the park's architecture—not even the fence—keeps visitors from City Hall. Indeed, it's the mayor who decides whether the park gates are open or stay locked. And for now, based on the most current assessment of the terrorist threat, large parts of the park are open but the zone immediately surrounding city hall is closed.

Actually, Hopper asserts, this is a brilliant design feature because it is so flexible. On 9/11, you could see this in action. Not long after the two planes hit the Twin Towers, all the gates to City Hall Park were shut and locked. They remained closed for months. By January 2002, however, city officials felt comfortable letting the public in to enjoy parts of the park again. The gates opened. Hydraulic bollards sank back into the ground. Hopper likens the design's flexibility to an onion. "You can peel back the layers as the threat level decreases," Hopper says. Should the terrorist threat drop to zero, everything can be opened up.

In the meantime, we'll have to get used to the idea that fountains may protect as well as romance us.

VIII. STATE COURTS

The third branch of state government, the judiciary, probably is the one part of state government with which most citizens would prefer not to interact. State courts handle the crimes reported in the news—drunk driving, child abuse, robbery, murder, and rape. Personal disputes, divorce cases, and other civil matters also are tried in state courts.

Despite the importance of the judiciary in state politics, it is perhaps the least visible branch. One reason is because citizens want it that way; they want the courts to be above the hurly-burly of politics. The legislature may conduct its business in a circus-like atmosphere and the governor may crisscross the state to keep an impossible schedule of appointments, but the courts must be a model of decorum, a place where the rational presentation of facts and arguments leads to truth and justice. But often there are breaches in this hoped-for decorum: the actions of defendants, lawyers, witnesses, aggrieved individuals, spectators, and even, in some people's opinion, the media can be disruptive to the pursuit of justice.

The Court System

The several levels of state courts each have different responsibilities. At the lowest level are trial courts, where cases are argued and juries may be called to weigh the facts presented. Intermediate appellate courts, the next level in many state judicial systems, are where the decisions of the trial courts and other lower courts can be appealed. Finally, each state has a court of last resort. It is usually called the supreme court, but in Maine it is called the Supreme Judicial Court; in West Virginia, the Supreme Court of Last Resort; and in New York, the Court of Appeals. Here, the final appeals to lower-court decisions are made unless a federal question is involved, which then means that appeal to the federal appellate courts is possible.

State court judges rule on a variety of concerns. Part of their workload is administrative

(for example, the probating of wills). Another part involves conflict resolution (for example, deciding which party is correct in contested divorce settlements and property disputes). And still another area of responsibility includes the criminal prosecution and appeals process.

In a broader sense, state court judges are policy makers. Court decisions, rather than legislation or constitutional amendments, often modify or set aside state policies. Courts are reactive institutions of government, and their decisions are limited by the nature and timing of the cases brought before them. Judges establish new norms of acceptable behavior and revise existing norms to match changing circumstances. Their interpretations of the law may or may not have the backing of the public or of the governor or state legislature. Nonetheless, what they say goes—that is, of course, unless it is overturned by another court decision or by another decision-making body. In some instances, court decisions simply are ignored because the judiciary has no bureaucracy or army of its own to enforce decisions.

Judicial Politics

The norm of separating partisan politics from the judiciary is part of our national and state political cultures. But judges must be selected in some manner, and inevitably politics becomes a factor.

The methods used to select judges vary from state to state. Sometimes judges are appointed by the governor and confirmed by the state senate. In three states, the legislature appoints the judges. In fifteen states, some or all of the judges are elected as Democrats or Republicans. In another nineteen states, judges are elected on a nonpartisan basis.[1]

Some states have adopted a variation of the "Missouri Plan" to remove politics from the selection process as much as possible. In this process, a nonpartisan group such as the state or district bar association screens candidates and recommends the top contenders to the governor, who then makes the final decision. The argument is that merit will be the foremost criterion in the screening and nomination process.

The Missouri Plan also provides that when their terms expire, judges can "run again" on their record. The voters are asked: Should Judge X be retained in office? If the voters say yes, the judge serves another term. If the voters say no, the selection process starts anew. In this way, the judiciary is accountable to the citizens of the state.

In the mid-to-late 1980s, the world of partisan elective judicial politics was in considerable ferment. Political observers were startled in 1986 when three states—California, North Carolina, and Ohio—all had well-publicized, negative, and very expensive partisan races for their state's chief justiceship. In California, the conflict revolved around the reelection of the chief justice, who objected to the death penalty; in North Carolina, it concerned the governor's choice of a new chief justice; and in Ohio, it centered around the very partisan and controversial style of the chief justice.[2]

In 1988, the entire Texas supreme court was up for election. Issues in those races included the governor's appointment of a new chief justice, charges of impropriety, controversy over the selection of judges, and the fallout from the major Pennzoil-Texaco lawsuit.

These campaigns, which cost an estimated $10 million, had "the nastiest, most negative campaigning I have ever seen," one Texas legislator told North Carolina's Judicial Selection Study Commission. "If you are before a judge in Texas now, you've got to be worried if you are a Democrat and he is a Republican."[3]

Is justice for sale, as some critics suggest? Giving money to political campaigns, even judicial campaigns, is legal and "that's the problem," according to a Texaco spokeswoman.[4] One Houston lawyer suggested that "it looks just as bad for a lawyer to give a lot of money to a judge as for a judge to take a lot of money from a lawyer."[5] This is all cannon fodder for those wanting to remove the judicial selection process from electoral politics.

In the nonpartisan reelection held for chief justice in Wisconsin in spring 1999, the politics turned inward as three of the other sitting supreme court judges endorsed Chief Justice Shirley Abrahamson's challenger. Then came negative campaign ads attacking Abrahamson, to which she responded with negative ads against her opponent.[6] While Abrahamson won reelection for her third term, the race for the chief justiceship cost around $1 million.[7]

The federal government is also involved in the politics of the states' judiciaries. In early 1987, a U.S. district court judge in Jackson, Mississippi, ruled that Section 2 of the Voting Rights Act of 1965 applies to judges elected at the state level. At issue was the question of whether electing judges from at-large, multi-member districts dilutes minority voting strength. The implications were very clear: state judges should be elected from single-member districts, thereby offering the possibility of greater minority representation in the state judiciaries.[8]

In December 1989, a three-judge federal appeals court upheld the concept that the Voting Rights Act applies to judicial election districts.[9] So, in those states covered by the provisions of the Voting Rights Act, any changes in judicial district lines or the addition of judges must be precleared with the U.S. Department of Justice before being implemented.[10] In April 1990, the Department of Justice threw out Georgia's system of electing judges because it was discriminatory against blacks. The problem with the system was the election of judges in broad judicial circuits by a majority vote, rather than by a plurality vote. This has the same effect that at-large elections often do: diluting the strength of minority groups.[11]

Sometimes the "minority" can be a political party. In January 1994, a federal district court judge issued a preliminary order declaring that all North Carolina trial-level superior court judges be elected in their home districts rather than statewide. The case involved a Republican Party lawsuit charging that the practice of electing these trial judges statewide leaves "islands of Republicans . . . unconstitutionally swamped in a sea of yellow-dog Democrats. Only one Republican has ever been elected as a superior court judge."[12] In the 1994 elections, the Republican judicial candidates won handily statewide, but the portion of this decision ensuring judicial elections to be counted in home districts allowed some Democrats to win!

Tides of Judicial Policy Making

A current issue in the states concerns who should take the lead in the judicial system—the federal judiciary interpreting the U.S. Constitution, or the state judiciaries interpreting the individual state constitutions. For decades, the loud cry of "states' rights" masked inaction by state courts on segregation, malapportionment, and other unconstitutional practices in the states.

During the 1950s and 1960s, under a broad interpretation of the Constitution (especially the Fifth and Fourteenth Amendments), the U.S. Supreme Court moved to upset the states' intransigence and, in some cases, illegal activities. Led by Chief Justice Earl Warren (the former Republican governor of California from 1943 to 1953), the U.S. Supreme Court overturned state laws upholding segregation; forced state legislatures to apportion themselves on a one-man, one-vote basis following each census; expanded voting rights; legalized abortion; and broadened the rights of the accused in the state criminal justice system. The Warren Court set minimal standards for the states to follow in these areas and often reversed state court decisions that narrowly construed the rights of individuals.

In recent years, the U.S. Supreme Court has become more conservative in its decisions. What this has meant in terms of the states is that the Court is deciding more cases in their favor, especially when the argument is over which level of the government—federal or state—should be considered correct in their argument.[13] And the Court has even backed away from some of the minimal standards it set earlier. Several state courts have decided not only to uphold these minimal standards but, in a new form of judicial activism at the state level, to exceed them.

Former U.S. Supreme Court justice William J. Brennan Jr. once described this trend as "probably the most important development in constitutional jurisprudence today."[14] Ronald Collins, an expert on state constitutional law, estimated that between 1970 and the mid-1980s state high courts issued approximately 400 decisions based on the higher standards of the state constitutions as opposed to the minimum standards established by the U.S. Supreme Court in interpreting the U.S. Constitution.[15] As New Jersey supreme court justice Stewart G. Pollock suggests, "Horizontal federalism, in which states look to each other for guidance, may be the hallmark of the rest of the century."[16]

Why does such activism develop in a state's supreme court? One study of six state supreme courts from 1930 to 1980 found that dramatic shifts by state high courts from a relatively passive role to an active role take place in a relatively short period of time and are due mainly to a change in the composition of the court. The appointment of a "maverick" judge to a state's supreme court begins a process in which that judge dissents from the previous consensual and passive court decisions, soon swaying some supporters to the minority position. With additional appointments of more activist-oriented jurists, the court changes direction. Of import is the fact that once a transition to activism occurred, none of these courts moved back in the direction of nonactivism, at least not during the period studied.[17]

However, there is a question as to whether federal or state court decisions will affect states more. In recent years the U.S. Supreme Court has been making significant decisions affecting state politics. For example, since 1986 the U.S. Supreme Court allowed losing political parties to challenge a redistricting plan;[18] threw out mandated closed party primary systems, thereby allowing independents to participate in the party nominating process;[19] upheld local government affirmative action plans favoring women and minorities;[20] ruled against the time-honored patronage system of governors hiring political supporters;[21] upheld a state's mandatory retirement age limit for its judges;[22] is knocking down state redistricting plans based on affirmative action or "racial gerrymandering, [and has tried to define how admission to state universities and their graduate programs can continue to bring in minorities without using too blatent an affirmative action factor in the process."]

The state courts addressed some difficult issues recently. The area of criminal procedure is in ferment now as more citizens seek stronger and more effective punishment of criminals and protection of victims. The recent spate of special legislative sessions and new and tougher state criminal laws passed in response to rising crime rates ensures that state courts will be handling challenges to these laws and their administration. In 1996 the California supreme court knocked down that state's "three strikes and you're out" law.

State courts are also involved in the process of addressing school finance issues. With so much of the K–12 education financed by revenue generated from local property taxes, parents find that where they live determines the quality of education their children receive. State court decisions are supporting lawsuits by parents from the poorer parts of a state and mandating that a new and more equitable school finance system be established. As governors and legislatures fight over how to achieve an equitable solution, the state courts often end up trying to develop ways in which educational equity can be achieved.

But the answers to this school equity problem are elusive and fraught with political problems. Two major approaches are available for governors and state legislatures to consider: an increase in a statewide income or sales tax earmarked for school equity purposes, or shifting money from affluent communities to poor communities and from rich school districts to poor school districts. Another option is to create a statewide property tax for education. Such actions will lead to conflict with the other two branches of government and some divisive politics.[23]

The abortion fight has also shifted in part to the states as a result of the 1989 *Webster v. Reproductive Health Services* decision. Some state legislatures and governors have developed abortion policies with no middle ground on which prolife and prochoice advocates can agree. Such efforts go directly into the state courts. The author of a controversial abortion judicial decision in Florida found his retention election much more difficult as anti-abortion groups sought to defeat him. He won, but the political message was clear: abortion politics can be lethal.[24]

In the spring of 2000 a crisis concerning the New Hampshire state supreme court shocked state observers and citizens. A report by the state's attorney general indicated potential criminal activity by members of New Hampshire's top court. At issue was the finding that some judges who had recused or disqualified themselves from certain cases because of a conflict of interest still attempted to influence the other judges in their decisions on those cases. One judge, who had done so on his own divorce case, resigned. The state house eventually impeached the chief justice on four counts over this breach of judicial ethics, but the state senate voted against impeaching him.

The articles in Part VIII explore different aspects of the state judicial branch. Christopher Swope of *Governing* discusses a growing movement in the state courts—"do-it-yourself defense." Pam Greenberg of *State Legislatures* examines a growing issue that state courts have addressed: e-mails as part of the public record. Alan Ehrenhalt of *Governing* addresses the amnesty binge that several states have undertaken recently to reduce the load on courts and prisons.

Notes

1. Henry R. Glick, "Courts: Politics and the Judicial Process," in *Politics in the American States,* 7th ed., eds. Virginia Gray, Russell Hanson, and Herbert Jacob (Washington, D.C.: CQ Press, 1999), 242.

2. Katherine A. Hinckley, "Four Years of Strife Conclude with Ohio Chief Justice's Defeat," *Comparative State Politics Newsletter* 8:2 (April 1987): 13.

3. Jane Ruffin, "Texan Warns N.C. Commission to End System of Electing Judges," (Raleigh) *News and Observer,* November 12, 1988, 3C.

4. Sheila Kaplan, "Justice for Sale," *Common Cause Magazine* (May/June 1987): 29.

5. Peter Applebome, "Texan Fight over Judges Illustrates Politics' Growing Role in Judiciary," (Raleigh) *News and Observer,* January 24, 1988, 14A.

6. Steve Schultze, "Three State Judges Endorse Rose in TV Ad," *Milwaukee Sentinel-Journal,* March 26, 1999, from stateline.org.

7. Tribune News Services, "Pricey Campaign Debated," *Chicago Tribune,* April 8, 1999, from stateline.org.

8. "Mississippi Ruling Could Aid N.C. Suit on Judgeship Elections," (Raleigh) *News and Observer,* April 5, 1987, 32A.

9. The Voting Rights Act of 1965, extended in 1970 and 1975, banned redistricting plans that diluted the voting strength of black and other minority communities. The law suspended literacy tests and provided for the appointment of federal supervisors of voter registration in all states and counties where literacy tests (or similar qualifying devices) were in effect as of November 1, 1964, and where less than 50 percent of the voting-age residents had registered to vote or voted in the 1964 presidential election. State or county governments brought under the coverage of the law due to low voter registration or participation were required to obtain federal approval of any new voting laws, standards, practices, or procedures before implementing them. The act placed federal registration machinery in six southern states, twenty-eight counties in North Carolina, three counties in Arizona, and one in Idaho.

10. "Federal Court Applies VRA to State Judicial Districts," *Intergovernmental Perspective* 16:1 (Winter 1990): 20.

11. Peter Applebome, "U.S. Declares Georgia Judge Selection Illegal," *New York Times* News Service, in (Raleigh) *News and Observer,* April 27, 1990, 3A.

12. Joseph Neff, "Ruling on Judges Cheers GOP," (Raleigh) *News and Observer,* January 4, 1994, 1A.

13. Joan Biskupic, "Viewing More as an Affair of State: Pay Case Shows High Court's Trend Toward Curbing U.S. Power," *Washington Post,* April 1, 1999, A10.

14. Quoted in Robert Pear, "State Courts Move Beyond U.S. Bench in Rights Rulings," *New York Times,* May 4, 1986, 1.

15. Cited in Lanny Proffer, "State Courts and Civil Liberties," *State Legislatures* 13:9 (September 1987): 29.

16. Quoted in Pear, "State Courts," 16.

17. John Patrick Hagan, "Patterns of Activism on State Supreme Courts," *Publius* 18:1 (Winter 1988): 97–115.

18. *Davis v. Bandemer* (1986).

19. *Tashjian v. Republican Party of Connecticut* (1986).

20. *Johnson v. Transportation Agency, Santa Clara County, Calif.* (1987).

21. *Rutan et al. v. Republican Party of Illinois* (1990).

22. *Gregory v. Ashcroft* (1991).

23. Lawrence Baum, "Supreme Courts in the Policy Process," in *The State of the States,* 3d ed., ed. Carl E. Van Horn (Washington, D.C.: CQ Press, 1996), 156–157.

24. Ibid.

Bellying Up to the Bar

by Christopher Swope

There's an old courthouse proverb almost every attorney knows: "He who represents himself has a fool for a lawyer and a fool for a client."

That adage may be as true as it is self-serving. Nevertheless, a growing number of Americans seeking justice are ignoring it. Courts in every state these days report seeing more and more people defending themselves without a lawyer, especially in divorce, child support and other domestic cases. Although national statistics are elusive, it's typical nowadays for more than half of all litigants in family courts to represent themselves. In Arizona, only one out of 10 family cases involves lawyers on both sides.

Why are Americans going it alone in court? Distrust of lawyers and the high hourly fees they charge are only part of the explanation. Reforms such as no-fault divorces have made some types of cases easier for laymen to handle. There's also the grim reality that more people are getting divorced for a second or third time—so they already know the ropes.

Most significant, however, is the nation's growing do-it-yourself culture. "We are in a self-help society," says Margaret Marshall, chief justice of the Massachusetts Supreme Judicial Court. "With the Internet, it's increasingly possible for people to access information hithertofore available only to professionals. You see it in medicine, home design, accounting and travel. The legal profession is no different."

For state and local courts, handling the boom in lawyerless litigants is an enormous challenge. The right to defend oneself is enshrined in the Constitution. Yet do-it-yourselfers are clogging up court dockets. They require loads of extra attention navigating the legal system, putting both clerks and judges in an awkward position. How much help can they give without sacrificing their neutrality?

Maricopa County, Arizona, took an approach that dozens of other court systems have since followed. Seven years ago, the county set up "self-help" centers at three courthouses where people can pick up all the information they need to handle their own cases. Forms were translated from legalese into simple English. Staff are on hand to answer procedural questions, but they are careful not to talk legal

Christopher Swope is a staff writer for *Governing*. This article is reprinted from *Governing* (December 2002): 18.

strategy. If litigants sense they are in over their heads, they are referred to a roster of lawyers. "If people are willing to take the time to sort through the information we've got, then there's a chance conscientious people can do it on their own," says trial court administrator Gordon Griller.

Some new experiments involve technology. Many courts are creating virtual self-help centers on the Internet. Waukesha County, Wisconsin, rolled out a new Web site in February with legal forms and instructions for filing a case. The site, *courtselfhelp.waukeshacounty. gov,* processed more than 6,000 "visits" in six months. In Orange County, California, the local legal aid society developed computer kiosks for the courthouse. The machines, known as I-CAN, prompt litigants with questions about their cases and automatically print out properly formatted court filings.

Decidedly low-tech approaches are working as well. Fresno County, California, has the "lawmobile," a self-help center on wheels that drives out to churches, senior centers and other locations. Some courts, often in collaboration with legal aid societies, are offering self-representation classes taught by volunteer lawyers. And for divorce cases, Kane County, Illinois, has given do-it-yourselfers a court of their own. Every Wednesday night, a judge presides over lawyer-free divorce court.

These efforts are helping to level the playing field somewhat. They're also helping the courts move the cases along faster. The only grumbles, not surprisingly, are from attorneys concerned that they're losing business. Bonnie Hough, who supervises a self-help Web site for California's administrative office of the courts, doesn't think the lawyers have anything to worry about. "I think we're tapping into a totally different market," Hough says. "One thing you can do with a court program is say, 'Look, I have no financial interest in your case. But you really need a lawyer.'

The Public Life of E-Mail

by Pam Greenberg

What's in a word? Or, more importantly, what's in the e-mail people use to chat incessantly across the Internet?

Plenty, say news organizations campaigning to make lawmakers' e-mail a matter of public record.

Four news groups have sued Utah Governor Mike Leavitt, saying he is illegally destroying his e-mail messages. The governor claims many of his e-mails are personal, which would exempt them from the public records law. But a Salt Lake newspaper requested the messages be released for the six-week period when the state's voting districts were redrawn. The newspaper is seeking access to messages that would fall under the public records law, which states that "correspondence . . . in which the governmental entity determines or states an opinion upon the rights of the state, a political subdivision, the public, or any person" are normally public. The matter has ended up in court.

In Indiana, the question of e-mail has stymied legislation on open records until the 2003 session. The General Assembly passed a measure that would have let lawmakers decide which of their records could be made public, but the governor vetoed the bill. The importance of the electronic messages was emphasized when an Indianapolis newspaper sought access to legislators' e-mail last year. During the 10-week 2002 session, House leaders and news organizations argued about whether lawmakers' mail and e-mail should be open to the public. Lawmakers insisted that it should be private to protect constituents who expect their personal correspondence to be kept confidential; media groups claimed the exemption was too broad.

Nebraska news organizations consider e-mail a public record, which means the messages should be available to anyone requesting them. Nebraska law states that information considered a public record in its original form is also a public record when maintained in computer files. However, when a district court judge ordered the state to produce e-mail about Nebraska's fight against a nuclear waste dump, officials said many messages had been deleted. The back-up tapes that should have contained the e-mail were subsequently taped over with other data as part of the recycling process in

Pam Greenberg is NCSL's expert on legislative technology. This article is reprinted from *State Legislatures* (September 2002): 27.

place in the secretary of state's records management division. The division is now setting up a formal process to retain e-mail.

In Arkansas, each agency and elected official decides which records to save and which to delete. The Arkansas Press Association, however, is deciding whether to seek legislation in 2003 to preserve government e-mail. The association contends that deletion of the messages could "impede criminal investigations and shield public officials from complaints against them."

Most states do not expressly define whether e-mail is a public record, leaving it to the record holders to decide for themselves or, if challenged, for the courts to decide. Some state open records laws include provisions that consider communications to be public record regardless of physical form. In other states, the laws apply only to executive branch officials and agencies, not legislators and legislative staff.

Only a few states have addressed the issue head-on. Colorado law provides that e-mail

messages sent or received by legislators are a public record; however, communications that a constituent "would have reason to expect to remain confidential" are exempt from public disclosure. Under Rhode Island's public records law, e-mail is considered a public record, but the law exempts messages between elected officials and those they represent.

Montana in 2001 enacted legislation that includes electronic mail as a public record, to be treated the same as other documents under the public records law. And Texas law explicitly states that public disclosure of electronic communications between citizens and members of the legislature and the lieutenant governor is prohibited unless the citizen authorizes disclosure.

Determining whether e-mail is a public record is a first step. States are only just beginning to grapple with the next: policies and procedures that outline how and what types of electronic communications should be preserved, and for how long.

Beware the Amnesty Binge

by Alan Ehrenhalt

Amnesty and forgiveness are two different things. Amnesty is indiscriminate—the canceling of debt, obligation or penalty not out of a desire for individual justice but out of a belief that there is something to be gained by simply wiping the slate clean.

It is a very old idea. The book of Leviticus commands that every 50 years, in the Jubilee Year, all personal debts shall be erased and every slave shall be free to go home. The moral condition of the beneficiary isn't an issue. Anybody who happens to be in the right place at the right time qualifies. "Even if he is not redeemed," the Bible says, "he and his children are to be released in the year of Jubilee."

In the three millennia since then, public authority has granted amnesties to an enormous variety of offenders—from captured revolutionaries and student protesters to illegal immigrants and violators of narcotics law. But it's doubtful the concept has ever been employed quite so freely as it is right now, by state and local governments all over the country. We are in the middle of an amnesty binge.

This year alone, Kentucky, Massachusetts, Missouri and South Carolina have all declared forgiveness of penalties for deadbeat taxpayers willing to come forward and make some form of restitution. Chicago, Philadelphia, Detroit and Dallas have done the same thing for parking and traffic offenses.

Every week or so, another new zone of forgiveness seems to be carved out. The village of Spring Valley, New York, recently offered amnesty to anyone who had illegally converted a single-family home into a duplex. Lakeland, Florida, offered amnesty for violations of its building code, such as bad plumbing, faulty wiring or too much junk in the front yard. Lakeland promised to waive fees for these offenses as long as the homeowner was cooperative—"even if it's just cooperation during the amnesty period," the chairman of the code Enforcement Board said.

There are many reasons for the current amnesty binge, but much of it can be explained in a very simple way: fiscal desperation. At a time of frighteningly large budget deficits, states and localities can make up some serious revenue this way. Nearly every tax amnesty in the past year has brought in more money than originally projected. Missouri planned on $20

Alan Ehrenhalt is executive editor of *Governing*. This article is reprinted from *Governing* (January 2003): 6, 8.

Crime and Courts

Illinois governor George Ryan made a dramatic decision in January to pardon four condemned men and commute the sentences of the 167 remaining on death row in the last days of his administration.

Ryan was the first state official to initiate a moratorium on executions for the length of his tenure in office. His action helped touch off a debate over the issue that continues in legislatures across the country.

The U.S. Supreme Court's June 2002 decision to outlaw the execution of the mentally retarded affects twenty states and, potentially, hundreds of death row inmates who could see their sentences commuted to life.

Besides Nevada, states affected by the Supreme Court ruling are Alabama, California, Delaware, Idaho, Illinois, Louisiana, Mississippi, Montana, New Hampshire, New Jersey, Ohio, Oklahoma, Oregon, Pennsylvania, South Carolina, Texas, Wyoming, Utah and Virginia.

Source: Kathleen Murphy, stateline.org, February 2003.

---

million from its three-month amnesty program this fall, and took in twice that much, giving virtually all of it to the public schools. Kentucky hoped for $20 million and received $80 million, rebating a portion of that back to local governments in previously uncollected property tax bills. The tax amnesty in Massachusetts turned up so many repentant scofflaws that acting governor Jane Swift decided to keep alive a $9 million infant care program, scheduled for elimination because of lack of funds.

The cities that have decided to forgive traffic offenses aren't dealing in sums of that magnitude, but the money isn't trivial there, either. Detroit's Traffic Court counted up last spring and realized it was carrying $93 million in unpaid tickets and misdemeanor citations on its books. It decided to take 50 percent off every ticket for anyone who would step forward. The result—about $1 million in revenue—wasn't exactly a total solution. But the city was glad to get it. "A 50 percent reduction is pretty drastic," the chief judge admitted. "But 50 percent of something is better than 100 percent of nothing."

Other local governments have decided to proclaim amnesty less for financial reasons than to bring some order to their accounting processes. DeKalb County, Georgia, found itself with 3,500 unresolved traffic citations dating back more than a decade. "It's just a monumental nightmare to keep processing these," said a municipal court judge. So DeKalb canceled all penalties for a month in exchange for payment of the original fee.

Washington, D.C., with $347 million in unpaid parking fines more than five years old, didn't even do that. It simply threw the cases out. "Very few people are going to pay those fines," one member of the city council argued, and it would be a waste of resources to chase after them.

But if the wave of amnesties is mostly a matter of money, it's not entirely so. There's clearly a moral component as well. A councilman in Nashville decided last October that the time had come to reinstate the driver's licenses of local residents who had lost them through failure to pay off traffic tickets. He said most of them were poor, and were losing out on opportunities for work because they didn't have transportation. A Circuit Court judge agreed with him. "Anybody who is honestly trying to straighten their lives out should receive some help," the judge said.

There is little doubt that amnesty—and forgiveness in general—are powerful ideas. They are also weapons that need to be invoked with extreme caution, lest they become dangerous. Physically dangerous, in some cases.

Thirty-seven years ago, Charles de Gaulle decided to spring a treat on the voters of France after they reelected him. He declared an amnesty on outstanding traffic offenses. It was a wildly popular scheme—and every French president since then has repeated the gesture.

These amnesties still serve to enhance the honeymoon effect for newly chosen chief executives. The only problem is that French drivers, knowing that they will be forgiven, drive like maniacs in the months leading up to the election. This isn't just a matter of anecdote: Highway deaths in France consistently increase by significant percentages just prior to an election. In May 2002, the month before France reelected President Jacques Chirac, there were 616 fatalities, compared with 553 during the same period the year before.

French safety experts have estimated that each amnesty costs roughly 600 lives. Last year, for the first time, there was a significant public outcry against the practice, and Chirac agreed not to apply it to offenses "that could endanger lives." But he refused to end the custom altogether.

The French example, bizarre as it might sound, points up precisely what is wrong about the use of amnesty on such a large scale. It ignores the concept that economists like to call "moral hazard." When people don't expect to be held liable for their mistakes, they take chances they otherwise wouldn't take. In the 1980s, savings and loan institutions in the United States made billions of dollars' worth of foolish and ultimately uncollectible loans, knowing that the federal government had promised to hold them harmless. It's not all that different from French motorists driving 150 kilometers an hour during an election campaign.

Perhaps the most important strategic point about amnesty is that it has to be unpredictable. You can't afford to create a sense of expectation. If you do, human beings will misbehave—sometimes disastrously.

In the current American amnesty binge, not every jurisdiction has learned this. Early in 2001, Macon, Georgia, announced it would soon hold a two-month parking and traffic amnesty. Local officials began advising citizens who called about their tax bills to hold off payment until the amnesty began. The callers may have taken that advice as a more sweeping gesture of forgiveness than was intended. After two months, the program had brought in only $80,000, out of a total of $11 million in unpaid fines.

Public libraries, which went in heavily for overdue-book amnesties in the late 1990s, have learned a similar lesson. They overdid it. By running several amnesty programs within the space of a few years, some libraries received back thousands of books that had been missing from the shelves for years. But they were also encouraging bad habits. "We all soon found out," said the president of the Public Library Association, "that people were holding on to their materials and waiting for the next one." In the past couple of years, libraries have been more inclined to turn hard-core scofflaws over to collection agencies than to try to lure them back with forgiveness.

Of course, there is a way around this problem: Use amnesty as an extremely rare event, and build in some serious consequences for those who fail to take advantage of it. This past fall, the city of Chicago announced its first parking amnesty in 15 years. Anybody with tickets more than two years old and totaling less than $5,000 could come in, pay the original fine and have the penalties forgiven. At the same time, the mayor announced that when the amnesty was over, anybody with three or more unpaid tickets could expect to have his car booted, and the 100 drivers who owed the most money would have their names posted on the city's Web site. When the amnesty window finally closed on October 15, nearly 70,000 taxpayers had come in to do penance, 242,000 debts were wiped off the books and $8 million had been raised.

So there are good ways and bad ways for government to conduct an amnesty. But even the good ways ought to leave those who promote them at least a little bit uneasy. People who send in their taxes and pay off their traffic fines do it on the implicit assumption that they are to be treated in a different way from others who evade those responsibilities. Whatever legitimate purposes an amnesty may serve, it is a breach of faith with the law-abiding. It turns the most conscientious citizens into suckers, one small step at a time. If there's anything more corrosive to citizenship than the feeling that government is taking you for a sucker, I can't imagine what it would be.

I can understand why states and cities are attracted to amnesty schemes that bring in millions of dollars at a time when money is scarce. But I'm afraid they are bad investments in the long run.

IX. LOCAL GOVERNMENT

Former U.S. House Speaker Tip O'Neill always reminded us that "all politics is local." This admonition cautions those who would read some national feelings or trends into voting results across the country. In much the same way, it is also true for many of us that "all government is local." People are more immediately affected by what goes on at city hall and the county courthouse than by what occurs in the statehouse or the White House.

Evidence of this is everywhere. Children attend local schools; local transportation systems help them get to school and their parents and others to work; local police and fire departments ensure our protection; city sanitation departments, or contractors hired by them, pick up our garbage and trash; recycling efforts are established locally; marriage licenses, divorce papers, and wills are filed with county courthouses; civil suits and criminal trials are carried out in those same courthouses; recreational facilities and programs are run locally—and the list goes on.

Just as each election and campaign was local or unique in O'Neill's view, so, too, is local government. A particular array of services and facilities provided to those living in one community may vary considerably from those provided in another. In some instances a state government mandates a certain level of service. Often, communities go beyond that level in areas such as schools or parks, if that is what the elected officials and citizens of the community want to support. The phrase "want to support" should be translated as what they are willing to be taxed for.

For those who have lived in several different communities in their lifetime, the observation that there are real differences between these communities in what they provide for their citizens is no surprise. This variation can be even more striking when compared across states. For example, someone accustomed to the efficiency with which communities in northern states cope with snowstorms is amazed at the chaos that reigns in southern communities at the mention of a possible snowfall, let alone what happens when the snow actually starts to fall.

Running Local Governments

The job of running local governments can be mind boggling to those who have sought and won a local elective position. Not only are they faced with trying to satisfy the demands of their fellow residents, but they must also answer to the demands of governments higher up in the federal system. These officeholders may have run on a platform with specific goals and may have made equally specific proposals and promises, but once in office they find severe restrictions on their ability to seek, let alone achieve, these goals.

Local governments are creatures of the states and are given a variety of responsibilities and tools with which to work. Some of these governments, such as counties, act more directly as agents of the state in carrying out certain state responsibilities. Others, such as cities, towns, and villages, are established to act as the general, local government of responsibility within a specified area. Still others are set up as special districts with some very specific responsibilities. School and fire districts are examples of these. Special district governmental units work in the same geographical areas as general governments, which can result in great confusion and overlapping of perceived responsibilities.

Unlike the very basic constitutional provisions that demand separation of powers in our federal and state governments, local governments may in fact concentrate authority in their legislatures. Mayors and chairs of county commissions are often selected from among members of the city council or the county commission. And while some mayors are separately elected, just as are governors, they lack the array of powers and institutional support that most governors have at their disposal. Generally, the larger the city or county, the more likely it is that the chief executive is elected separately. In many cities and towns, the mayor is the local chief executive, heading the administration of city government. In other municipalities (and in an increasing number of counties), there is *no* elected executive. Instead, the local council or commission hires a professional manager to act as the chief executive official of local government.

Policies and budgets wind through a tortuous course at the national level, as the president and the two houses of Congress pull and push in an attempt to achieve their goals. Each has the ability to stall, even stop, initiatives. So, too, at the state level: the governor and the houses of the legislature struggle with each other over policies and budgets. A stalemate often results. Yet this is an anticipated product of a concept dear to our constitutional framers: the separation of powers.

There can be stalemate at the local level, too, but it is usually the result of political and policy differences within the one local legislative body, the council or commission. Even when a mayor or county chief executive is elected separately, all of these officials will often meet together and attempt to work out their differences. Only a minority of mayors have the power to veto council actions. Policy and budgetmaking are generally the responsibility of a single government body, and the participants are expected to work out their differences within it.

In a way, this is considerably neater and more efficient than the national or state models. But it is also more vulnerable to manipulation, lacking the protection of other institutional power bases to intervene or check misuse or abuse of power. In response, some states have established oversight agencies and processes as a check on such potentialities.

Yet all this is still only a part of the story. The governing boards of the special district governmental units operating in the area must also be considered. For example, school boards and transportation authorities make policy decisions that have budgetary and tax consequences that the general government must fold into its overall local government budget and tax structure. These special district units possess a separate base of real or potential power, which adds to the political calculus of the local governmental process.

At this level, much is made of the "weak" and "strong" mayor models, with the difference based on whether a mayor is elected separately or selected by vote of a governing body, and whether a mayor has sole power of appointment, veto power, and so on. What is important to remember is that individual mayors often define whether they are weak or powerful. While formal structure does define the formal bases of power, it leaves out the many informal bases of power that an individual may or may not bring to the office. It is common to find an individual in a structurally strong situation acting as a weak leader, and vice versa.

What are these informal bases of power? They can vary by individual, by city or county, and by situation. Among them are an individual's personality and style, the strength of the political parties within a locality, the ability to access and use the media to an advantage, the size of the voter mandate received at the polls and the size of the citywide or countywide mandate received from the voters relative to the district-by-district mandate of the local legislators, the strength of ties to major nongovernmental institutions and other power bases in a community, and the realization by those involved in the governing process that an individual "is going places" and could be (should be, probably will be) a candidate for higher office.

In 2002 we all saw how one big city mayor parlayed his ability to work with many players and citizens in a time of crisis elevate him to a high status. New York City Mayor Rudi Giuliani worked so hard to help those in the city cope with the September 11 terrorist attack on the World Trade Center that he became a symbol of the city's ability to rebound from such a disaster. While limited to run for a third term because of term limits, there was an effort to repeal that limit so that he could run for mayor again. While that didn't work out, he began working on the larger national stage by helping fellow Republicans in their efforts to win election in 2002. Giuliani is also considered a potential candidate for several higher offices such as U.S. senator or governor. His personality, style, and presence has overcome what has been the potential roadblocks to such political advancement.

There is one other major distinction of local government that is not seen at either the national or state levels. A rapidly rising number of local governments are run on a day-to-day basis by professionally trained administrators. Even many of those localities with mayors or commission presidents as CEOs now employ full-time professionals as chief *administrative* officers. These administrators, with master's degrees in public administration or business, bring to government a series of learned approaches and well-tested processes geared toward making government work as efficiently and effectively as possible. They are generally nonpartisan and outside of the regular political process and politics of the community.

However, because of their unique position in government, these administrators often gain considerable power at the local level. They know what is happening, what it costs, and how effective it is. They know where the problems are. They handle the budget and work with the bureaucracy and those served by it on a daily basis. And they take the lead in developing next year's budget. In a very real way, they set and spell out the agenda for the local elected leaders.

All this power notwithstanding, these administrators are also vulnerable to political changes within the community and among elected officials. They are responsible for any errors or miscues that occur in the government. It should be no surprise, then, that there is considerable turnover among these professional administrators, as only a very few have a strong political base of their own. Their power base is usually the vote of the council, commission, mayor, or commission president. When that support is gone, they are, too. While hired administrators are not out of the political system, they are very much a part of the politics of local government.

A Political Entry Point

Local government can serve as an entry point into the political system for those who are politically ambitious. While many enter local politics for specific reasons, such as to improve the schools or promote economic development or environmental protection, they often find their work as elected officials very rewarding. A strong performance can expand an official's political base and can open up the opportunity to seek higher office. In a few words, these local units in our system are at the base of the political ambition ladder in the states, and many individuals take advantage of this.

Being elected mayor of a state's largest city will automatically place that mayor's name on a list of potential candidates for higher office. If nothing else, other serious candidates for higher office will usually try to obtain the support of the mayor in their own quests. When there are many good-sized cities in a state, however, being mayor of one may not open up such opportunities.

However, in California, the former mayor of San Diego, Republican Pete Wilson, was able to use his position as a starting point from which to move up the political ladder to a seat in the U.S. Senate and then the governor's chair.

After winning reelection in 1994, he decided to move toward seeking the Republican nomination for president in the 1996 election, although the campaign turned out to be an unsuccessful effort that damaged his previous reputation as a consistent winner. In 1998 George Voinovich took the next step in his move up the Ohio political ambition ladder when he was elected to the U.S. Senate. He had previously served as mayor of Cleveland for ten years, and was governor of Ohio for eight.

But there are other realities to serving as an elected official in local government. One is the closeness of the official to the problems and the people being served, a closeness so intense as to cause burnout in some. Another is being tagged with the problems or errors of others in the governmental units—a sort of guilt-by-association situation. And all too often there is a need to obtain more revenue to finance citizen wants—a need that translates into raising taxes. All of these and others can quickly shorten an individual's political career.

Still, the ongoing flow upward to other levels of government of many locally elected officials keeps alive the notion that "all politics [and government] is local."

The People Problem

All of the above omit an important aspect of what goes on in local governments: the people and what they are about. Throughout our history the migration of people has been a major factor in our nation's development. This migration has also had a major impact on local governments. The cities have been the focus of those wishing to move off the land and into a different sector of the economy. They are also the destinations of those coming from other countries. Individuals feeling disenfranchised from the society, economy, and political culture around them made the cities their jumping-off boards for new starts. Then, as mobility increased and individual wealth grew, people

began moving out of the cities and into the suburbs to get away from the growing problems of decaying urban areas.

In recent decades, two national regions became target destinations of migration. People living in the colder and harsher climates of the Northeast and Midwest began to move southward and westward. Economic factors abetted these moves as the older, Rust Belt economies began to falter just as the newer, Sun Belt economies began to grow and expand. Ongoing developments in transportation and information exchange continue to fuel the movement of people across the nation's landscape, as the results of the 2000 census so dramatically demonstrate.

All this has a major impact on local government and public policy. At one extreme are those governments presiding over failing economies that have led to an exodus of wealthy and productive citizens, a rise in the numbers of people requiring assistance, and a continuing need to increase taxes just when the tax base is eroding. At the other extreme are governments coping with rapid and often uncontrolled growth that puts facilities and services, if even provided, at risk. Lack of tax revenues are not necessarily the problem here. Even where growth is generating more income in increased revenue, the problem is trying to direct this growth and make some sort of coherence out of how the future community should develop.

In between these extremes are a variety of situations with which local governments must cope. For example, there are one-industry towns that suddenly find their industry gone with nothing to replace it; small farm-to-market towns that find their youth departed and farms bought out by large landowners using migrant labor; strip city developments where the only way you know you have left one city and entered another is by the signs saying "Good-bye" and "Welcome to"; and cities where never-ending development around their edges leaves the one-time heart of their metropolitan areas depleted and empty, like the hole in a doughnut.

Many would argue that the states are where the action is. But try telling that to some local elected officials. States are relatively well-defined cultures with their own established systems of politics and higher education, and are easily found on the Rand-McNally maps. Cities and other local governments often lack such definition; if it *does* exist, it is usually in flux. That is what makes working in local governments, whether elected, appointed, or as part of the bureaucracy, so challenging.

Now there is worry in local government circles, considering the changes being made at the national and state levels recently, that there will be more action at the local level than officials can cope with. Governors have made a strong pitch to congressional leaders not to balance the national budget on the backs of the states. Local leaders have a double fear facing them: that both the national and state budgets will be balanced on the backs of the local governments. Their worst fear is the adoption of tax cuts and program reductions at higher levels of government that will place unbelievable demands for services and programs, and the necessary tax increases to pay for them, on the desks of local officials. Now, in the economic recession of the early 2000s, states are cutting back on funding what local communities need as state revenues have faltered. Thus local leaders are faced with the need to raise local taxes—mainly property taxes—just to keep the level of services as they are already. To the local officials, such decisions can lead to shortened political careers.

The articles in Part IX focus on some of these very difficult situations at the local level. Alan Greenblatt of *Governing* provides perspective on how some local areas are trying to cope with too many governments—merge them into one larger metropolitan government. Greenblatt also looks into the fears that local government officials have of the states trying to balance their budgets on the backs of the local governments. Greenblatt also indicates that local officials are now working harder to "squeeze" more money out of the federal government to help the localities. Christopher Swope of *Governing* reports on some significant changes in the type of big-city school chiefs that are being chosen. Finally, Alan Ehrenhalt of *Governing* looks at the safety problems that so many local governments face, especially those who live in the suburbs and must commute to work.

Anatomy of a Merger

by Alan Greenblatt

In 1938, some of Louisville's bourbon distillers decided they didn't want their South End neighborhood to be annexed by the city, because that would force them to pay higher taxes. They persuaded the Kentucky legislature to allow small cities veto power over annexation and then quickly created a new jurisdiction called Shively, as a kind of tax shelter. The idea soon spread and before long every subdivision in Jefferson County that wanted lower taxes or its own one-man police force chose to incorporate. By the 1970s, the county had more than 80 municipalities. Their proliferation was a source of frustration for everyone, from engineers laying down sewer lines to developers trying to figure out which building codes applied where.

Worse still, the region had a mayor running Louisville and a judge-executive in charge of Jefferson County, more often than not with wildly different agendas. Business leaders complained that trying to get the two levels of government to agree on anything made them feel like children trying to wheedle a joint decision out of parents who refuse to talk to one another. "When you think about trying to make deals with companies," says Bill Summers, a former Louisville deputy mayor now with the local economic development agency, "you often spent more time negotiating with the two governments, trying to get them to agree on what we wanted to offer, and who was going to take credit and how they were going to take it, than actually negotiating with companies to get them here."

Next month, however, the days of duplication and rivalry will end. As a result of a ballot initiative passed two years ago, Louisville and Jefferson County will be combined into one metropolitan government, implementing a merger of a size that no city in America has pulled off since Indianapolis did it in 1970. Already, scout ants from Memphis, Milwaukee, Rochester, Buffalo, Cedar Rapids and Fresno have come sniffing around, hunting for strategies they can use in their own nascent moves toward merger. "The model of what Louisville is doing would be ideal for us," says Fresno councilman Brian Calhoun.

Despite all the interest and attention, the architects of Louisville-Jefferson Metro Government, as the new entity will be officially

Alan Greenblatt is a staff writer for *Governing*. This article is reprinted from *Governing* (December 2002): 20–22, 24–25.

known, are trying to avoid promising too much. They are not claiming that the merger will be an economic development panacea, that Louisville will become America's new hot city, a Seattle or Austin that spawns trendy industries, or an engine of growth along the lines of Atlanta.

People in Louisville tend to regard their city realistically, as a comfortable, solid, unspectacular place. Louisville and Jefferson County still contain two-thirds of the people and 80 percent of the jobs in the seven-county metropolitan area—job suburbanization has taken place largely within the Jefferson County lines—but the trend is that both jobs and people are moving farther out. If the merger can help Louisville maintain a decent mix of jobs and industries, while preserving the importance of the merged city in the larger area, that will be triumph enough.

The Born Closer

One of the important aspects of the Louisville merger that may not be easily duplicated elsewhere involves a cult of personality. Jerry Abramson, who served as mayor of the "old" Louisville for a dozen years before he was term-limited out in 1999, won the newly created office of metro mayor last month with 74 percent of the vote against three opponents. Abramson is the closest thing Louisville has to a resident rock star. Steve Higdon, president of Greater Louisville Inc., the local chamber and economic development agency, says "there's not one better person on the planet" to lead the area politically. That kind of hyperbole isn't uncommon. "I would not underestimate the urge to throne him again," says Mike Herrald, regional president of PNC Bank. "People had the belief, rightly or wrongly, that if only he were in charge of the whole thing it would be better."

The 56-year-old Abramson is a legendary salesman, a "born closer," in the words of one associate, who can drive around his city and point with pride to all the successful projects

built during his previous tenure: the minor league baseball field; the riverfront reclaimed and revitalized east of downtown; and the 1,400-unit public housing disaster that was remade into a New Urbanist mixed-income neighborhood. Abramson is also is a true policy wonk who likes to hold Clintonesque bull sessions with his staff and can discuss drainage problems in the far corners of the city without notes.

Abramson is taking an almost Mussolini-like approach to the details of the merger, devoting himself to making sure that all of the managerial trains run on time. Ask him what he plans to do once he takes office, and rather than revealing any grand blueprint, he talks about changing the radio systems of the city police and county sheriff's departments so that officers in the combined jurisdiction can actually talk to one another. He'll go on at length in public forums about the $400,000 software package he wants to buy for county human resources personnel so they can team up easily with their city counterparts.

Abramson understands that the merger will not be a hit with the public unless the trash is carted away on the usual day and citizens can connect with the right person when they call to get a stray dog picked up. But simply providing the accustomed level of services without a tax increase will be a challenge in itself: As a result of city and county tax code differences, the new Louisville government faces an immediate shortfall of at least $44 million. "There's a good reason why people aren't lined up to be the first mayor of the new city," Abramson says. "There'll be a cavalry charge to be the second."

A Tough Sell

Discussions of regional governance generally take two forms nowadays. In areas that have experienced rapid growth, such as Denver and California's Silicon Valley, political leaders—generally prompted by local business interests—are recognizing that issues such as transportation and the environment don't honor political boundaries. This leads to a kind of ad hoc approach in which regional solutions are discussed for individual problems—water management, for example—but the idea of actually merging governments is barely a blip.

Serious merger discussions usually happen in less vibrant areas, where metropolitan government is viewed as a way of shaking things up and cutting down on costs. If matters are difficult, the urge toward a grand solution is stronger. But merging governments is always a tough sell. While regionalism is often portrayed as the cure to a lot of urban ills, from traffic congestion to wasteful duplication of resources, few localities are eager to sacrifice their autonomy merely in the hope that it might lead to a more efficient combined water district. Municipalities, even small and inefficient ones, like to be able to provide their own services without having to be dependent on someone else.

Merger is an especially tough sell in declining areas where fights over diminishing resources have, perversely, made cooperation more difficult. In Milwaukee County, for example, where consolidation is being pushed by a local economic development agency, there is great distrust between the city of Milwaukee and the suburbs, growing out of a decade-long fight over who would pay for court-ordered city sewer improvements. The city won that fight, but may have lost the war when it comes to looking for further help from its neighbors.

Suburbanites want to maintain their friendly local police and fire departments, and don't want their tax dollars sent to prop up ailing downtowns. Cities might cry that the suburbs should help finance the urban amenities that their residents enjoy, but suburbs like to complain that cities talk to them only when they need money. When Fresno's Brian Calhoun put a resolution before the city council calling for a commission to study merger ideas,

it passed unanimously, only to be shelved by the county board of supervisors. "The pressure was coming from all these smaller communities that somehow thought big bad Fresno would step on their turf," Calhoun says. Memphis Mayor Willie Herenton has been pushing for a referendum on merger, but polling indicates the idea has a long way to go before residents of surrounding Shelby County will embrace it. "Does the phrase 'D.O.A.' mean anything?" asks John Ryder, Republican National Committeeman from Shelby County.

In Erie County, New York, County Executive Joel Giambra has backed away from his earlier calls to fold the city of Buffalo into the county, which has about 60 separate governments. "There are not many people in the suburbs who have much confidence in the city government," Giambra admits. Having no hope of a full-scale merger, Giambra has been taking an "inch by inch" approach, setting up agreements for the county to share purchasing, assessing and water management with some of the municipalities, and facilitating shared services, such as law enforcement, between neighboring towns and villages. With several of Erie's smaller governments having raised tax rates by double-digit percentages in recent weeks, Giambra hopes his call for abolishing duplication will take on greater urgency. Even in Milwaukee County, savings from merged fire districts in smaller North Shore communities have kept hope of merger alive.

Falling Behind

As dramatic as Louisville's move may seem, the truth is that consolidation has been happening on a piecemeal basis between the city and Jefferson County for years. The water and sewer authority has answered to both jurisdictions since shortly after World War II, and the school systems merged in 1975. In the early 1980s, Abramson negotiated a deal with the county that combined administration of the park, zoo and library systems, and put an end to annexation wars by establishing a permanent proportional split of occupational tax revenues. This year, Jefferson County will write a check to Louisville for $11 million to keep the county at its codified 58 percent of the occupational tax take.

Even so, proposals to merge Louisville and Jefferson County failed three times, in 1956, 1982 and 1983, before finally winning approval in 2000. This was in large part because they spelled out too much of the detail in advance. Plans to abolish local fire districts, for example, drew plenty of fire themselves. This time, merger proponents were careful to give voters few specifics to worry about. The ballot measure simply provided that the city and county would become a single unit, with a metro mayor taking over the responsibilities of the previous city mayor and county executive, and one metro council replacing the board of aldermen and the county's fiscal court. Beyond changing the nature of these elected offices, nothing was settled as to whether agencies or even administrative functions of the city and county would be consolidated. All those 80-odd municipalities within the county and the 21 fire districts outside the city of Louisville could remain intact (although a dozen or so of the smaller cities have chosen to merge with each other in recent months to have more of a voice in metropolitan affairs).

For most proponents, the reason to merge this time was more economic than political. Louisville has a relatively stable employment base, headed by manufacturing companies (among them Ford and General Electric) which still account for about 20 percent of the jobs. The city and county are home to a growing health services sector. The airport is the overnight hub for United Parcel Service, Kentucky's largest private employer, which recently completed a billion-dollar expansion of its facilities. And Louisville has long been a fast-food paradise, spawning Kentucky Fried Chicken, Papa John's pizza, Rally's, Chi Chi's, Long John Silver and several other chains. The mix of junk food, tobacco and bourbon leads locals to joke that they don't engage in healthy living but "happy living."

Still, the national economic boom of the 1990s largely passed Louisville by. Young people have been leaving steadily for the past 30 years—a net loss of 35,000 people in the current 25- to 34-year-old age group since 1970. Elderly residents comprise 14 percent of Louisville's population, among the highest proportions of seniors in the country. Academic studies place the region at the bottom of the list of technology-friendly metropolitan areas. "Ultimately," says Steve Higdon, the president of Greater Louisville Inc., "what is at stake for any community is whether you can attract and retain the brightest people. And we have not done well at that at all for decades."

Louisville boosters never tire of trumpeting the fact that merger will vault their city from the 64th largest in the country to the 16th largest, the highest ranking it has held in more than a century. Greater Louisville Inc. recently launched a quarter-million-dollar public relations campaign to get that word out nationally. "From an economic development standpoint," says Higdon, "perception is reality. Period."

When companies look for a "Top 20" city, or one that's home to more than 500,000 people—which many of them do—Louisville will now make the cut. Higdon and other business leaders believe that the city-county merger will end 40 stagnant years by creating the sense that the city finally has regained some ambition. If Louisville can change the entire government structure for 700,000 people, this line of thinking goes, it can shake off its historic complacency and insularity. "We are now looked at as a community that's ready to embrace change," says Rebecca Jackson, Jefferson County's outgoing judge-executive.

Ready for Change

During nearly a decade as county clerk, Jackson watched as a succession of mayors and county judge-executives pursued conflicting agendas and maneuvered for power. She herself voted against merger in the 1980s but ran for judge-executive in 1998, she says now, in order to make merger happen. She was a major public face of the 2000 campaign, posing for pictures with Louisville Mayor Dave Armstrong, who had hoped to run for the new metro mayor job himself. (He eventually bowed out in favor of Abramson.)

Organizers of the "unity" campaign, as the merger supporters called themselves, also managed to shepherd every living person who had held the mayor or county judge-executive position onto a single stage for a news conference announcing their unanimous support. All this symbolism and political theater were important, because the earlier merger attempts were widely perceived to have foundered in part because they were driven strictly by the business establishment.

Even with so many stars in alignment for merger, however, the key factor was Abramson. Polling—done by consultants hired from both major parties—showed that Abramson's regular public appearances and starring role in television ads made the difference. The new city has a strong-mayor structure, and voters seemed reassured by the near-certainty that Abramson would be the mayor, lending his experience and political skill to the newly elected 26-member metro council, which will be made up overwhelmingly of political novices.

Because his election was a foregone conclusion, Abramson has been planning the transition for months, meeting with citizens in each of the 26 new council districts and strategizing with key decision makers such as Greater Louisville Inc. and the Louisville *Courier-Journal* editorial board. Weeks before the November election, outgoing Jefferson County

BIGGER AND BETTER?

Louisville before and after the merger

	BEFORE	AFTER
Area in square miles	60	386
Population	256,231	693,784
White	64%	79%
African American	34%	19.5%
Hispanic	2%	2%
High school graduates	76%	82%
Bachelor's degree	21%	25%
Graduate degree	9%	10%
Median household income	$28,843	$39,457
Median home price	$82,300	$103,000
Homeownership rate	52.5%	64.9%
Median age	35.8	36.7
Unemployment rate	7.4%	5%

Source: U.S. Census Bureau, 2000

Commissioner Dolores Delehanty said, "People are now talking about 'WWJD'—What would Jerry do? People immediately think, how is this going to fly with Jerry?"

But what does Abramson actually want to do with his home city, now that it has nearly tripled in size and abolished some of its long-standing habits of institutionalized parochialism? Abramson says that the merged city-county governments of the 1960s and '70s—Nashville, Indianapolis, Charlotte, Jacksonville and nearby Lexington, Kentucky—offer little guidance in putting together Greater Louisville. Those mergers took place before the modern era of information technology and under different public employee union contracts. Suburban growth wasn't as advanced as it is now, meaning issues of drainage, sewer lines and permits are quite different.

A more useful and up-to-date model, Abramson says, comes from corporate mergers.

He jokes about meeting with an alphabet soup of CEOs, CFOs and COOs who talked with him about their mergers, how they had done months of preparation and due diligence and when they switched on the lights the first day, it was all a big mess anyway. But their failures were mostly private affairs. Abramson knows he'll make plenty of mistakes, and he knows that each will be treated as breaking news.

Trucks and Squad Cars

Still, the city and county seem far closer to being ready for this merger than even supporters of the idea dared hope two years ago. Only a few technical issues, regarding such matters as Social Security and bank forms, actually have to be taken care of the first day, January 6, but city and county departments have proven surprisingly cooperative in planning for the new world they're about to enter, and the public works, information technology, human resources and finance departments are preparing to consolidate as of day one.

Final decisions about the shape and scope of larger government changes will have to wait for the mayor and council to be sworn in, but the outlines of many of those are clear as well. There had been a lot of debate in Louisville whether to follow the Indianapolis model, under which the city and county public safety agencies remain separate, three decades after consolidation, but a police-sheriff merger in Louisville/Jefferson County appears all but inevitable. The current arguments focus on what color the squad cars should be.

But Abramson and the council will have plenty of difficult questions to cope with, such as balancing city-run versus county-privatized emergency medical services, reconciling different pay scales for everyone from custodians and secretaries on up, and negotiating with the different unions that represent public works employees. Abramson always got a laugh during the campaign by comparing the different

ways the city and county classify trucks. The city, he says, has 12 separate truck classifications, while the county has only two—big and little. "I like two," he says.

In the beginning, city, suburbs and unincorporated areas will receive essentially the same services they are receiving now. The old city will retain its boundaries as an "urban service district," with higher taxes and more services. Whether people outside the former city limits will come to expect more services, and will be willing to pay more in taxes for them, remains to be seen.

Kentucky's legislature has given the new government five years to work out differences between pre-existing city and county statutes. After that, laws that haven't been reconciled will simply expire. In the meantime, the rules are that if both the county and the old city have a law addressing a given topic, the county law prevails. Where the city has a law and the county doesn't, such as a curfew ordinance, the city law takes effect throughout the county.

In some cases, the differences aren't worth much bother. In September, a Louisville alderman dropped his plan to ban roosters from the city when he realized a county ordinance would soon make his bill redundant. But other differences will matter a great deal, from inconsistencies in tax rates to the fact that the much weaker county housing code, meant for a rural area, will suddenly apply in the city. "The first year is going to be fair chaos," says Mike Herrald, the bank executive, "but the person who goes to the zoo, the person who goes to the library, the person who calls the police with a fender bender, they aren't going to notice the change and, God knows, that's the object."

Even while trying to make good on Herrald's premise, though, and preventing any disruption in core functions, Abramson wants ultimately to bring about real restructuring. When he built the downtown baseball park, during one of his earlier terms as mayor, he visited parks in five other cities and stole the best design elements from each of them. He hopes to do the same thing with ideas for delivering services, combining and experimenting wherever it makes sense to try something new. Abramson told one audience recently that, if the city has 20 garbage trucks and the county has 20 garbage trucks, "and we merge them and have 40 garbage trucks and call it consolidation, we will have missed that opportunity to remake local government."

Driving past the ballpark, Abramson still sounds a little bitter about the trouble he had raising money to build it. He raised millions from private sources, but it took him forever to score the last $3 million he needed because county officials wanted no part of the deal—even though their constituents would take advantage of the new park, just as they were prime users of a $4 million swimming complex and other facilities that the city of Louisville had built. "I could have built that park a year and a half earlier," the mayor recalls, if it had not been for the jurisdictional rivalry.

After January 6, Abramson will no longer have to wait to get the county to sign off on his favored projects. "We'll have a single public-sector agenda," he says. "We should be able to make economic development decisions faster. That's the hope, anyway."

Enemies of the State

by Alan Greenblatt

Imagine yourself watching a sexy television ad about municipal finance. If you're having a hard time with that, imagine trying to write one. That's Mike Madrid's job. A longtime Republican political consultant, Madrid is working on a campaign to persuade voters in California to protect the finances of cities, counties and special districts from poaching by the state. His polls suggest voters are sympathetic—most of them believe local taxes should stay in the hands of local governments. But the complexity of the financial machinations involved makes it very hard to get their attention, let alone persuade them to support an initiative on the subject. "When we would break the money out into different, specific revenue streams," Madrid says, "the voters' eyes would glaze over in focus groups."

The League of California Cities, the major force behind the initiative campaign Madrid is running, wanted at first to place its initiative on this year's state ballot. Now it has backed off and is trying for March 2004. The whole process has been frustrating for the league—even many local officials are dubious about the ultimate prospects for passage. But then, feelings of frustration are something that California's cities and counties have grown used to.

A quarter-century of prior initiatives and policies have left localities here at the financial mercy of the state. Cities control less than half of their discretionary spending—the state tells them what they can do with the rest. The situation is even more desperate for counties, which have final say over less than one-third of the money they spend. The League of Cities initiative wouldn't change any of that. It would simply lock into place those revenues that localities still do control, using the year 2000 as a baseline.

Whatever happens with the initiative, localities in California don't expect things to break their way significantly anytime soon. All the many billions of dollars that the state has taken from them over the years, they figure, are gone for good. The state government, for instance, has shown little inclination to return to localities the property-tax dollars it has shifted to the K-12 education budget over the past decade. So the locals, at this point, simply hope that no more is taken away.

But the threat of further losses is all too real. The state of California is facing a deficit in

Alan Greenblatt is a staff writer for *Governing*. This article is reprinted from *Governing* (June 2002): 26–28, 30–31.

the neighborhood of $20 billion. Localities know they are going to get hit again. The only question is, how hard. "The governor and legislature have said that they are not going to balance the budget on the backs of local government this time," says Steve Szaley, executive director of the California State Association of Counties. "Of course, none of us are buying that."

What the localities fear most is that when the moment to balance the budget actually comes, the legislature will stiff them on car-tax revenue. Back during the flush days of 1998, the state decided to slash vehicle license fees, promising to make good the lost dollars this tax cut would mean for local governments. But the state has to appropriate that payback each year. This year, that gesture would cost $4 billion. The suspicion that the legislature ultimately will refuse to pay up haunts city and county officials all over the state. "They have their budget to balance," says Jake Mackenzie, a city councilman in Rohnert Park, a small Northern California town. "It's sort of tough luck in terms of local government."

If localities in California are starting to flinch, they are not alone. Forty-three states are grappling with revenue shortfalls this year, which leaves governors and legislatures with three choices: cut state spending, raise taxes or shift the burden onto somebody else. Given the political unpopularity inherent in the first two options, it's no wonder many states are looking to squeeze as much money out of local government as they can.

Last year, as a candidate for governor, New Jersey's Jim McGreevey criticized his predecessor for stinginess in offering state aid to towns and school districts. But he froze that aid in his own budget this year. Wisconsin Governor Scott McCallum went much further—he proposed to end the state's 90-year tradition of sharing revenue with localities, a move that would eventually have cost the localities $1 billion a year. North Carolina Governor Mike Easley is withholding $209 million in payments owed to local governments in shared tax income and reimbursements.

"It was painful," says Fred Terry, an alderman in Winston-Salem, which lost $7.2 million out of its $200 million budget. "It may not sound like that much, but when you're counting on that money and it doesn't arrive, it puts you in a pinch."

There have been some victories for localities in state capitals this year. Most notably, the Virginia legislature voted to allow the Washington-area suburbs to hold a referendum that would raise local sales taxes to pay for more roads, ending the state's decades-old stranglehold on transportation policy. For the most part, though, the state legislatures have been looking at localities as if they were ATMs.

It's not that local officials quarrel with the need to freeze aid payments or make one-time cuts to grapple with a gaping deficit. Their worst fear is that such short-term fixes won't do much to solve chronic budget problems next year, or the year after that. If the red ink continues to flow another two or three years, locals worry, the cutbacks inflicted on them won't be quick or simple ones. They are likely to be deeper structural cuts with the potential to cripple the capacity of local governments for a long time to come.

No doubt some of the fears are exaggerated, but what they reveal is that many years of heavy-handed treatment, in California and other places, have left localities wary of the legislatures and governors they must report to. It's a wariness that spreads beyond the fiscal arena, into such areas as transportation and land use, in which any state needs the full cooperation of localities to put its policies into place. The requisite goodwill is no longer there. "The state has, from our point of view, been such an unreliable partner that it's hard for us to trust them," says Chris McKenzie, executive director of the League of California Cities.

California's local strategists, as they search for ways to win sympathy and support for their cause, might want to examine the successful public relations campaign waged by localities in Wisconsin against McCallum's budget proposal. That state has a shared-revenue system that is a remnant of the Progressive Era, designed to equalize payments across the state on a per capita basis, so that even residents of property-poor areas can count on a minimum level of services. It's separate from money the state grants to localities for roads, computers or other specific programs.

McCallum threatened earlier this year to do away with the entire system, and not just because Wisconsin was looking at a $1.1 billion deficit. The governor said his ultimate purpose was to get rid of wasteful layers of local government. He complained that there were 54 units of government within a 10-mile radius of where he stood in downtown Madison. McCallum figured if he cut off one of their major funding sources, some of those units would be forced to consolidate, thus reducing duplication. "People here agree there ought to be consolidation," he says. "It's just that they want to have control after they consolidate—not the other guy."

Wisconsin cities used a number of tactics to challenge McCallum, attacking the honesty of his numbers and describing services they would be forced to cut if the governor's plan went through. For weeks, those budgetary horror stories seemed to turn up in the lead of just about every newspaper story about the controversy. Then the stories were featured in a series of television ads the League of Wisconsin Municipalities ran knocking McCallum's ideas—the first such direct-to-voter ads that the league had ever run.

The strategy worked spectacularly, aided by the governor's own failure to recommend specific steps that would help towns to merge. The plan reached the legislature "dead on arrival," in the words of one legislative aide.

But while Wisconsin's shared-revenue system may have survived McCallum's assault this year, its long-term prognosis is still shaky. One portion of the program has not been granted an increase in seven years (it's due for one this year), while the other major portion has been frozen since 1981. The fact that it shuttles money from one unit of government to others with few strings attached puts it at risk politically. "People don't like to run for office to be a tax collector for somebody else," says Dan Thompson, executive director of the Wisconsin municipal league. "That's always a hard sell."

The shared-revenue system is certain to face renewed attacks in coming years, and local officials will spend a considerable amount of time trying to repel them. "When the livelihood and survival of your community depends on the funding of state shared revenue," says Jane Wood, city manager of Beloit, "that becomes your consuming priority."

Beloit, just north of the Illinois border, receives the most shared revenue in the state on a per capita basis. Its local government has produced a brochure suggesting that if that state money were taken away, it would be able to meet its bond obligations and retiree health insurance payments, but then would have only $4.6 million left to fund nearly $30 million worth of current services. Beloit, in other words, would go broke.

Perhaps the most important lesson of this year's state-versus-local war in Wisconsin was the ability of the local forces to turn the public argument around, suggesting that instead of accusing cities and counties of waste, McCallum should get the state's own house in order first—getting rid of the swimming pools and planes that it owns before cutting off funding to localities for the parks, libraries, police and fire service that everybody loves.

It is a tactic that local officials in other states are likely to turn to as they become more desperate. In California, local governments are already starting to train their ammunition on the state's management problems, from the electricity deregulation debacle to the fact it managed to dig itself a $20 billion hole.

There is a historical irony in all this, because California used to be one of the strongest home-rule states in the country. Communities can enact charters and ordinances, change their names and annex their neighbors without the permission of the legislature. They used to have control over their own budgets and property taxes as well. All that changed in 1978, when the statewide Proposition 13 ballot measure not only cut property tax revenues roughly in half but also gave the state authority over their distribution.

This became a crucial power in the 1990s, following passage of another ballot initiative requiring the state to devote 40 percent of its general fund to elementary and secondary education. The property tax that had once funded basic county services became, in essence, a state tax used to finance K-12 education. "Since 1993," says Alameda County Supervisor Keith Carson, "when the state started shifting more dollars into the Department of Education, just our county alone has lost $1.48 billion in revenue."

Several legislators have proposed giving back to the localities a portion of the money the state has transferred to education, but even those proposals would put strings on almost all the dollars involved. Tom Torlakson, chairman of the Senate Local Government Committee, concedes that his bill, which would give localities transportation money if they build more affordable housing, has no chance to succeed in a deficit year.

As a candidate for governor in 1998, Gray Davis sounded pretty friendly to the local cause. "We will give the money back," he said, "because it wasn't ours to start with." Two years later, however, when the state was enjoying a surplus of more than $12 billion, Davis vetoed

a measure, passed unanimously in both legislative chambers, which would have allowed localities to keep the increased property tax revenue they received because of rising home values.

The state did compensate for much of the money it had shifted to schools, but provided most of that money in the form of grants tied to a specific purpose and unavailable for other needs. Sacramento has been making decisions about funding priorities in communities located hundreds of miles away. Meanwhile, the more mundane and sometimes less visible costs of local government receive scarcely any state help at all. "We can't stop putting out fires and filling potholes just because the state decides it wants to spend money on something else," says Margaret Clark, a member of the Rosemead City Council in Southern California.

It is California's counties that fare worst under this system of earmarked grants: Counties provide more than $13 billion worth of state services annually, but the money the state sends them does nothing to help fund many less glamorous programs and services they are expected to handle purely as a local matter. "What we have in California," says Marianne O'Malley, of the state Legislative Analyst's Office, "is local administration. We don't have real local governance."

Cities have things a little easier, in large part because they still have a dedicated funding stream they can count on, namely, the sales tax. Of the 8 cents or so that the state collects on every dollar of sales, one penny of purely discretionary money makes its way back to the city of purchase. Naturally, this has led to a mad rush on the part of cities to land major retailers within their borders, notably big-box stores and car dealers. More than in any other state in the country, local planners court retail business in preference to residential development, and even to new industry.

The textbook example is Monrovia, a Southern California town that passed up a

Kodak plant a few years ago, even though it would have brought several hundred manufacturing jobs to the city. All those employees, Monrovia's government reasoned, would cause wear and tear on the local roads, while the tax benefits from the plant would go largely to the state. The city wanted the site used instead for a Price Club discount store, even though it would generate far fewer jobs at much lower salaries, because a reliable portion of the sales-tax dollars generated would stay in Monrovia.

Other communities have been making the same seemingly perverse decision. "It may not be best from the perspective of smart growth and creating high-paying jobs," admits Jake Mackenzie, the city councilman in Rohnert Park, which recently sold some city land to attract a Costco warehouse store. "But we tend to act rationally under these circumstances." What's rational for a city in the short term, though, obviously can be irrational for the state as a whole.

An obvious solution to this problem would be some sort of revenue-sharing agreement between the locals and the state. But local governments in California are increasingly wary of such an agreement: They fear that their financial dependence leaves them in a weak negotiating position. They also worry that the legislature and the governor will change the terms of any deal after the fact. "There's not in this state the sense that we're all in this together," says Diane Cummins, fiscal adviser to state Senate President John Burton. "It's 'I don't trust what you're going to do to me.' "

This year, however, a bill to force some limited tax sharing within six counties in the Sacramento area did pass the Assembly. The bill, sponsored by Assemblyman Darrell Steinberg, would force localities inside the area to divvy up a portion of their future sales tax revenue growth. The city of sale would be guaranteed one-third of the money, and would be eligible for another third if it met stated housing and planning goals. The remaining third would be redistributed throughout the Sacramento area on a per capita basis.

Steinberg argues that since a limited number of Wal-Marts and Costcos are going to locate within the region anyway, it doesn't make sense for the local communities to fight over them, wooing developers with subsidies that they don't need and the communities can't afford. His critics counter that it is merely a backhanded way of transferring funds from Sacramento suburbs to the central city, where Steinberg himself once served on the city council.

But the real significance of the bill could be as a possible precedent for future statewide action. Steinberg's proposal has attracted support from diverse elements within the state but also has been derided by dozens of cities, many of which are lobbying hard against it even though they are located far from the affected area. "Any formula contained in state law to change the allocation of local revenues could easily be changed by a new state law," says Matthew Newman, director of the California Institute for County Government, "and that makes the locals nervous."

So the most important obstacle in the path of Steinberg's bill may simply be the mutual suspicion that hovers over the entire state-local relationship at this point. "Local government has good reason not to trust the state," says Patricia Wiggins, who chairs the Assembly's Local Government Committee. "The pressure on these communities to build housing without being able to use the property taxes from the housing is almost like an unfunded mandate."

The heated reaction to Steinberg's fairly modest bill suggests that any wholesale change to the state-local fiscal relationship may be a long time coming. In a climate of distrust, sweeping changes usually don't occur until the crisis is imminent.

There's one other factor, of course, that prevents a more rational distribution of funds between state and local government in California. That is the fact that the state benefits from the present arrangement. When times are good, the legislature can afford to be generous to localities, as it was in the immediate aftermath of Proposition 13. When times are tough, it can turn off the spigot, forcing the locals to take the blame for any resulting cuts in services. There is little incentive for state policy makers to abandon a system that grants them power through control of the dollars.

Squeezing the Federal Turnip

by Alan Greenblatt

Alan Autry, the mayor of Fresno, California, steps out of his Washington hotel into a bright, cold winter morning. "It's a great day to beg," he declares.

Today he will be begging at high levels, pleading with his state's congressional delegation for money. Autry takes this part of his job seriously, both in D.C. and in Sacramento. He's hired a lobbyist to work the California legislature for Fresno, after the city went a decade without one, and he's rejoined the U.S. Conference of Mayors after an even longer absence. In Washington, he's retained the services of Leonard Simon, one of the many lobbyists who specialize in guiding local governments through the federal policy thicket.

Autry understands that cities come to Washington for the same reason Willie Sutton robbed banks—because that's where the money is. Fresno, a fast-growth city that's now up to almost half a million people, is burdened by a long list of problems, including a 15 percent unemployment rate, air quality that's among the worst in the nation and enough crime to justify spending three-quarters of the city's general fund on public safety. That anti-crime concentration doesn't leave Autry much money to fund economic development efforts,

or any other policy innovations, for that matter. In his quest for new revenues, Autry is hoping that Washington will help.

As it happens, the federal government is not in a particularly generous mood toward cities or counties just at the moment, with war and tax cuts dominating its agenda. Local officials complain that Washington is involving itself intrusively in issues such as public safety, education and election procedure, normally the province of state or local government. Moreover, the feds are mandating costly changes without offering sufficient help to enable the localities to pay for them. Autry and his counterparts around the country worry that further changes in federal health and welfare programs might lay more responsibility at their feet.

It appears that the agenda of cities and counties is more at odds with that of the federal government than it has been for a long time. "You get the feeling sometimes that the feds are just not on the same map as state and local governments," says Lynn Cutler, who worked in the White House intergovernmental affairs office during the Clinton administration and now

Alan Greenblatt is a staff writer for *Governing*. This article is reprinted from *Governing* (March 2003): 26, 28–30.

lobbies for the city of Cleveland. "And—hello—I thought they all represented the same people."

But if states and localities are finding the feds unresponsive to the larger items on their agendas, earmarked funding for local programs remains a growth industry in Congress, with members eager to support projects that can earn political credit for all involved. If only the strongest dogs are going to get scraps in the present budget environment, it may be more important than ever for local governments to hire their own lobbyists if they want to stay in the hunt.

Fresno has been averaging more than $3 million a year in earmarked appropriations, which is pretty good, and as Autry makes his rounds on Capitol Hill, he takes pains to sound grateful. He thanks the city's three U.S. representatives—Fresno is split into three districts—for their help in securing money for transit and an industrial park. Autry is thrilled when Senator Barbara Boxer looks him in the eye and pledges her support for a half-million dollar study that may lead eventually to a major mass transit system in the San Joaquin Valley. "When you sit face to face to get a commitment, that's huge," he says.

Fresno's mayor has some advantages in working Capitol Hill that other mayors do not possess. When he walks down the hall with a congressman, Autry is the one guards and tourists recognize. Not many recall that he was a backup quarterback with the Green Bay Packers, but nearly everyone seems to remember his role as Lieutenant Bubba Skinner in the TV series, "In the Heat of the Night." While dining at his Washington hotel, in fact, Autry is recognized by the ambassador from Uganda, who says after the ice is broken that he'd like to come study the cotton fields outside of Fresno.

Double Teaming

While the mayor shakes hands, poses for pictures and compares notes on football games,

Simon stays in the background, checking appointments on his portable Web device. ("I have a deep passion for anonymity," he says.) But Autry plays up the veteran lobbyist's connections in an effort to score points himself with members of the delegation. He tells Devin Nunes, Fresno's 29-year-old freshman congressman, that Simon (who spent a decade lobbying for the U.S. Conference of Mayors and has been in private practice 15 years) will be available to help explain the players and the process on Capitol Hill. Over lunch, Simon points out some of his new congressional colleagues to Nunes and advises him to play pickup basketball in the House gym as a way of making contacts.

However helpful a service this may be, the fact remains that Autry, not Simon, is the city's most effective lobbyist. So why does Fresno need to pay Simon $24,000 a year to advance its interests? The answer is fairly simple: The money buys persistence. Autry will fly home the next day, but Simon will be walking the corridors over and over again, reiterating the same points to the same members, staff and executive branch bureaucrats. It is an article of faith on Capitol Hill that members of Congress respond to repetition—they believe that if a city keeps asking about a project, it must really want it. The more visits, phone calls and e-mails from Simon that are logged into a congressional office computer, the better Fresno's chances of seeing its projects through to completion. "I make a good pitch, then I go back and run a city," Autry says. "Any endeavor's going to take a sustained effort to push things through."

Or so everyone believes. "If you leave it just to the members and the senators," says Cutler, "they've got a whole lot of folks they have to take care of, and they're picking among their children in a way."

Only the largest cities—Chicago, New York, Los Angeles—have their own Washington lobbyists on staff, but hundreds of cities, counties and transit authorities contract out such services. Most of them rely on small-shop lobbyists such as Simon, Carolyn Chaney (who, like Simon, represents several cities in the West) and Virginia Mayer (who works for Boston), or big law firms with municipal practices, such as Patton Boggs or Holland & Knight (where Cutler works). It's impossible to guarantee results, however, and some mayors question whether the expense is worth it. Cincinnati, for example, recently cut its Washington lobbying budget by 17 percent and may eliminate such spending altogether. "I don't think we're getting the kind of service we should for that amount of money," Mayor Charlie Luken, a former congressman, complained to his local newspaper recently. "I plan to do a lot more of the lobbying for the city myself."

Other mayors are just as convinced, however, that the money is well spent. The city of St. Joseph, Missouri, shares a federal lobbyist's time with the local college, hospital and chamber of commerce, an investment that Mayor David Jones says has paid off in additional highway money. "They know how to play the game better than us," Jones said during a recent visit to Washington. "Within an hour of a vote, we know how it affected St. Joseph. Having them up here to inform us is a huge benefit every day." Alan Autry agrees. "If you had to pick one or the other, an active mayor or a lobbyist," he says, "you better pick the lobbyist."

Strained Relations

These days, hiring a friend in Washington may be about the only way a city can ensure that it will have one. Local officials are coming to town with low expectations and then finding even those too optimistic. Issues of the greatest importance to cities and counties barely register as a concern in the capital, even among members of Congress who used to be mayors or

county commissioners themselves. When the problems do register, the first instinct often is to punt to the states, who can act as middlemen with the locals. The federal government has a constitutionally based relationship with states, and policy makers find it easier to keep an eye on how programs are doing in 50 states than tracking them through 19,000 local entities.

There is a widely stated notion that Republican control of both the White House and Congress makes federal relations even tougher for cities, whose political leadership is heavily Democratic. But municipal-federal relations seem to ebb and flow in ways that have more to do with institutional roles than with which party is in power. "Our membership is about half Democrats and half Republicans," says Larry Naake, executive director of the National Association of Counties, "and I don't think the Republicans are getting any more help than the Democrats from the federal level."

Bush administration officials, from Homeland Security Secretary Tom Ridge on down, have offered repeated assurances to local officials that Washington will send them billions of dollars for police, fire fighters and other so-called first responders. But those checks have yet to be put in the mail. Meanwhile, according to the U.S. Conference of Mayors, localities are out $2.6 billion in additional security costs for the year following the attacks of September 11, 2001. If the feds refuse to pay for a heightened state of alert for foreign terrorism, mayors complain, what would they pay for? "The perception is, here we come again with tin cup in hand," says Carol Kocheisen of the National League of Cities. "The other side of the equation is, we wouldn't be here again if you didn't want us to do X, Y and Z by yesterday."

There are other complaints as well. Because of accounting problems, the U.S. Department of Housing and Urban Development plans to cut aid to public housing by 10 percent from the amount promised earlier. That figure was itself a reprieve of sorts; the reduction was originally supposed to be 30 percent. New federal education testing and reporting requirements are going to cost state and local governments billions, and the hopes of additional federal funding for that purpose are becoming ever more dim. Last year's federal election law allotted $4 billion to help pay for new voting machines and other improvements, but local officials doubt that much money will actually be appropriated.

Cities, meanwhile, are suing the Federal Communications Commission to reverse a ruling last March that declared cable modem service to be an "interstate information service." That means that cable companies providing this service don't have to pay fees to cities, as cable TV franchises do, or reimburse them for tearing up rights of way. The loss in fees to local governments could add up to about $200 million a year. Ken Fellman, the mayor of Arvada, Colorado, and chairman of an FCC advisory committee on intergovernmental relations, says his state's congressional delegation is sympathetic to the cities' plight in the matter. But, he says, it's simply not an issue that distracts their attention from matters such as Iraq and homeland security. "Public safety and transportation are much higher on their priority level than consumer privacy or local revenues," Fellman says.

Banding Together

To cope with the FCC ruling and other telecommunications matters, more than 100 cities have formed a lobbying alliance. That kind of response is necessary, they say, because of the generally poor coverage of communications issues: Of four federal lobbyists at the National League of Cities, only one-third of the time of one of them is devoted to communications. The industries that cities are competing

against, meanwhile, maintain some of the best-funded lobbies in Washington.

Local officials often feel outgunned in lobbying competition with private industry on many issues besides communications. For instance, cities and counties have not succeeded in several attempts at persuading Congress to pass legislation allowing them to force garbage haulers to take some of their waste to local facilities. (The Supreme Court ruled such requirements illegal in 1994.) "All the counties in the country couldn't defeat waste management companies," says one former city lobbyist who now works for Congress. "They don't pass out $100 bills."

Anyone who lobbies for local governments in Washington will tell you it's difficult right now to win any policy change aimed at helping cities in general. Decisions once made at the Cabinet level are now under strict White House control in the Bush administration. Where once the HUD secretary, for instance, was an internal advocate for more public housing funds, now he is more likely to toe the line in support of White House policies. "For all Andrew Cuomo's faults, he did have a relationship with the White House, one that was characterized by a robust debate with OMB over funding levels," says Kurt Creager, head of the Vancouver, Washington, housing authority, referring to Clinton's HUD secretary. "We don't have that anymore."

And—mostly under cloak of anonymity—local officials and lobbyists say that within the White House, the Office of Intergovernmental Affairs, which was never terribly powerful to begin with, has further diminished in importance. Director Ruben Barrales has been moved out of the West Wing and split off from the domestic policy operation. Barrales' role is to be a facilitator, presenting local concerns to federal policy makers and explaining consequent policies to cities, counties and states. Barrales says he's doing just that. "We spend a lot of time advising the president and others in the White House about concerns of mayors and local officials at all levels," he says. "In many ways, a lobbying effort is always involved in wanting more."

Many local officials, however, complain that communication flows only in one direction, with the administration handing out marching orders and not listening to their arguments. "Ruben was given less resources to engage with local officials than were provided to me," says Mickey Ibarra, who ran the Office of Intergovernmental Affairs during the second Clinton term and now lobbies for cities and corporate clients. "In the current administration, they have lost their place. There's no pretense of involving them." For all of his insistence on White House openness to city and county concerns, even Barrales has a hard time listing many Bush administration programs or policies of specific benefit to localities.

Location and Luck

And so the best thing for a mayor to do in Washington right now may be to avoid the broader policy questions and instead focus on specific projects, coming up with a strategy for converting them into earmarked dollars. Then he or she can present that strategy on the Hill and work the phones until it bears fruit.

It's a cliché that much success in life springs from the mere act of showing up, but it's a lesson that cities far from Washington for-

get at their peril. A few weeks ago, Autry and Simon sat in the office of U.S. Representative George Radanovich, hoping to persuade him to keynote a regional clean air summit in Fresno in April. Local governments from eight counties, along with farmers, environmentalists and business leaders, will be gathering to formulate a plan for cleaning up the stagnant air in Fresno and California's San Joaquin Valley, which the EPA is about to downgrade from "severe" to "extreme," a move that will do nothing to burnish the city's image. Autry hoped Radanovich, who represents parts of Fresno, would lend his congressional imprimatur to the resulting plan.

As it turned out, he got more than that. While Autry and Simon were talking to Radanovich, four officials from the federal Environmental Protection Agency were cooling their heels in the congressman's cramped reception area. Radanovich brought them into the meeting, and won a promise that a top-level EPA official would attend the summit. That was important because it would tacitly link the Bush administration to whatever plan might emerge, which in turn would help assuage the concerns of corporations looking for a place to locate.

It was a small but significant victory—and one that was achieved essentially by coincidence. The right people turned up in the right place at the right time. "We plan everything meticulously," says Leonard Simon, "and then let life take over. Location and timing are just extremely important."

Hail to the School Chiefs

by Christopher Swope

When Joel Klein took charge of New York City's schools on August 19, there was no mistaking the symbolism. If Klein could take on a leviathan such as Microsoft Corp. as an antitrust lawyer—something he did as assistant U.S. attorney general during the Clinton administration—he could certainly handle reforming the nation's largest school district. Klein is a new actor to the school stage, but the storyline is becoming increasingly familiar: Cities are turning to people from outside the education establishment to run school systems.

Since Minneapolis experimented with hiring a consultant to run its schools in 1993, at least a dozen cities have turned to "nontraditional" superintendents. Seattle, New Orleans, Jacksonville and Washington, D.C., hired military figures. Chicago and Baltimore tapped financial officers. San Diego hired a federal prosecutor and Los Angeles, a former governor.

Cities are looking for fresh blood to tackle one of the toughest, most politically charged job titles in public service. "Particularly in very large urban districts, there's a growing sense that the superintendent's job is about politics and management as much as it is about education," says Paul Houston, executive director of the American Association of School Administrators.

The non-educators have had some success, none more than in Seattle. In 1995, Seattle hired John Henry Stanford, a former Army general who later died in office and was replaced by Joseph Olchefske, a former investment banker. Both won wide acclaim for improving instruction along with test scores while trimming fat from the schools budget. Most important, they compensated for their biggest weakness—their lack of classroom experience—by surrounding themselves with knowledgeable educators.

San Diego took that idea to a new level in 1998 when it split the top schools job essentially in two. Alan Bersin, the federal prosecutor who served as "border czar" on immigration and drug issues, became the school CEO, while a position akin to "chief academic officer" went to a school reformer from New York City. National experts credit Bersin for firing languid principals and focusing on improving teaching. Locally, he's more controversial. Teachers and principals criticize his management style as heavy-handed. Bersin's two opponents on the five-member school board are always one vote away from ousting him.

Christopher Swope is a staff writer for *Governing*. This article is reprinted from *Governing* (September 2002): 62.

In his first two years as superintendent of the Los Angeles school system, Roy Romer's political skills have won him support from the school board. Just this June, the board voted unanimously to extend the former Colorado governor's contract through 2005. It's too early to rate Romer's performance, but even the *Los Angeles Times,* which at first called him a "bad fit" for the schools, is upbeat about him—for now. Romer won a 15 percent pay hike for teachers, something that was needed to attract more and better teachers to Los Angeles. Test scores in the city's elementary and middle schools are rising.

In other cities, non-educators have found out why urban superintendents get chewed up and spit out an average of once every two-and-a-half years. Previous hires in Baltimore, New Orleans and Washington, D.C., found they either lacked the drive to take on unwieldy urban school districts or fell prey to school board politics. That's a fate Joel Klein will try to avoid in New York. Klein has the strong support of Mayor Michael Bloomberg and a public that seems willing to give him a shot. Soon enough, he will be able to judge which is harder: educating 1 million kids or fighting Bill Gates.

The Deadly Dangers of Daily Life

by Alan Ehrenhalt

Even in an era of declining urban crime rates, Houston is a dangerous place. Its toughest neighborhoods, such as the notorious "Bloody Fifth" Ward, continue to rank far above most of the country in every category of violent offense. This past May alone, the Fifth Ward police district experienced 27 aggravated assaults, 18 burglaries, 23 car thefts and a rape. Every few months, there is a murder on the street.

The city as a whole is doing much better; its homicide rate has fallen to less than a third of what it was just 10 years ago. But people make decisions based not so much on the latest numbers as on longstanding perceptions and on the scenes of violence that confront them on the 11 o'clock news. In Houston, as in every other metropolitan area, families rank safety above all other considerations in choosing a neighborhood. In surveys by the National Association of Homebuilders, more than 80 percent place it at or near the top of their priority list.

For much of the past decade in the Houston area, that steered them to Montgomery County, the huge stretch of suburban territory northwest of the city whose population grew by more than 60 percent—to nearly 300,000—in the 1990s. The Woodlands, a meticulously planned community started in 1974 on 27,000 acres of forest land in the county, now has 70,000 residents all by itself. And most of them report safety as a major attraction that drew them there—safety for themselves and especially for their children.

For quite a few, however, the quest for safety dictates moving even further out of town, into the Texas countryside. Houston expatriates are becoming a familiar phenomenon on the far eastern edge of the region, in old cattle towns such as Liberty, Hankamer and Anahuac. Chambers County, of which Anahuac is the quiet county seat, is now up to 26,000 people, the most it has ever had.

To the families who have made moves like this, the question of whether their lives are safer is a silly one. They have left crime-plagued urban America for a refuge in which crime scarcely exists. Despite Montgomery County's rapid growth, there were only 10 homicides there in 2000, among more than a quarter-million people. In Chambers County that year, there were no homicides at all.

Alan Ehrenhalt is executive editor of *Governing*. This article is reprinted from *Governing* (August 2002): 6, 8.

That would appear to settle the safety issue once and for all, if it even needed settling, were it not for some ingenious research by William Lucy, a professor of urban planning at the University of Virginia. Lucy posed a simple inquiry about American metropolitan areas that, to my knowledge, nobody else has bothered to pose before: What if, instead of being measured by itself, homicide were to be measured along with other forms of violent fatality—specifically, automobile accidents, the second major category of violent death in the United States.

In other words, if your goal is not just to avoid being murdered but to avoid being killed, period, where are you safest and where are you most at risk?

Lucy compared the combined fatality rates from homicide and car accidents in eight U.S. metropolitan areas, in places as diverse as Houston and Milwaukee. His results, released earlier this summer, amount to an actuarial bombshell.

In 2000, to cite just one example, Houston suffered 230 murders, 57 of them in the most frightening category—"random" killings by persons unknown to the victim. It also recorded 248 traffic fatalities. The chance of an individual Houstonian dying during the year either at the hands of a murderous stranger or as the victim of an automobile were about 1.5 in 10,000. Montgomery County, in the same year, recorded 10 random homicides and 72 traffic deaths. Adjusting for population, that gave Montgomery a combined violent death rate of 2.5 per 10,000 residents—more than half again as dangerous.

Even more remarkable, bucolic Chambers County, while murder-free, had 13 traffic fatalities in a population of barely 25,000. Those 13 deaths alone gave it a combined rate of 4.9—more than three times as high as Houston's figure. As Lucy puts it, "What we're dealing with is a huge misperception of risk."

There are arguments one can launch against his numbers. It might be objected, for example, that the accident record reflects only the location of a crash, not the victim's place of residence. The number of fatalities in the suburbs might be inflated by truck drivers and tourists who crash while passing through on the interstate highway.

It might be—but it isn't. Lucy found that barely 10 percent of the fatal accidents in suburban and exurban counties take place on interstates. The vast majority happen on two-lane local roads. That means most of the victims are local as well.

Or one can argue, taking a more subjective approach, that feeling secure is as much perception as reality, and that when people worry about safety, they are worrying about deliberate acts of aggression, not accidental collisions. People buying a house often look at the local crime rate. They don't look at the accident rate. And they don't lie awake imagining that they will drive off a road and into a tree some rainy night. When a community is not threatened by menacing strangers on the streets, residents regard it as safe. Therefore, it might be said, lumping murder and accidents into the same category is arbitrary and unwarranted.

Against this criticism, I can't improve on the response Lucy makes: It's true, people don't spend much time worrying about accident rates in prosperous suburbs, but then again, maybe they should. After all, as he puts it, "you're dead either way."

The failure of Americans to appreciate the actual danger built into their daily lives may be surprising, but it's not really out of character. When you get right down to it, hardly any of us are good at evaluating risk and making intelligent decisions about it. That is just as true of public officials as it is of ordinary citizens.

In the months since last September's terrorist attacks, communities all over the country have been calculating what they need to do—and how much they need to spend—to feel secure from future attack. They don't know for sure, obviously, and they never will. Terrorists can attack anywhere. But the whole society has a big stake in seeing that these calculations of risk at least bear some relationship to probability. Given the emotion of the issue, that may not be easy to achieve.

Big cities are worried about becoming terrorist targets, and that's understandable. If I were the emergency communications director in Chicago, I'd have to assume some level of danger: A terrorist organization that fixated on the World Trade Center might develop an interest someday in the Sears Tower or the John Hancock Building, or failing that, in the urban water supply or the utility network. It may be a long shot, but it's one that no wise urban leader can afford to dismiss.

On the other hand, how far does a given city's potential vulnerability extend throughout its metropolitan area? During the recent U.S. Conference of Mayors meeting in Madison, Wisconsin, some of the mayors representing Chicago suburbs sounded as if they considered themselves prime targets. The mayor of Oak Brook theorized that her town could be in danger because it has a huge shopping mall and is headquarters for McDonald's and the manufacturer of Beanie Babies, both symbols of American consumerism. "Which is easier to hit," the mayor asked a *New York Times* reporter, "something in Chicago or something out here? Which is going to put Middle America in a tailspin, big city or supposedly safe suburbia?"

Schaumburg, Illinois, a few miles down the road from Oak Brook, is equally worried about the security of its big shopping mall. The mayor of Bartlett, Illinois, a small exurb just beyond Schaumburg, is concerned that her town might get caught up in the aftermath of an attack on Schaumburg's commercial center, or in the evacuation of Chicago itself following a chemical or biological attack.

Could those things happen? Well, sure. Anything can happen. But given the number of cities in this country, the number of suburbs, exurbs, shopping malls and capitalist corporate headquarters, any small-town mayor would be morally justified in reacting to a future terrorist attack with the numbing disbelief that Humphrey Bogart displayed upon seeing Ingrid Bergman again in *Casablanca*: "Of all the gin joints in all the towns in the world, she walks into mine." No sensible person would bet on it.

The bottom line is that governing one of the hundreds of affluent American suburbs in the 21st century justifies a reasonable amount of prudence and precaution. It doesn't justify sleepless nights or emptying the local treasury. Anybody tempted to overreact needs to stop and look at the numbers.

If you're still not convinced of that, let me pose one final question: Purely on a statistical basis, what's more likely to get you killed during the course of this year: (A) living in Israel, in the midst of the Intifada, or (B) living 40 miles outside Houston or Los Angeles and commuting to work on the freeway every day? The correct answer, once again courtesy of William Lucy, is (B). It's not even close.

That doesn't mean you should move to Jerusalem to be safe. But if you're a long-distance commuter living in an American exurb, and you have a choice, you might at least ponder the wisdom of moving back into the city. When it comes to the hard facts of human risk, things are not always what they seem.

X. STATE AND LOCAL POLICY ISSUES

One might think that the goal of state government is to provide the services that citizens need and then raise the money to do so. Actually, the governor and state legislature see just how much money will be available under the current tax structure and then decide the extent of services the state can provide. It comes as no surprise, therefore, that financial issues are at the top of state policy agendas. If additional funds are needed, how should the revenues be raised—taxes, user fees, bonds, lotteries? What kinds of taxes should be imposed—sales, income, inheritance, property? Who will bear the burden of these taxes—the rich, the poor, the consumer, the property holder? These are the most important questions state governors and legislatures address.

The 1980s presented the states with a roller-coaster ride in their budgets. In the early 1980s, there was a recession and state revenues dropped precipitously. The fiscal crisis necessitated layoffs, hiring limits, travel restrictions, and delays in expenditures. The budget crunch of the early 1980s greatly lowered expectations of what state government could and would do.[1]

At the same time, the states were waiting to see how the national government would handle the federal deficit, and how that decision would affect state and local finances. Then, in the mid-1980s, a major fear of state leaders came true: the president and Congress decided to solve part of the national deficit crisis by letting the states pay for a considerable part of it. Saving a program that formerly was funded in whole or part with federal funds meant increasing state and local taxes. And to many lawmakers, increased taxes can mean defeat at the polls.

During this time, however, the economy recovered and revenues flowed into state treasuries. No matter what the governor proposed and the legislature adopted, there was always a surplus at the end of the fiscal year. State decision makers were confident despite the major changes going on within the federal system.

However, by the end of the 1980s another problem developed in many states: their fiscal health began deteriorating from reduced tax revenues as the nation's economy seemed to be slipping into a recession. The states faced a new budget problem: keeping their budgets balanced.

What could the states do? As already noted, one option would be to raise taxes. States also could seek new sources of tax revenue. For example, more and more states considered instituting a state lottery, which seemed to be a painless way to raise money. But research on state lotteries indicates that they amount to a "heavy tax"—one that is sharply regressive—because it is levied in part on those who cannot afford it.[2]

After a couple of years of economists arguing whether the country was moving into a recession, it became clear that we had. This translated into decreasing state tax revenues or a decline of the revenue growth state leaders had experienced in the mid-1980s. Deficit reduction became the byword rather than just balancing the budget. This often meant tax increases had to be considered seriously and often adopted if programs were to be maintained at their current levels, let alone starting new initiatives. And, in some situations, services still had to be cut to close the deficit.

There were few states not facing serious budget problems. The budget deficits in some cases were enormous; California's for 1992–1993 was over $14.2 billion, and even shutting down the state's entire higher education and correctional systems would still have left a large deficit to handle. Governors and legislatures tried to erase these deficits with all types of "revenue enhancements," program and governmental cutbacks, and they even reverted to what the federal government had been doing: shifting some responsibilities downward, toward the local governments. However, by fiscal year 1994 the severe instability in most state budgets was subsiding.[3]

But following the 1994 elections, a new set of priorities began to come into focus: cutting taxes and reducing the size of government and its programs. This was most evident at the national level as Congress worked through the Republican "Contract with America." But it was also happening at the state and local levels as elected leaders tried to outdo each other in their calls for cuts. The economy-based money problems that had been evident at the outset of the 1990s were being replaced by ideologically and politically based money problems in the mid-1990s.

However, by the late 1990s, the national economy and all but a few state economies were healthy and growing, a situation that translated into surpluses in state budgets. In some states the budget surpluses were substantial; in others they were not as great, but there still was "extra" money available. Thus, everyone with an interest in state government and politics was looking hungrily at how these "extra" funds might be directed toward their own needs. Schoolteachers wanted higher salaries; so did those in higher education and state government employees in non-education positions. There were also environmental issues that needed funding in the states, and calls for tax cuts were ringing out in the state capitals.

Now, at the outset of the twenty-first century, monetary concerns are again the top issue for the states and their local governments. As it appears that the dark days of the early 1980s and '90s are revisiting us, leaders at the state and local levels are facing some tough decisions as revenues are not reaching the goals these leaders had set. Many probably wish they had stashed more of those surpluses away in a "rainy day fund" as they now look out their windows and see increasingly inclement weather. But the lure of providing tax cuts

often proved irresistible to elected officials in those bygone days.

After money, what are the issues of greatest concern to the states? Education at all levels—K–12, community colleges, universities—is demanding greater attention and funding to keep the upcoming workforce ready for the jobs that will be out in the economy when they graduate. And the need to keep the technology used in these institutions up to speed is costly and constantly changing. Health and environmental issues are also high on most states' agendas. These issues are often very complex and need sophisticated approaches to address them. This too translates to expensive outlays of money.

Of course, different regions of the country have different priorities. In the Southwest, water policy dominates. In the Midwest, farm problems, the declining industrial base, and lack of economic development are of concern. In the Northeast, an aging infrastructure must be rebuilt so the economies can recover. And in California, a region unto itself, the state must cope with both in and out migration, a multicultural population, unpredictable weather pattern shifts and earthquakes, and a shifting economic base in addition to a myriad of societal problems.

Then there are the unforeseen events that intrude into the normal flow of politics and policy concerns in our state and local governments. In the 1990s, much was said and written about the effect of the El Nino and La Nina weather patterns across the nation that created many major and minor disasters with which individuals and state and local governments must cope. These governments often have to contend with the effects of earthquakes, floods, hurricanes, tornadoes, and other natural disasters. Even though there may be federal disaster aid available, the first call for help, and for continuing assistance, goes to these lower-level governments in our federal system. Now with the threats of man-made disasters such as the terrorist attacks of September 11 followed by the erratic anthrax mailings, a whole new approach to something called "homeland security" has been developing with all levels of government involved.

Setting the Agenda

How do particular concerns become priorities on states' agendas? Although state constitutions provide for the education, health, and safety of citizens, events can trigger new interest in issues. For example, the collapse of financial institutions such as insurance companies or state-chartered banks can lead to a crisis and action by state regulators. Campaign promises and court decisions also influence policymaking. A gubernatorial candidate promising to lower utility rates or cut out the car tax will try to keep this promise once elected. And if a state court finds that some citizens, such as the mentally handicapped, are not receiving the state services to which they are entitled, the governor and state legislators will have to address this issue.

Provisions of the U.S. Constitution also can force issues onto a state's policy agenda. Since the 1950s, there has been a series of U.S. Supreme Court decisions on "separate but equal" education, reapportionment, and criminal justice based on lawsuits challenging state and local government policies and actions as violations of the plaintiffs' constitutional rights. These decisions have caused state and local lawmakers considerable anguish as they address and adopt often controversial and expensive new policies, which usually translate into tax increases.

Federal program requirements also can play a role in state policy making and administration. For example, in the early and mid-1980s the states had to raise the legal drinking age to twenty-one and limit interstate highway speeds to 55 miles per hour or face the loss of federal highway funds. However, federal encroachment on setting speed limits came to a head in a highly publicized and controversial vote to override President Ronald Reagan's veto of a multibillion-dollar transportation bill in March 1987. The override allowed those states that so desired to raise the limit to 65 miles per hour on rural interstates.

Innovations and programs in other states can influence a state's agenda, as a new form of activity in one state may lead to similar action elsewhere. This "copycat" method of decision making has proved to be very popular: How did State X handle this problem? However, as some have noticed, what is "reform in one state may be the exact opposite of reform in another." For example, California made its insurance commissioner an elected official the same time that Louisiana sought to make that office appointive rather than elective; and Georgia repealed no-fault auto insurance the same time that Pennsylvania added it.[4]

Events not only in another state but in another part of the world occasionally determine the issues that state governments must address. Although the recent decrease in tension between the United States and the former Soviet Union has raised hopes of a "peace dividend"—a budget windfall from cuts in the defense budget—some states bore more of the costs of that dividend than did others. Cuts in the defense budget meant closing military bases in some states, reducing military personnel, and cutting back or cancelling contracts for military hardware and weapons systems and funding for military research. Many states and localities greatly benefited from the defense budget in years past. Then, as times and concerns changed, so too did their economies and fiscal health. Now that we have entered the new era of anti-terrorism efforts in international affairs, there will probably be some additional "winners and losers" in defense budget decisions.

Implementation

Once policy goals and priorities are set by governors and legislators, important decisions must be made concerning who will implement them. This not only means which agency in state government will have the responsibility, but which level of government—state, local, or both.

Implementation decisions are often made with the considerable interest and involvement of the federal government. State and local governments administer some federal programs: food stamps, child nutrition, social services, and senior citizen centers. In other areas federal and state governments *share* administrative and fiscal responsibility: Medicaid, interstate and federal highways, hazardous waste, and water supply and sanitation. And in the new welfare reforms, all three levels are sharing the responsibilities. Leaders in the states are becoming very upset over their part in the Medicaid program as the state-level costs involved are mounting at a rapid rate and adding considerable stress to the already overburdened state budgetary situation.

The federal system is in a continual process of change. The results of the 1994 elections escalated the velocity of the process and the nature of these changes. As already noted, the debates and conflicts in Congress are centering on how to cut back the national government's role in domestic policy. When politicians debate the role of the federal government in domestic policy, for the most part they are referring to the extent to which the federal government will work with state and local governments in a wide range of policies. But for state officials and their counterparts at the local

level, the outcome of these debates will have a direct impact on their own jobs and responsibilities. By extension, the outcome of these debates will have considerable impact on citizens and on what they can expect from their state and local governments.

The articles in Part X focus on some of the policy concerns states are facing. Melissa Conradi of *Governing* analyzes the why, who, where, and what aspects of ten issues currently on the state agendas. Chad Foster in *State Government News* points out the problems that states are having with paying for homeland security measures. Ellen Perlman of *Governing* shows how many states are exploring legalizing or expanding gambling to raise revenues. Charlotte Postlewaite of *State Government News* indicates just how public education is being squeezed in the current fiscal crisis the states are facing. Christopher Swope of *Governing* presents two perspectives on how the states are faring in getting sales taxes levied on Internet purchases—a pact simplifying sales taxes across the states and a pact with a band of large retailers. Swope also looks at how the states are saving money by reducing the cost of corrections.

Notes

1. National Governors' Association, *The State of the States,* 1985, 6.
2. Peter Passell, "Duke Economists Critical of State Lotteries," *New York Times News Service,* reported in the *Durham Morning Herald,* May 21, 1989, 11A.
3. "Severe Instability in State Budgets Subsiding," *Governors' Bulletin,* November 8, 1993, 1–3.
4. Hal Hovey, "Ebb and Flow in State Policy," *State Policy Reports* 9:18 (September 1991): 12.

Ten Issues to Watch

by Melissa Conradi

Budget Shortfalls

Why is this an issue?

Fiscal 2003 is the worst year for state budgets since WWII. Most states face big budget gaps—more than $17.5 billion at last count—and the future isn't looking any brighter. One-time fixes and reserves have already been tapped and revenues are still slumping.

Who are the main players?

Everyone. Tax watchdog groups, for example, are working with government to restructure tax systems. Public health groups are fighting the use of tobacco money as a cure-all for budget holes, and religious leaders oppose gambling expansion.

Where will it be debated?

Only a handful of states aren't hurting. Gambling expansion will be on the table in Pennsylvania, Maryland and Ohio. Florida's class-size initiative will cost money. Thirty-one states signed a streamlined sales tax act, which will go into effect after 10 pass it.

What can we expect?

All areas of spending will be subject to cuts. Some states will work on revising their tax structures with the help of commission/task force reports. Sin taxes will be a first line of defense but can't solve all these problems—expect increases in sales and income taxes.

Homeland Security

Why is this an issue?

States are waiting for up to $4 billion from Congress for homeland security. Public health preparedness has been tested with anthrax and West Nile, but how ready are we for a full-scale bioterror attack?

Who are the main players?

Cities and counties need money for first responders. Public health departments will help craft emergency plans. Latino activists have been fighting new restrictions on driver's license requirements for immigrants.

Where will it be debated?

In New Jersey, a bill offers a contingency plan in case many legislators die at once. Wyoming plans to update quarantine laws dating back

Melissa Conradi is research coordinator for *Governing.* This article is reprinted from *Governing* (January 2003): 32–33.

to 1903. Bioterrorism legislation is being pushed in New Mexico. Georgia will revisit its licensing laws.

What can we expect?

States will prepare their security spending wish lists but must work on updating and tightening old systems even before federal help arrives. A draft Model State Emergency Health Powers Act might prove helpful in planning for the worst.

Health Costs

Why is this an issue?

Medicaid is the fastest growing portion of state budgets, and prescription drug and health insurance costs are soaring. Last year, 39 states considered proposals aimed at reducing pharmaceutical costs, but hospital spending is emerging as a major issue as well.

Who are the main players?

Prescription drug companies don't want to lose profits under extreme state cost-cutting plans, and health providers want to be sure they're reimbursed enough. Advocates for the beneficiaries will argue against decreasing eligibility or raising prices.

Where will it be debated?

The largest and most complex problems are found in California, Florida, Massachusetts and Texas. A number of states are doing a top-to-bottom review of their Medicaid programs. In Kentucky, state employees have the legislature's ear about rising insurance costs.

What can we expect?

States will look at every possible option to reduce costs, including cutting back on programs that were added in the flush times but are not mandatory, and tightening eligibility requirements. There will also be emphasis on ensuring that health care is delivered efficiently.

Education Standards

Why is this an issue?

It all revolves around No Child Left Behind. Standards are the focus at every level—assessing students and schools for proficiency, ensuring quality teaching, providing school options, and funding and enforcing changes at the worst schools.

Who are the main players?

Education associations will lobby against vouchers. State Supreme Courts are forcing legislators to fix unbalanced school financing formulas. State education departments are crafting the plans for approval by the federal government.

Where will it be debated?

At least eight states have expressed intent to introduce voucher legislation; Louisiana will be a battleground. Alabama and Mississippi will work on getting schools up to standards. School financing litigation will play a role in Tennessee and Ohio.

What can we expect?

GOP wins and court rulings give school choice momentum. The feds will return states' education proposals to them on January 31st, when they'll scramble to adapt laws to those plans. States facing funding-formula overhauls or huge new expenses will be hit especially hard.

Air Quality

Why is this an issue?

The absence of federal action has set the stage for state regulation.

Who are the main players?

California's ground-breaking CO_2 legislation is being challenged by the Bush administration, automakers and the state's chamber of commerce and farm bureau. Power and energy companies have a stake, as do renewable energy providers and environmentalists.

Where will it be debated?

New Jersey considered several alternative-fuel bills in 2002. Western states will draft regional haze legislation as deadlines approach on a federal rule. New York will revisit multipollutant strategies.

What can we expect?

States will continue looking for ways to make alternative energy sources more appealing. Tax breaks for renewable power and new fees to finance energy conservation projects have proven popular. Strict emissions-capping programs are more controversial.

Insurance

Why is this an issue?

Tight market conditions lead to higher rates, which lead to greater legislative attention. Homeowners' and medical malpractice insurance are in the spotlight. In addition, states are worried about federal preemption, so are working to streamline regulation.

Who are the main players?

Homeowners and doctors rebel against soaring rates, and AARP and the National Partnership for Women and Families seek to protect vulnerable customers. Trial lawyers oppose tort reform. Insurance groups are involved in crafting responses to the problem.

Where will it be debated?

Texas is the hot spot in the homeowners' insurance crisis; eight bills slated for this year's session target rates. Medical malpractice insurance reform is on the table in West Virginia and Pennsylvania. Nevada is looking at tort reform.

What can we expect?

Options will include new forms of insurance regulation, already happening in a dozen states; alternatives to litigation, such as reporting programs to quickly identify problems; and tort reform. An interstate compact that streamlines insurance regulation is in the works.

Welfare

Why is this an issue?

Since the feds didn't reauthorize the welfare program in 2002, states are trying to prepare for changes when TANF is eventually approved. Some also are looking at revamping their programs to reflect new or emerging priorities and problem areas.

Who are the main players?

Marriage and family programs could be the only source of new money coming from the federal government. Substance-abuse and mental-health advocates will try to guide new state attention toward long-time welfare recipients.

Where will it be debated?

All states will be affected once Congress reauthorizes TANF. Arkansas is exploring how to provide services to families that have left welfare. Arizona and Nevada saw caseloads rise dramatically this past year, so will look at backing off programs that had been added.

What can we expect?

States are taking on some of the harder cases—people with severe barriers to work, and post-welfare conditions that make it hard to survive without benefits—as well as reexamining what they can do with their money in tough budget times.

Privacy

Why is this an issue?

The proliferation of information available through computers has become a major concern.

Identity theft is one of the most severe consequences, but business use of personal data for marketing or other purposes is also a problem.

Who are the main players?

Insurers use credit reports to determine rates, which is raising the ire of consumer-protection advocates such as the U.S. Public Interest Research Group. Direct-marketing trade associations worry about their livelihood. AARP has vowed to fight for seniors' privacy.

Where will it be debated?

Thirty-two states already have no-call lists; New Jersey's governor is pressing for the strongest possible no-call law. An Ohio bill would restrict credit scoring. Indiana's property tax reassessment sparked debate over public access to home-sales information.

What can we expect?

Business groups will defend their right to use information, but increasing security concerns will give citizens the upper hand for now.

Election Reform

Why is this an issue?

Federal election law shifts the burden to the states, which will have responsibility for ensuring that certain requirements are fulfilled but will have almost $4 billion of federal money to do it.

Who are the main players?

Voting machine vendors want to get a piece of the action. Voters rights groups will play a part in states where there is concern of disenfranchisement—the NAACP and Common Cause have both issued report cards on election reform.

Where will it be debated?

Massachusetts is among the states that have done nothing and now face looming federal deadlines. Wisconsin and New York will have to make voter databases from scratch, while Pennsylvania and Louisiana must reexamine provisional voting rights.

What can we expect?

Last fall's elections offer some guidelines for the future. Georgia's bid to become the first in the nation with all new voting machines was a success and will no doubt spark followers. Training poll workers will have to be a key element, as demonstrated in the Florida primaries.

Medical Worker Shortage

Why is this an issue?

Nurses, technicians, dentists and home- and community-based service aides are in high demand, and the field is not attracting enough workers. Low salaries, poor working conditions and mandatory overtime have become chronic problems.

Who are the main players?

Nurses' groups and dentist associations have been rallying for higher pay. Hospitals and other health-care providers are concerned about getting and keeping enough qualified staff.

Where will it be debated?

Wyoming will consider establishing a nursing education loan program in an attempt to retain nurses. Wisconsin formed a committee to recommend ways to close the gap between supply and demand. Georgia hopes to expand home- and community-based care.

What can we expect?

California is the first state to mandate nurse-patient ratios. More states will look to career ladders and staffing plans to improve morale on the job, as well as financial incentives. Licensing reciprocity between states will also be pursued.

Homeland Security: Who Pays?

by Chad S. Foster

As many states face tight or shrinking budgets, they find themselves struggling to meet new responsibilities for ensuring homeland security. Throughout the past year, securing the homeland has become an increasingly difficult challenge. Slow federal action and lack of internal resources are keeping the states from making bold moves toward homeland security preparedness.

President Bush's *National Strategy for Homeland Security*, released in July, details many of the roles and responsibilities of the federal, state and local governments and private-sector partners. But it falls short of spelling out current and future funding sources, avenues and mandates. Without clear financial support and guidance from the federal government, state and local leaders are wrestling with complicated issues as they attempt to fund necessary homeland security measures.

New Responsibilities, Costs

After the September 11, 2001 terrorist attacks, states immediately began to assess their threats and vulnerabilities and to formulate long- and short-term strategies and plans. Many states quickly realized that:

• they lacked manpower, equipment and training for all first responders;
• their public health communities and abilities to respond to terrorist acts involving biological agents were insufficient; and
• they lacked adequate protection for public and private sector infrastructures, and communication gaps prevented cooperation and collaboration between these entities and state and local leaders.

The plans to address these and many other shortcomings created significant new costs for the states. Before September 11, most states did not have a line item in their budget for homeland security. Now, they face new line items with the potential for substantial spending.

Who Should Fund Homeland Security?

More than a year after the September 11 attacks, there are still more questions than answers when it comes to funding homeland

Chad S. Foster is a public safety and justice policy analyst at The Council of State Governments. This article is reprinted from *State Government News* (January 2003): 23–24, 28. Copyright 2003 The Council of State Governments. Reprinted with permission from *State Government News/Spectrum*.

security efforts. Should the federal government take a lead role? Should it simply give state and local entities funds to use as they deem necessary, or should it provide funding for specific and mandated reasons?

Should the federal government mandate states to match grants, or should there be "no strings attached? What type of funding policy should the nation use, and what type of policy is it currently using?

Many people believe that the federal government should take a lead role in funding homeland security. They argue that although state and local governments must shoulder a great portion of responsibility for protecting residents, they simply do not have the resources to provide upfront costs to fix the high-priority security measures.

Studies soon after the September 11 attacks showed that the states alone were expected to spend roughly $6 billion the first year to address homeland security needs. Data showing actual expenditures by states on all facets of homeland security is currently not available. It is safe to assume, however, that federal and state funding during the first year fell far short of the expected $6 billion.

Consequently, states face the dilemma of trying to meet urgent homeland security needs with inadequate resources. Federal grant funds are making their way to the states at a much slower pace than was first expected. By waiting on federal grants for first responders and other high-priority needs, states are accepting high levels of risk, thus temporarily sacrificing preparedness.

Furthermore, states have many high-priority needs that the federal government will not fund. For example, some states have created new positions and offices for homeland security.

In addition to slow federal funding streams, a lack of state resources complicates the homeland security puzzle. Many states were already facing tight budgets or budget shortfalls before the September 11 attacks. Now they have a new line item in their budget that requires hefty upfront costs.

As budget forecasts continue to worsen in many states, policy-makers find themselves facing difficult choices. They not only face the question of whether to wait for federal funds or try to self-fund high-priority needs; they also face the thorny dilemma of where to find additional state money. Should they cut budgets of other departments or programs? Should they use state reserves or rainy-day funds? Or should they raise taxes?

Some states have already made difficult policy decisions. In 2002, for example, Pennsylvania increased taxes on its gaming commission to fund first responders and homeland security initiatives. Similarly, Minnesota increased the surcharge on phone use in the name of homeland security.

What Can States Do?

One way or another, states will face difficult homeland security decisions this year. A timely decision and turnaround on federal funds will surely assist the states in focusing their efforts, time and resources on internal needs. Regardless of federal policy, states can take several measures to help prepare for these upcoming decisions:

• share and study other state practices and innovative funding solutions for homeland security;

• collaborate with other states and regions to create mutually beneficial solutions;

• increase collaboration with federal, local and private partners;

• use higher education institutions within the state to assist in research and development, self assessments and other homeland security needs; and

• explore all potential money-making and cost-saving options at the state and local levels. Methods for raising revenue might include increasing or imposing new taxes, surcharges or fees. Options for realizing cost savings might include cross-border resource sharing.

Unfortunately, there is a price tag for preparedness. Funding homeland security will likely challenge all the states in the year to come.

Gaming the Budget

by Ellen Perlman

The sun is shining and the breeze is warm as the boat pulls away from the Florida coast, packed with people out for a pleasure cruise. But these passengers aren't planning to relax in deck chairs or watch dolphins leap from the waves. Rather, they have come aboard for the chance to feed money into loud-clanging, lights-flashing slot machines and, if they're lucky, win back their investment and more. These hours-long jaunts are called "cruises to nowhere," but they actually do have a destination. It's an invisible line in the ocean, where Florida waters become international waters, and the gambling that is illegal in the Sunshine State becomes a permissible activity. Once the boat crosses that spot, the fun begins.

It isn't much fun for the Florida treasury, however. With the state's 2004 fiscal year budget $2 billion in the red, the idea of all those dollars lost at sea does not sit well with state officials. The simple fact is that Floridians are gambling—not only on boats off shore but in nearby states as well. And the way it works now, Florida gets no financial benefit from it. Some state legislators are out to change that this year.

They'll have lots of company. In the midst of tough economic times, officials in many states that don't currently sanction gambling operations are increasingly concerned about their residents routinely augmenting the coffers of neighboring states. "Cross-border casino shopping is a catalyst for many states," says Andrew Zarnett, a gaming analyst and managing director of Deutsche Bank. "You can't say they're not playing, they are," he says. "So states think, 'Why don't we just capture our own revenue back?'"

Like swallows to Capistrano, states return to the idea of "easy money" from gambling whenever there is a major fiscal crisis. Yet with so many—and such large—budget shortfalls, some policy makers who opposed gambling in the past now feel under pressure to sing a different tune, particularly if they promised during campaigns not to raise taxes.

Although it's difficult to put an exact number on how many are seriously contemplating the issue, discussions are taking place in at least 18 states about allowing or adding new types of gambling, as well as increasing the number of electronic devices in existing

Ellen Perlman is a staff writer for *Governing*. This article is reprinted from *Governing* (March 2003): 32–35.

venues. The only state actively considering a halt to the expansion of gambling this year is Connecticut, which already has two popular Indian casinos.

Into the Mainstream

It's not hard to understand why gambling is a tempting budget fix: A lot of revenue flows from one of the country's highest-taxed industries. In Illinois, for example, the top tax rate on casino revenues now is 50 percent—and that's in addition to other corporate taxes. Rhode Island gets close to a 55 percent cut from jai alai and dog racing. "It certainly is a convenient way for people in politics to obtain revenue without seeming to impose higher taxes," says Bennett Liebman, coordinator of the racing and wagering law program at the Albany Law School.

Since the period between 1989 and 1993, when states last looked en masse to gambling as a budget savior, it has become more palatable and mainstream. In 2002, several gubernatorial candidates actively supported gambling. "Before, it was a political hot potato politicians tried to avoid," says Bill Eadington, professor of economics and director of the Institute for the Study of Gambling and Commercial Gaming. But this time, he notes, " 'If I get in it will be part of my program,' was the line."

Last year, gubernatorial candidates in several states ran successfully on the issue of gambling. Robert Ehrlich campaigned for slot machines at Maryland horse tracks, and Oklahoma's Brad Henry promoted a state lottery. In Pennsylvania, both new Governor Edward Rendell and his opponent, Attorney General Michael Fisher, backed putting slots at the state's four racetracks. New governors in Alabama, Arizona, Kansas, Massachusetts, New York and Wisconsin favor some form of gambling.

And despite continued vocal opposition from religious leaders and other anti-gambling groups, the general public has shown increasing acceptance of gambling as a legitimate form of entertainment. Idaho voters approved allowing Indian tribes to have 3,000 video lottery terminals. In Iowa, where gambling was an issue on the ballot in 11 counties, voters chose by a landslide to keep casinos and "racinos" (slot machines at racetracks) for eight more years.

Hawaii and Utah are the only states remaining that do not have some form of legalized gambling. Tennessee left the dwindling group last year after voters removed the constitutional ban on a state lottery with 58 percent of the vote. The legislature now is mulling how to structure a lottery.

Another difference in the gambling resurgence this time around is that few states are proposing casinos that would be owned by large private companies, the way it's done in Las Vegas, Atlantic City and Mississippi. Just about everything else is on the table, however, from Indian gambling to allowing electronic gaming devices at casinos to increasing taxes on existing gambling and renegotiating the state's share of what it takes from casinos.

California wants to allow an expansion of gambling devices at Indian casinos in exchange for a larger slice of the revenue pie. Missouri is looking at raising taxes on casinos. The Massachusetts legislature is considering allowing slots at the commonwealth's four horse and dog tracks. Ohio lawmakers also are mulling slot machines at horse tracks.

Casino Cannibals

If the primary reason for choosing to go the gambling route is to repair budgets, then the obvious questions are how well does it do that and at what cost? Opponents are quick to point out that Nevada, despite being home to Sin City, has a huge budget hole, possibly as large as $700 million, according to recent estimates. "How can it have a budget crisis? It's got gambling," scoffs Tom Grey, executive director of the National Coalition Against Gambling Expansion. "Show me where states have gambled themselves rich."

Connecticut allowed Indian gambling back in 1991 as a solution for budget problems then. Yet, it is projecting a shortfall of between $1 billion and $2 billion for fiscal year 2004. "Initially, these things are a panacea for budget problems in the future," says Paul L. Dion, an economist in the budget office in Rhode Island, which is considering allowing casino gambling. "When money comes in, it gets spent, it's that simple. That's not a knock on Connecticut. Every government works that way."

With the exception of Nevada, gambling is never going to boost a state's general fund revenue by more than a few percentage points—and that won't happen overnight. "If this was really what they say it is, every state with a deficit should be jumping at it," Grey says. "That's not what's happening. The battle is still going on."

What's more, one state's revenue increase may be another state's loss. When new casinos are built, there is great potential for them to cannibalize other states' gambling revenues— as well as harm their home state's lottery. At the extreme end, if every state legalized gambling, markets would likely become saturated and profit margins squeezed.

In the Northeast, there appears to be a race to capture the hearts and pockets of gamblers. Last year, New York approved joining a multi-state lottery, tribal gambling and slots at racetracks and casinos. If slots are added in New York, Pennsylvania and Maryland, it could lessen anticipated revenues for all. And it likely would suck $750 million, or 14 percent, from Atlantic City's gambling revenues by 2006, according to a Bear, Stearns report. But as one Maryland racetrack owner told the *Washington Post,* "when one side has all the ammunition and the other side's got nothing, we can hardly spend time worrying about an arms race."

But what about shooting oneself in the foot? Last year, the Massachusetts State Lottery generated about $899 million in profits, which went to cities and towns. Tim Cahill, the new state treasurer, worries that this money would be at risk if the Bay State were to bring in casinos. In written testimony submitted to a gambling commission formed by then-Governor Jane Swift, Cahill pointed out that in Connecticut, the sales growth for the lottery for the years 1982 to 1991, before casinos were approved, was 212 percent. Since 1992, sales growth has been only 54 percent. "We cannot lose sight of these numbers when discussing the potential impact of casino gambling on our own lottery revenues," Cahill declared.

Nervous Neighbors

States that already have gambling are apprehensive about the marked interest in expansion elsewhere and are watching to see what neighboring states do. "We have some concerns about Massachusetts adding video lottery terminals at the greyhound tracks," says Rhode Island's Dion. Currently, Rhode Island gets 52 percent of the adjusted gross revenue from its greyhound park and 57.5 percent from its Newport Grand Jai Alai Fronton, and those percentages are slated to increase each year, to 55 percent and 59 percent, respectively, by 2006. If a casino were to open on Massachusetts' southeastern border, as has been discussed, "it would clearly affect us," Dion adds.

It's not a given, however, that when one state opens the door to slots, neighboring states automatically start trying to generate such revenues for themselves. "There are too many political issues involved for there to be a direct effect," says Liebman. "We aren't going to find how this falls out until the first state moves ahead." But he also believes that thus far, the demand for gambling, especially slot machines, has generally exceeded the supply.

Raising taxes on existing gambling might seem like the least controversial option, but there are consequences to consider. Missouri is thinking about raising its flat 20 percent gross receipts tax levied on casinos. But Jim Oberkirsch, chief financial analyst for the Missouri Gaming Commission, suggests that a sharp increase in taxes may not be the best bet. He cites neighboring Illinois as an example.

When Illinois brought in gambling, there was a flat 20 percent tax rate and a $2 casino admission charge. Effective July 1, 2002, that changed to a graduated tax rate ranging from 15 percent on the first $25 million in gross receipts to 50 percent on takes of more than $200 million. That has had a negative economic effect on the communities where gambling is located, argues Tom Swoik, executive director of the Illinois Casino Gaming Association, who used to be deputy administrator of the Illinois Gaming Board, the state's regulatory agency.

To protect their bottom line, given the higher tax hit, Illinois casinos have reduced the giveaways and promotions at casinos that attract some customers and cut back on capital expenditures. Harrah's, located in Joliet and Metropolis, was going to expand one facility and build a hotel at the other but decided not to. Empress in Joliet reduced a $70 million planned renovation to $40 million. Another casino closed a restaurant and laid off staff.

Neighboring Indiana's graduated tax now tops out at 35 percent and Missouri's at 20 percent. "We're in competition with both of those states," Swoik says. "If you were a business, would you renovate where the taxes are 20 percent or 50 percent?"

Revenue and Responsibility

While many states are still struggling with the gambling issue, others have made their peace with it. Not only has Oregon permitted slots for more than a decade, the state lottery actually runs the operation. By doing so, it gets at least 50 percent of the take from slot machines operating in bars, taverns, bowling alleys or other places that are licensed for liquor and have age-controlled areas where only those 21 years old and up are allowed. If a commercial outfit were involved, the take would be more like 35 percent.

A decade ago, Oregon conceded that people enjoyed playing slot machines. They played "gray machines" at arcades where they weren't supposed to win money, but some illegal machines were returning money. Rather than outlaw slots completely, Oregon decided to outlaw the gray machines and put in "real" ones it could regulate and get the financial benefit from.

While the state-run model does transfer more money from the machines to the state than if a commercial operator were running the games, the state also has added responsibility. "You do end up building up an entity of the state," says Don Robison, Oregon's video lottery product manager. "We have 417 employees throughout the state. There are operational issues associated with that."

How gambling might be instituted and who would run it are among the many facets that Florida lawmakers could debate in the coming months. In light of the state's budget woes and the need to fund a new class-size reduction initiative, gambling looks mighty enticing to some legislators. But others remain adamantly opposed.

Florida Senate President Jim King takes a dim view of full-blown casinos but wants to give citizens the choice whether to legalize video lottery terminals at ailing racetracks rather than raise taxes to fill the state's gaping budget hole. "I believe, and I haven't been proven wrong yet, that citizens would say let's go the VLT route with some guarantee there will be no expansion beyond that," King says.

"It's not an expansion of gambling issue, it's a revenue-production issue."

His counterpart in the House, Speaker Johnnie Byrd, is dead set against gambling. So if the state doesn't have enough money to do everything it wants to do, then some hard choices will have to be made. "We should build on the strength of Floridians," he says, "rather than on their weaknesses through some expansion of gambling or get-rich scheme."

Education Funding Squeeze

by Charlotte Cornell Postlewaite

Talk is cheap. School funding is not. As the bedrocks of school funding formulas—property, sales and income taxes—were beginning to crumble under the weight of budget shortfalls last November, they became the focus of state elections.

This month the debates move from the campaign trails to the state capitols where legislators will have to find sources for school funding at a time when polls indicate the public supports education at all costs, but wants lower taxes.

In one poll, nearly three-fourths of respondents opposed reducing state spending for education as a means of dealing with the budget crises many states face. The 34th annual *Phi Delta Kappan*/Gallup Poll of attitudes toward public schools released last August reported 58 percent of the respondents would favor increases in state taxes to avoid cuts in education while 78 percent would support avoiding cuts in education spending by making cuts in other areas. The entire poll results are available at *http://www.pdkintl.org*.

November's elections proved something of a litmus test for public support of education. In the Northeast, voters in New Hampshire elected a governor who denounced income tax as a means of supporting education and who also indicated plans to cut the state's property taxes. State Treasurer James H. Douglas won his race for governor after campaigning to dismantle Act 60, the state's education funding law that pools property tax money from wealthier communities and channels it to poorer ones.

Nowhere was the public's school funding paradox more dramatically apparent than in Florida, where voters mandated early childhood education for all 4-year-olds, placed a cap on class sizes, and reelected fiscally conservative Gov. Jeb Bush, who did not support class-size limits because of the price tag.

In California, voters approved Proposition 49, the After School Education and Safety Program Act of 2002. That program will not begin until 2004, giving the economy a chance to recover and state officials time to coordinate the logistics of dispensing money to as many as 6,600 public schools.

Charlotte Cornell Postlewaite is the chief education policy analyst at The Council of State Governments. This article is reprinted from *State Government News* (January 2003): 16–18. Copyright 2003 The Council of State Governments. Reprinted with permission from *State Government News/Spectrum*.

Federal Mandates Costly

Elsewhere, school funding continues to invite debate and litigation as the focus shifts from equity to adequacy everywhere from New York to North Carolina.

Election results followed on the heels of federal legislation that requires states to close the gap between poorer students' achievement and their opportunities to achieve. That legislation is more than just talk. It requires extra help for students at risk, for students with limited-English proficiency, and for students with physical or mental handicaps. But local and state education agencies have found that the price tag requires a great deal of complex financial maneuvering in times of shrinking state revenues.

States provide nearly half the funding for all public education, according to Dr. John Augenblick's report, *The Status of School Finance Today,* prepared for the Education Commission of the States. Augenblick, principal consultant for Augenblick & Myers Inc., said that state funding for public elementary and secondary schools typically accounts for 25 to 40 percent of state general-fund budgets and is the largest general-fund item in state budgets.

So when state legislators return to their committee work and roll calls this month, they face the task of trying to deliver to constituents a federal mandate for better schools with equitable and adequate education for all, while tempering constituent desire for lower taxes. For legislators looking to deliver all the goods, it is almost like pulling a rabbit out of their hats.

Funding Education Initiatives

Florida's Amendment 8 is likely to cost between $400 million and $650 million a year. Elected leaders will head to Tallahassee in 2003 with the task of putting together a financing package to pay for the pre-kindergarten programs, slated to begin in 2005.

Support for limiting class sizes, Amendment 9, remained strong until opponents began saying it would force a major tax increase. Amendment 9 narrowly passed 52 percent to 48 percent to the dismay of re-elected Gov. Bush. Throughout his campaign, Bush said the state would not be able to build schools fast enough or sustain services if the amendment passed. After his re-election, Bush said he would ask an advisory group to help devise a means for funding Amendment 9.

Florida does not assess income tax, and legislators now must find a way to finance both amendments. Sen. Mandy Dawson does not favor taxing the public. "Ultimately, Florida's tax dollars belong to its taxpayers and it is their needs which must be addressed," she said.

Prior to the election, Dawson advocated revoking tax breaks for corporations and putting that money back into classrooms to address class size and higher salaries for teachers, counselors, aides, cafeteria and janitorial employees. "I believe Florida's tax system can be fixed simply by taking a 2-year break from corporate excise incentives to really look at logic and evaluate the results of losses or gains," she said.

In Vermont, Gov. Douglas said he sees two things that he can do to help correct the problems associated with Act 60 if he can gain support in the state legislature. First, he cited a State Superior Court ruling on Act 60. "It said that the methodology for appraising property is so flawed that it's unconstitutional, and we need to deal with that. Second, we want to work toward eliminating the sharing pool that towns have to pay into. If they want to spend over the amount of the block grant, they have to pay multiples based on their situation."

Douglas said many property owners in the state call the sharing pool the Shark Pool. "It's really offensive and divisive," he said.

What began as a boon to Oklahoma's economy in the late 1980s and early 1990s has become a bust to local school districts. In 1986, voters approved a constitutional amendment that authorized counties to grant five-year ad valorem tax exemptions to new or expanded manufacturing companies. Today, the reimbursement fund has shrunk with the economy. "The state told the local school districts they'd hold them harmless with the reimbursement fund back in 1986, and now the fund can only pay 50 cents on the dollar because state income taxes are down," said Rep. Ron Peterson.

In districts like Peterson's, cash flow remains weak. "It's an injustice to the school districts and it remains a hot issue," he said just days before his re-election. "We'll have to restructure the existing budget, and it's going to be a fight."

Under Oklahoma's school funding formula, wealthier districts like Bixby and Broken Arrow share their tax revenues with poorer districts, but the weakened reimbursement fund has allowed those former boom districts to take a larger share of the state's education revenue pool.

It has also reduced those districts' contribution to poorer districts. "Its impact will flow out to every school district in the state if we don't fix this," Peterson said. School districts stand to lose millions of dollars over the next three years unless Oklahoma legislators find a solution. Prior to the November election, Peterson worried that voters might blame the issue on him and other legislators who inherited the problem, but he regained his seat.

In Plano, Texas, incumbents and challengers alike campaigned against the state's school finance plan. The system, sometimes called The Robin Hood Plan, requires that property-wealthy districts such as Plano's must transfer property-tax revenues to districts that are less affluent. The current formula seeks to equalize school funding statewide, but wealthier districts have formed advocacy groups to gain support for school finance reform in the 2003 Texas Legislature. Called the Texas School Coalition, the group supports an initiative that encourages Legislators to address problems in the current formula. The wealthier districts are circulating a resolution calling for changes prior to the upcoming session.

Courts Play Role

Tennessee's funding mechanism, called the Basic Education Program, also provides extra state funds to systems in counties with smaller tax bases, but the state Supreme Court ruled in October that the same type of inequities exist today that existed in 1988 when litigation over equity first began. It has ordered the Legislature to achieve equitable funding for teacher salaries in rural and urban districts.

In a state that does not levy state income tax, legislators are hard-pressed to find ways to support the court's decision. Tennessee charges the highest sales tax in the country at nearly 10 cents on the dollar, and legislators there do not expect to raise it more.

The West Wants Compensation

In Utah and other Western states, legislators would like the opportunity to have more property to assess for taxation. Sounds ironic? Unique to that region of the country, massive federal land holdings thwart state endeavors to fund education a rate comparable to other parts of the country, said Utah Rep. Steve Urquhart. He and Utah House Speaker Marty Stephens and Rep. Tom Hatch spearheaded CSG-*WEST*'s Resolution 2002-01: "Resolution Urging the United States Congress to Compensate Western States for the Impact of Federal Land Ownership on State Education Funding."

The Apple Initiative, as it is called, "will unify the West," Urquhart said. "The West is being educated to the fact that all Western states are falling behind in education, and we will have to speak with one voice in the future."

Representatives delivered the resolution last summer to the U.S. Department of the

Interior, U.S. Department of Education and the National Education Association. Urquhart plans to run the resolution through the Utah House and expects similar resolutions to move through Western legislatures this year. They hope the resolutions will gain the attention of the U.S. Congress and also capture the attention of the next presidential candidates.

In Oregon, residents will vote this month on a proposed temporary 3-year state income tax increase. Legislators decided last fall to place the fate of school funding and other state services in voters' hands. If the proposal fails,

schools and other public and human safety services are likely to absorb $310 million in cuts for the biennium. Last October, 55 percent of those polled in *The Oregonian* newspaper said they were in no mood for a tax increase.

These debates are sure to continue when legislatures across the country convene this month and November's winners are likely to arrive at state capitols armed with what they believe is a mandate by their constituents to either cut back school spending or increase it by raising or introducing new state taxes.

States Approve Sales-Tax Pact

by Christopher Swope

Is a Hershey's chocolate bar a candy or a food? A group of 34 states that want to levy sales taxes on Internet and catalog purchases took a big step forward in November when they settled upon an answer: candy. This and dozens of testy sales-tax issues were addressed, clearing the way for the next step in tax simplification: approval of the simplified rules by state legislatures.

It took three years for state revenue officials to hammer out their simplification plan. The motivation was there: e-commerce is eating up as much as $14 billion a year in state and local revenues. Technically, when consumers buy online they owe sales or use taxes, but states can't always make retailers collect the tab. The U.S. Supreme Court has said the taxes are too complex to administer nationally—some 7,600 jurisdictions each have their own rates and rules. In simplifying the system, states are wooing retailers and a skeptical Congress into letting them collect.

The states' 70-page agreement spells out common definitions for goods from candy to clothing; states and localities still decide for themselves whether or not to tax a category of items. States would pick one tax rate—the same goes for local governments—although

both would be allowed a different tax rate for food and medicine.

Nothing takes effect until 10 or more states pass laws bringing their tax systems in line with the agreement. Moreover, those states must represent at least 20 percent of the population of the 45 states that levy sales taxes.

It won't be easy. The sales taxes took on complexities as states poked holes in the tax code as favors to powerful home-state business interests. "This is the hard part," says Neal Osten, who follows the issue for the National Conference of State Legislatures. "All the complexity—the exemptions, the definitions—occurred over 70 to 80 years of sales-tax history. It's going to take some work."

Simplification will create winners and losers in every state—and any business or industry that suspects it may lose can be expected to fight it. The agreement could also wreak political havoc in other ways. Maryland and Ohio, for example, would both lose revenue simply because they would have to start rounding numbers down, rather than up. New York, Massachusetts, Connecticut and Vermont would have

Christopher Swope is a staff writer for *Governing*. This article is reprinted from *Governing* (January 2003): 44.

to give up "thresholds" whereby consumers pay no sales tax on, say, the first $100 or so of clothing. Local governments in Alabama, Arizona, Colorado and Louisiana would have to hand over responsibility for administering their local-option sales taxes to their state governments. In Arkansas, North Dakota and Tennessee, local governments may collect more sales taxes when local tax limits go away.

State officials involved in the sales-tax project predict 20 to 30 legislatures will debate the agreement this year. They hope 10 to 15 states pass it. "Having state budgets in the poor condition they're in adds some weight to the effort," says Scott Peterson, director of business taxes in South Dakota. "It's going to be an interesting year."

Online Sales Tax Is for Real

by Christopher Swope

In February, an anonymous band of large retailers struck an unusual deal with 37 states. The sellers, which reportedly include Wal-Mart, Target and Toy 'R' Us, agreed to begin collecting sales taxes from their customers who make Internet purchases. In exchange, the states promised not to sue them for back taxes. They also agreed to ignore the retailers' past ploys in which many large brick-and-mortar stores set up Internet shops as separate divisions. For behemoths such as Wal-Mart, with stores in all 50 states, the old structure paid big rewards: Walmart.com, for instance, could largely avoid the hassle of collecting sales taxes, except in the nine states where the dot-com side of the business owned an office or warehouse. Now that will be impossible.

Why the deal? For their part, big retailers have a new business model in mind. They want their Internet units to be closely integrated with the brick-and-mortar side, and the need to maintain separate subsidiaries for tax purposes is getting in the way. Walmart.com was already testing the limits of separation when it began allowing customers to return purchases made online at a Wal-mart store. Now it may blur the lines further by letting customers buy products online and pick them up at a store. "There will

no longer be a need to keep those businesses separate," says John Coalson, the Atlanta attorney who represents the group of retailers and who initiated discussions with the states.

The states that signed on to the deal did so to help stem their tide of red budget ink—now and in the future. Not that the agreement, which will pump perhaps $25 million into state coffers this year, comes close to solving their budget woes. But with states facing a combined 30 billion in shortfalls this year and an estimated $80 billion next year, they figure every little bit helps. More important, the deal mitigates future losses as the retailing giants' online sales grow in the coming years.

Not all the states are going along with the deal. Three states—Arizona, California and South Carolina—have rejected the offer, while several other states are weighing their options. Illinois is suing Wal-Mart and Target, among other retailers, for nonpayment of taxes. South Carolina isn't planning any lawsuits, according to state revenue director Burnie Maybank, but auditors there are pursuing an "aggressive

Christopher Swope is a staff writer for *Governing*. This article is reprinted from *Governing* (April 2003): 52.

nexus program" seeking back taxes from retailers. "We don't enter into agreements to wipe out back taxes on an anonymous basis," Maybank says.

Still, the deal gives momentum to proponents of taxing all Internet sales. Some 34 states are moving toward the goal after signing an agreement in November to streamline and simplify their sales tax structures. As state lawmakers debate the pact this spring, opponents are finding their arguments undercut by the big retailers' willingness to deal with the sales tax: Perhaps collecting it online wasn't so complicated after all.

Another argument—that forcing retailers to collect taxes will hurt their sales—isn't bearing out, according to Wal-Mart. "We haven't seen an impact on our online sales," says Cynthia Lin, a spokesman for Wal-Mart, which began collecting taxes for all states on February 1. "Our sales continue to be strong and continue to grow."

Taking Aim at Correction Costs

by Christopher Swope

With their finances under pressure and prison budgets skyrocketing, a growing number of states are trying to shrink costs by reducing the number of prisoners under their care.

Louisiana is a prime example. With the highest rate of incarceration in the country, the state's corrections budget took on weight as its prison population grew during the 1990s from 20,000 to 35,000. Many of the new inmates were low-level drug offenders, put behind bars by a wave of tough-on-crime laws passed in the height of the early 1990s crack cocaine epidemic.

Now that the state's budget is tight, Louisiana wants to tame prison costs. The most immediate method is to set inmates free. The state this winter set up "risk review" boards. The boards evaluate whether certain nonviolent inmates are safe enough to recommend for pardon or parole. As many as 800 inmates—who currently cost $23 each per day—are expected to pass muster and be released this year.

Louisiana lawmakers also took steps to stanch the flow of new inmates. They cut mandatory sentences for some drug-related offenses in half and eliminated mandatory minimums for other crimes. They also amended the state's "three strikes" law so that only those convicted of three violent crimes are locked away for life. "The legislature was asking a legitimate question," says corrections chief Richard Stalder. "Are there more cost-effective ways to deal with these problems?"

It isn't only Louisiana. The crime rate is down from its soaring levels of the early '90s, giving politicians wiggle room on crime policy. Lawmakers can now ease sentences without fear of being labeled "soft on crime." In Mississippi, lawmakers scaled back the state's "truth-in-sentencing" law, giving first-time nonviolent offenders a shot at parole once again. Connecticut changed its mandatory minimum sentencing law to give judges discretion to issue shorter sentences for nonviolent drug offenders, while North Dakota repealed mandatory minimums altogether for first-time drug users.

Meanwhile, the 1990s boom in prison construction is crashing like dot-com stock. Illinois, Ohio and Michigan are all closing prisons, while Missouri is putting off opening a

Christopher Swope is a staff writer for *Governing*. This article is reprinted from *Governing* (April 2002): 54.

new 2,000-bed prison because it can't afford to run it.

Troubled finances are a motivation to act, but there is also evidence of a philosophical shift. The criminal justice pendulum may be swinging away from incarceration and toward rehabilitation. In California, which built 12 new prisons in the 1990s, nonviolent drug offenders are now getting treatment, rather than being locked up. The change, a result of a ballot initiative, is expected to save as much as $150 million a year and avoid some $500 million in costs for new prisons.

Indeed, saving money is not even a goal of one proposal working its way through the Washington legislature. Lawmakers are likely to pass a measure that will shorten the sentences of low-level drug offenders but pump the savings into drug treatment. Three-quarters of the money would go to counties to run increasingly popular "drug courts." The rest would fund rehab programs in state prisons. "I see us moving away from a drug policy that just focuses on law enforcement," says King County prosecutor Norm Maleng. "We can keep the tough laws but also have education and treatment."

Index

Homeowners insurance, 45
Homicide, 183
Hopper, Len, 138
Hough, Bonnie, 147
Housing and Urban Development Department,
  177–178
Houston, Paul, 180
Houston, Texas, 182, 183
Hovey, Harold A., 15
Hovey, Kendra A., 15
Hunt, Guy, 103
Hutchison, Asa, 28

Ibarra, Mickey, 179
Idaho, 29
Illinois, 108–110, 135, 201
Immigrant workers, 116
Implementation, 190
Incumbency, 6, 11, 24
Independent candidates, 5, 37–38
Independent voters, 4–5, 41, 49
Indian gaming, 30, 199, 200
Indiana, 86
Industrial hemp, 28
Information technology, 92–95
Infrastructure protection, 134–138
Initiative & Referendum Institute, 28–30, 31–33
Initiatives, 23
  animal rights, 29
  cost of, 25
  drug policy, 28–29, 31
  education reform, 29
  election reform, 29
  gaming, 29–30
  impact of money, 31–33
  interest groups and, 31–32
  process, 69
  regulating, 32–33
  states' rights and, 26–27
  tax reform, 30
  term limits, 6, 24, 25, 29
  in 2002, 28–30
Institute for Legal Reform, 44
Insurance, 44, 45, 83, 116, 193
Interest groups, 31–32, 39–40, 49
Internet sales tax, 209–210
Investment banking, 116
Iowa, 84, 94

Jackson, Gregory, 93
Jackson, Rebecca, 165–166
Jefferson-Pilot, 66
Jeffords, Jim, 4
Jennings, Ed, 95
Jewell, Malcolm, 37
Johnson, Gary, 84, 133
Jonas, Michael, 46–47, 87–91
Jones, Bradley, 90
Jones, David, 177

Jones, Robert, 27
Journals, 16
Judicial activism, 143–144
Judicial elections, 141–143
Judicial policy making, 143–145
Judicial politics, 141–143
Judiciary, 141. *See also* Courts
Justice Department (DOJ), 98, 99, 142
Justus, Margaret, 45

Kastick, Brian, 114
Kaufman, Jay, 90
Kelley, Steve, 93, 94, 95
Kentucky, 67, 84, 162–168
Keough, Robert, 71
Kerr, Michael, 132, 133
Kessel, Roy, 133
Key, V. O., Jr., 59
King, Angus, 5, 38
King, Jim, 201–202
Klein, Joel, 180, 181
Kniss, Chad, 45
Kocheisen, Carol, 177

Labeling of genetically modified foods, 30
Labor groups, 39
LaBrant, Bob, 43–44
Large states, and presidential elections, 7, 8
Latino voters, 99
Lauer, Nancy Cook, 70
Lawmaking, 53
Lawsuit abuse, 45
Lawsuits, 43–44
Lawyers, 45, 146–147
Lay, Kenneth, 45
League of California Cities, 169
Leavitt, Mike, 93, 148
LeBlanc, Jerry Luke, 86
Lees, Brian, 87
Legal drinking age, 189
Legislation, enacting, 85
Legislative campaign committees, 51
Legislative candidates, 5–6
Legislative elections, 10–12
  leaders, 12
  mid-term election trend, 10–11
  redistricting, 11–12
  regional analysis, 11
Legislative leaders, 12
Legislative parties, 48–56
  accountability, 52
  affiliation, 49
  assessing, 48–49
  campaigns and, 50–51
  choices for voters, 51
  competition and, 49–50
  consensus-building, 54
  fundraising by, 52–53
  governance and, 52, 55